Asia Meets Europe

To M&P, G&A

Asia Meets Europe

Inter-Regionalism and the Asia-Europe Meeting

Julie Gilson

University of Birmingham

Edward Elgar
Cheltenham, UK • Northampton, MA, USA

Published by
Edward Elgar Publishing Limited
Glensanda House
Montpellier Parade
Cheltenham
Glos GL50 1UA
UK

Edward Elgar Publishing, Inc.
136 West Street
Suite 202
Northampton
Massachusetts 01060
USA

A catalogue record for this book is available from the British Library

Library of Congress Cataloging in Publication Data

Gilson, Julie.
    Asia meets Europe : inter-regionalism and the Asia-Europe Meeting /
    Julie Gilson.
        p.cm.
    Includes bibliographical references and index.
        1. Asia–Economic policy–Congresses. 2. Europe–Economic
    policy–Congresses. 3. Regionalism–Congresses. 4. Asia-Europe Meeting.
        I. Title.

HC412.G558 2002
337.405–dc21   2002016654

ISBN: 1 84064 108 8
Printed and bound in Great Britain by MPG Books Ltd, Bodmin, Cornwall

Contents

List of Tables

Abbreviations

ACP	African, Caribbean and Pacific countries
ADB	Asian Development Bank
AEBF	Asia–Europe Business Forum
AECF	Asia–Europe Cooperation Framework
AEPF	Asia–Europe People's Forum
AEETC	Asia–Europe Environmental Technology Centre
AEH	ASEM Educational Hubs
AETLS	Asia–Europe Young Leaders' Symposium
AFTA	ASEAN Free Trade Area
AIPO	Asia–Europe Parliamentary Organisation
AMF	Asian Monetary Fund
APEC	Asia Pacific Economic Cooperation forum
ARF	ASEAN Regional Forum
ASEAN	Association of Southeast Asian Nations
ASEAN PMC	ASEAN Post–Ministerial Conference
ASEF	Asia–Europe Foundation
ASEM	Asia–Europe Meeting
BC–NET	Business Cooperation Network
BRES	Bureau de rapprochement des Entreprises
BIS	Bank for International Settlements
BOJ	Bank of Japan
CAEC	Council for Asia–Europe Cooperation
CAP	Common Agricultural Policy
CBMs	Confidence–building measures
CCP	Common Commercial Policy (of the EU)
CEPT	Common Effective Preferential Tariff (of AFTA)
CER	Closer Economic Relations
CFSP	Common Foreign and Security Policy

CLONG	NGDO–EU Liaison Committee
CP	Common Position
CSCAP	Council for Security Cooperation in the Asia Pacific
CSCE	Conference on Security Cooperation in Europe
CTBT	Comprehensive Test Ban Treaty
DG	Directorate-General (of the European Commission)
EAEC	East Asian Economic Caucus
EAEG	East Asian Economic Grouping
EARN	Europe–Asia Education and Research Network
EBRD	European Bank for Reconstruction and Development
EC	European Community/Communities
ECB	European Central Bank
ECHO	European Communities' Humanitarian Office
ECIP	European Community Investment Partners
ECSC	European Coal and Steel Community
ECU	European currency unit
EDC	European Defence Community
EEC	European Economic Community
EFEX	European Financial Expertise Network
EFTA	European Free Trade Area
EIB	European Investment Bank
EP	European Parliament
EPC	European Political Community or European Political Cooperation
ERM	Exchange Rate Mechanism
EMI	European Monetary Institute
EMM	Economic Ministers' Meeting
EMS	European Monetary System
EMU	European Monetary Union
EP	European Parliament
ESDF	European Security and Defence Forces
ESDP	European Security and Defence Policy
ETP	Executive Training Programme
EU	European Union
EURATOM	European Atomic Energy Community

Euro	Single European currency
FCO	Foreign and Commonwealth Office (UK)
FDI	Foreign direct investment
FPDA	Five Power Defence Arrangement
FRY	Federal Republic of Yugoslavia
G7/G8	Group of 7/8 industrialised nations
GATS	General Agreement on Trade in Services
GATT	General Agreement on Tariffs and Trade
GDP	Gross domestic product
GNP	Gross national product
GSMs	Global social movements
GSP	Generalised System of Preferences
IBRD	International Bank for Reconstruction and Development
ICCPR	International Covenant on Civil and Political Rights
ICESCR	International Covenant on Economic Social and Cultural Rights
IEG	Investment Experts Group
IFI	International financial institution
ILO	International Labour Organisation
IMF	International Monetary Fund
IPAP	Investment Promotion Action Plan
IPE	International political economy
IPR	Intellectual property rights
IR	International relations
IT	Information Technology
ITTO	International Tropical Timber Organisation
JETRO	Japan External Trade Organisation
KEDO	Korean Peninsula Energy Development Organisation
KFOR	Kosovo Force
KMT	Kuomintang (Taiwan)
LAFTA	Latin American Free Trade Area
M&As	Mergers and acquisitions
MAI	Multilateral Agreements on Investments
MEP	Member of the European Parliament
MERCOSUR	Common Market of the South/Southern Cone (Mercado Común del Sur)
MFN	Most-favoured nation status
MNC	Multinational corporation

MRA	Mutual Recognition Agreement
NAFTA	North American Free Trade Agreement
NAM	Non-Aligned Movement
NATO	North Atlantic Treaty Organisation
NGO	Non-governmental organisation
NIEs	Newly Industrialising Economies
NLF	National Liberation Front (Vietnam)
NMD	National Missile Defense
NPT	Nuclear Non-Proliferation Treaty
NTBs	Non-tariff barriers
ODA	Official development assistance
OECD	Organisation for Economic Cooperationand Development
OEEC	Organisation for European Economic Cooperation
OSCE	Organisation for Security and Cooperation in Europe
PAP	Political Action Party (Malaysia)
PBEC	Pacific Basin Economic Council
PECC	Pacific Economic Cooperation Council
PMC	Post-Ministerial Conference
PRC	People's Republic of China
R&D	Research and development
ROC	Republic of China, on Taiwan
RRF	Rapid Reaction Facility
S&T	Science and technology
SEA	Single European Act
SEANWFZ	Southeast Asia Nuclear Weapons Free Zone
SEATO	Southeast Asian Treaty Organisation
SEM	Single European Market
SLORC	State Law and Order Restoration Council (Myanmar)
SMEs	Small and medium-sized enterprises
SOEs	State–owned enterprises
SOM	Senior officials' meeting
SOMTI	Senior officials meeting on trade and investment
SPS	Sanitary-phytosanitary standards
STMM	Science and Technology Ministers' Meeting

TAM	Trade Assessment Mechanism
TC	Trilateral Commission
TEU	Treaty on European Union ('Maastricht Treaty')
TFAP	Trade Facilitation Action Plan
TNC	Transnational corporation
TNI	Transnational Institute
TRIMS	Trade-Related Investment Measures
TRIPS	Trade-Related Intellectual Property Rights
UDHR	Universal Declaration of Human Rights
UMNO	United Malays National Organisation
UN	United Nations
UNAMET	United Nations Mission in East Timor
UNCED	United Nations Conference on Environment and Development
UNCTAD	United Nations Conference on Trade and Development
UNMIK	United Nations Mission in Kosovo
UNSC	United Nations Security Council
UNTAET	United Nations Transitional Administration in East Timor
VER	Voluntary export restraint
VIE	Virtual Information Exchange
VRA	Voluntary restraint agreement
WB	World Bank
WCO	World Customs' Organisation
WEF	World Economic Forum
WEU	Western European Union
WTO	World Trade Organisation
ZOPFAN	Zone of Peace, Freedom and Neutrality

Preface

> ... as soon as an idea, fragmentary though it may be, has been realised, however imperfectly, in the domain of facts, it is no longer the idea that counts and acts, it is the institution situated in its [own] plane and time, incorporating within itself a complicated and mobile network of social facts, producing and undergoing a thousand diverse actions and a thousand reactions. (Lucien Febvre, *Pour une histoire à part entière*, 1962)

The Asia–Europe Meeting (ASEM) brings together in one forum of 'equal partners' heads of state or government from ten countries of Asia and from the fifteen member states of the European Union (EU).[1] Despite the EU's own long history of inter-regional arrangements, which include the Lomé, EU–ASEAN and EU–MERCOSUR agreements, ASEM represents a novel form of inter-continental interaction for a number of reasons. First, it links the participating members of Asia and Europe within an explicitly inter-regional framework, in which Asian and European collective responses respectively are solicited and developed prior to formal ASEM encounters. This is particularly interesting in the case of Asia, which, in spite of attempts at creating an East Asian Economic Caucus (EAEC), has no EU–like mechanisms for sustaining institutionalised regional integration. Second, ASEM is a product of the post-cold war period, in which former alliances are no longer clearly defined. Third, unlike arrangements such as the ASEAN Regional Forum (ARF) and Asia Pacific Economic Cooperation (APEC) forum, ASEM's agenda covers a range of economic, political and other issues in a broad dialogue (see Chronology). Finally, the developing and original nature of this meeting also poses interesting theoretical questions regarding the nature of inter-regionalism, especially in relation to regional integration and globalisation. To date, it has been somewhat awkwardly accommodated within existing International Relations (IR) and International Political Economy (IPE) literature, where it tends to be regarded simply as a stepping-stone or body of resistance to globalisation. This book seeks to examine the origins and effects of region-to-region engagement through the lens of inter-regionalism itself.

The idea for ASEM itself originated within a private organisation – the Geneva-based World Economic Forum – and was advanced subsequently by Singapore's Prime Minister Goh Chok Tong in 1994, on the occasion of an official visit to Paris during the French Presidency of the EU (Camroux and Lechervy 1996, p. 443).[2] The French Presidency accepted the summit in principle, and Prime Minister Goh secured ASEAN participation, although not without reservations. In particular, ASEAN member states could not agree upon the membership of the meeting, and eventually decided against Australian participation, in spite of Japanese lobbying on Canberra's behalf (*Asian Wall Street Journal* 23 February 1996). Once the membership question had been decided, foreign ministers of the participating Asian member states met in Phuket, Thailand, in February 1996, to negotiate a pre-summit position. The first ASEM summit subsequently took place in Bangkok in March 1996. ASEM 1 was hailed as a successful attempt to introduce previously distant interlocutors, and, in the eyes of certain observers, established the format for a 'whole new game' in international relations (*The Economist* 9 March 1996). The new partnership embodied in the ASEM process was designed to be based upon a common commitment to a market economy, to the open multilateral trading system, non-discrimination, liberalisation and 'open regionalism' (Chair's Statement at ASEM 1). It was built expressly upon pre-existing channels of inter-regional communication, such as the EU–ASEAN and EU–Japan dialogues and cooperation within the ARF, as well as pledges, like the EU's 1994 'New Asia Strategy', to improve mutual relations. In so doing, participants recalled ASEAN's original commitment to 'maintain close and beneficial co-operation with existing international and regional organisations with similar aims and purposes', and the EU's external goal to 'assign considerable weight to undertaking collective steps' vis-à-vis third countries in fields other than trade (Edwards and Regelsberger 1990, p. 12). Growing intra-regional developments continued alongside global pressures to consolidate region-to-region relations as part of the Europe–US–Asia trilateral schema, which has formed the basis of many attempts to interpret the rationale for Asia–Europe relations. While the first ASEM summit set the inter-regional tone of the multiple activities to be held in its name, ASEM 2 – despite the shattering effects of the Asian financial crisis – further embedded the idea that Asia and Europe were now meeting one another regularly. ASEM 3 saw attempts to return to issues that could be addressed mutually, and the timely North–South Korean *rapprochement* enabled leaders to discuss means of opening a broad security dialogue.

A number of works have examined the various forms of relations among countries of Asia and Europe (see, for example, Bridges 1999b; Chia and Tan 1997; Drifte 1996; Forster 1999; Gilson 2000; Palmujoki 1997; Smith,

M. 1998), and a few have concentrated uniquely on the role of ASEM (see Camroux and Lechervy 1996; Dent 1999a and 1999b; Maull et al. 1998; McMahon 1998; Okfen 1999; Pelkmans and Shinkai 1997; Rüland 1996; Serradell 1996; Stokhof and van der Velde 1999; Yeo 1997, 2000). Most interest in Asia and Europe has focused upon their developing economic and financial exchanges (Aggarwal 2000; Bridges 1999a; Dent 1999a and 1999b; Lee and Ruffini 1999); and a few have examined particular political (Bridges 1999b), security (Mahncke 1997; Shin and Segal 1997), human rights (Amersfoort 1998; Freeman 1998) and cultural interests (Hernandez 1997). Broader assessments have been provided from an international system perspective (Drysdale and Vines 1998), while there has been some attention to the nature of inter-regionalism (Cammack and Richards 1999; Gilson 1999; Richards and Kirkpatrick 1999) and to comparative studies involving the regions (Desthieux and Saucier 1999; Higgott 1998a; Minton 1999; Preeg 1998).

Since it only began in 1996, it remains difficult to make a full assessment of the impact of Asia–Europe relations within the context of ASEM. With that in mind, this book nevertheless begins with the premise that it is misleading to assume that ASEM is merely a counter-force to, or a repeated form of, other regional endeavours such as APEC. Rather, it aims to illustrate and examine the potential influence of inter-regionalism upon sub-state and supra-state actors, by examining how mutual historical experiences and multi-level interaction have begun to (re)define notions of 'region' in this novel context. Chapter 1 explores various key approaches to the study of regions and offers possible interpretations for examining inter-regionalism as a unique and alternative path for international exchange. Chapter 2 offers an overview of Asia–Europe historical relations as they have shaped mutual (sic) interpretations of one another. The following three chapters each take a 'pillar' of the ASEM format to examine, in turn, the economic (Chapter 3), political (Chapter 4) and socio-cultural (Chapter 5) aspects of Asia–Europe dialogue within a contemporary, international context. The Conclusion considers the extent to which Asia–Europe relations throw light upon inter-regionalism as a discrete level of analysis, and suggests possible avenues of future research on region-to-region relations.

This book would not have been possible without generous grants and enthusiastic support from the British Academy and the Nuffield Foundation, and editorial advice and assistance from Jo Betteridge at Edward Elgar. Innumerable individuals from national government agencies, non-governmental organisations and business also provided me with materials and advice along the way. Particular thanks go to: Paul Lim and Willem van der Geest for letting me spend time at their well-stocked European Institute for Asian Studies; Andy Rutherford at One World Action; Duncan Jackman and all the staff at the Asia–Europe Foundation, who provided financial support and constant assistance; Thomas Leeb and the Herbert Quandt Stiftung for inviting me to two Europe–Asia Forums; the School of Social Sciences at the University of Birmingham for allowing me time to focus on this project; and my graduate students in the Department of Political Science and International Studies, who challenged me along the way. As always, Simon makes this all possible. Naturally, I remain solely responsible for the contents of this book.

Notes

1. The Asian contingent comprises China, Japan and South Korea alongside seven member states of ASEAN: namely, Brunei, Indonesia, Malaysia, the Philippines, Singapore, Thailand, and Vietnam. The fifteen member states of the EU are: Austria, Belgium, Denmark, Finland, France, Germany, Greece, Ireland, Italy, Luxembourg, the Netherlands, Portugal, Spain, Sweden, and the UK. The European Community was renamed European Union in 1993, following the Treaty on European Union (Maastricht Treaty). In addition, the president of the European Commission also attends. Since ASEM began, three new countries have joined ASEAN (namely, Burma, Cambodia and Laos) but they have no automatic right of participation in ASEM.
2. The Presidency of the EU refers to a six-month period when one member state assumes responsibility for representing the EU and for organising its schedule. It is assisted by the Troika system, whereby the previous, current and next Presidencies work together in order to maintain a level of continuity in EU affairs.

1. Concepts of Inter-Regionalism

Quand l'Europe regard l'Asie, égoïstement, elle s'interroge d'abord sur elle-même. (Lechervy 1998)

'Asia' and 'Europe' are slippery characters. Comprising at different times and for different purposes local, interest-specific, sub-national, national, sub-regional, regional, trans-regional, international or global agents and structural boundaries, the possibilities for their definition are seemingly endless. This chapter adds further to this confusion, by bringing into greater relief the level of *inter-regionalism*, which is not only a theoretical construct, but also exists as a contemporary form of activity. Why, you may (indeed) ask, do we need yet another promontory from which to observe the already rough seas of international relations? Quite simply because times, conditions, agents and the whole structure of contemporary affairs have changed and continue to change. The ending of the cold war eroded old political and economic alliances, as new kinds of groupings came to the fore, rendering still more complex today's interdependent engagements and intensifying the need to resolve major problems collectively. The very nature of those problems has also changed, as ecological issues and ideas of conflict prevention and resolution supplement previously salient military, nuclear and weapons-based concerns: global warming, forest fires, water pollution, nuclear leaks and acid rain know no boundaries. One result of these changes is that regions are assuming more varied and pronounced identities and in their mutual interactions open up new spaces as agents within the international system. This development, in turn, has repercussions for the ways in which participants within a given region come to view themselves. In other words, a region may feel its 'regionness' in large part through interaction with other perceived regions. To date, the few existing forays into inter-regional analysis have tended to define this level of action as the sum of interacting regions, or else as an (inevitable?) stage towards the process of globalisation. In contrast, this chapter explores the value of analysing inter-regionalism in its own right.

Asia–Europe relations can be, and are, approached from a number of perspectives. For example, neorealists may view ASEM as 25 self-interested power-maximising states engaged in an essentially political exchange. In the

Asia–Europe context, the force of the United States that 'looms large' is seen to stabilise this inter-regional balance within the international system (Maull et al. 1998, p. xiv). By contrast, neoliberal frameworks may regard regions as a form of regime, whose boundaries constitute 'sets of mutual expectations, rules and regulations, organizational plans, energies, and financial commitments that have been accepted by a group of states' (Ruggie 1998, p. 56). Such boundaries also act as an institutionalised means of reducing transaction costs (Keohane et al. 1993, p. 175), and/or embedding new discourses among participants, and therefore require states to agree a joint obligation to norms of compliance. In this way, even a loosely institutionalised process like ASEM has the potential to create a body of rules, norms of behaviour, and in-built rewards and sanctions, which act to standardise the behaviour of constituent participants. In addition, a growing number of cognitive theorists emphasise the impact of the process of social interaction itself upon what constitutes a region, and inter-regional exchanges. In their cognitive role, regional groupings can be seen to provide the locus in which the practices that drive them also create norms for behaviour, thereby delineating 'the social script through which institutional participants communicate and ... the basis upon which fixed and readily identifiable idea-sets for an institution's practices are founded' (Wendt and Duvall 1989, p. 60). In this rendition, Asia and Europe will in part be defined by the very process of their mutual interaction. These different approaches will be examined below.

This book aims to demonstrate that the inter-regional level per se needs to be taken seriously, since it has repercussions on a number of levels: for the ways in which the EU engages with the rest of the world; for the possible impact of future North American participation in the international system; and for the very definition of the 'Asian' region (defined, inter alia, in its East Asian, Southeast Asian or Asia Pacific incarnations) in its global reach, all in the absence of clear cold war boundaries. The first part of this chapter examines ideas of 'region' in their 'autonomist', 'integrating' and 'defensive' forms. Following this, the main section of the chapter focuses upon the level of inter-regionalism itself: in so doing, it examines the structures, processes and cognitive factors which may inform its development. Finally, the chapter considers how this theoretical framework may be applied to the case of Asia–Europe relations.

UNDERSTANDING REGIONS

Regions are seen to derive from the misty processes of regionalism and regionalisation: the former term tends to depict state- (or other agent-) led efforts actively to create a region; and the latter tends to present the organic development of a sense of 'regionness'. Regionalism, then, may be viewed as a top-down, (generally) state-led attempt to define a functional regional identity and/or regional body in a 'formal' manner (Grugel and Hout 1999, p. 10; Ravenhill 1998, pp. 250–51) and may be incarnated in the 'creation of preferential-trading arrangements' (Paik 1998, p. 49). In contrast, regionalisation tends to be regarded as a bottom-up, 'natural' or de facto process, that issues from 'combinations of historical and emergent structures' (Gamble and Payne 1996, p. 250), without necessarily involving the efforts of the participants of the given region, and which may be driven by the effects of growing economic and political interdependence. While both forms may be seen to respond to global changes and (limited) actor preferences, their different perspectives can result in the dichotomy of 'external' and 'internal' region formation. Using this distinction, the case of the EU suggests that both regionalism and regionalisation occur simultaneously: the Union represents a 'natural' geographical trading region upon which is built decisive efforts to impose structures through institutional development. Within Southeast Asia, on the contrary, one may say that neither regionalism nor regionalisation has occurred until recently, because historical, religious and cultural disparities provide no 'natural' regional glue, while efforts to institutionalise relations, either through ASEAN or more recently the ARF, are stymied by national resistance. Not only is this region-to-region distinction difficult to sustain, but when it comes to super-imposing these different forms of 'region' upon an Asia–Europe canvas, an apparent lack of common heritage means that only regionalism is possible. Rather than adopt such inconclusive terms, therefore, this book prefers to present 'regionalisation' in a broader sense: to reflect not only the simultaneously overlapping processes of international systemic pressures upon entities which are also internally coming to regard themselves in new and particular ways, but also to examine how mutual processes of interaction serve to shape ideas of self and other as 'regions'. It is this focus on the impact of region-to-region responses that enables us to break down some of the either/or distinctions which tend to prevail when determining when and how a 'region' comes into being, and to consider how regions come to be defined according to the needs of their interpreters. The following section examines how regionalisation is generally interpreted as an autonomist, integrating or defensive development, and explores some of the pitfalls of these more prevalent approaches to regions.[1]

'Autonomist' Regionalisation

Autonomist regionalisation focuses on the development of an organic, incremental and ad hoc collection of interests, without necessarily involving the active engagement of individual states towards region building. The various characteristics which cause interests to cohere may include common historical experience, geographical proximity or a shared commitment to a specific set of issues, and may derive from 'tangible economic, historical, ethnic, administrative, planning or political units' (Keating and Loughlin 1997, p. 5; see also Buzan 1998, p. 70; Mattli 1999; Wriggins 1992, p. 4). The coincidence of interests may lead to a spillover into new areas of cooperation (Haas 1964), or may intensify cooperative arrangements for particular issues at the sub-regional level. Sub-regionalism follows a similar organic trajectory, whereby proximate labour and material resources are pooled for local benefit, in the face of a changing international environment that necessitates a greater push for competitiveness. The 'growth triangle' comprising Singapore, Johor state in peninsular Malaysia and Indonesia's Riau Islands offers one such example: the skilled human resources of Singapore, Johor's land and unskilled labour, and Riau's low-cost labour combine for mutual benefit (Mittelman 1997, p. 13). This level of activity, which embeds its own uniqueness (Buzan 1998, p. 69), does not simply replicate regional development, however, since the very idea of sub-*regionalism* implicates and further embeds the notion that a region either pre-exists, or subsumes, this more localised level.

Increasingly, these organic interests have come to be articulated by civil society groups representing ecological as well as geographical concerns (see Lähteenmäki and Käkönen 1999, pp. 214–15). These groups have been incorporated with some success within the 'new regionalism' of Hettne et al., who examine those political, economic, social and cultural dimensions which engender regionalisation-from-below (1999). However, rather than following a Coxian call to comprehend how people also create structures (Cox 1981), Hettne et al. (like Gamble and Payne before them, 1996) continue to regard regions as groups 'of countries with a more or less explicitly shared political project', and in so doing retain the idea that a region represents the sum of its parts (Hettne 1999, p. 1). Such postulating accepts only one 'reality', and leads to a standardised account of what a region should represent, with the effect of setting 'Asia' and 'Europe' into fixed moulds.

In terms of defining regions, autonomist approaches tend to evoke the sense that cumulative historical actions develop into 'natural' regions; thus the EU could 'legitimately' be refused observer status in the APEC forum, while in ASEM the question of the membership of Australia, India and Pakistan has important implications for the definition of the Asian region in that context, as well as for the excluded parties themselves. What is more, these definitions of region lead to a reification of often organic processes, with the result, for example, that *in comparison* to other (Western) regions, the Asia Pacific is seen to suffer 'from an excess of rhetoric over reality'

(Buzan 1998, p. 85). In other words, autonomist notions of regionalisation provide a normative framework of inclusion and exclusion. With regard to inclusion, such 'natural' regional affiliation may induce 'a sense of solidarity', which is then instrumentalised to emphasise uniqueness or difference when compared with other regions (Wesley 1997, pp. 525–6). As far as exclusion is concerned, economic and political linkages may not provide sufficient justification for membership if 'cultural' attachments are used as criteria. In the case of ASEM, this issue has arisen most saliently with regard to Australian membership, which to date has been opposed by Prime Minister Mahathir of Malaysia on the grounds that Australia is not an 'Asian' country. This issue will be examined in more detail in Chapter 4. As these points suggest, autonomist renditions tend to reify the region and to argue that a sense of 'regionness' will only derive from the organic coincidence of interests and needs. In contrast, an 'integrating' approach to regionalisation introduces the possibility of actor-led, strategic region creation by heads of state and government and their representatives.

'Integrating' Regionalisation

Unlike autonomist regions, which resemble to some extent the above-mentioned notion of 'regionalisation', integrating regions issue from the amalgamation of collective voices joined in political expediency. In other words, regions from this perspective are created through intent, and represent constructions of 'collective human action' (Gamble and Payne 1996, p. 17). Neorealists and their neoliberal counterparts share this platform; for, while the first group of scholars analyses the role of national governments in the development of regional groupings (Moravcsik 1998; Sandholtz and Zysman 1989; Stone Sweet and Sandholtz 1997), the importance of leadership, from individuals, epistemic communities, non-governmental actors, states or regional institutions, and the successful establishment of inter-regional groupings (Cooper et al. 1993; Haas 1992; Higgott 1993; Young 1991), the second focuses upon the mediating role and utility of institutions in region formation.

Neorealist interpretations show how state representatives may choose the path of integration in order to advance individual state concerns and maximise rational actor interests. During the immediate post-World War Two years in Europe, for example, there were calls from within France and Germany to cooperate in the name of mutual economic reconstruction (in order to enjoy the fruits of the Marshall Plan as a member of Europe, and later as part of a legalised set of institutions in the form of the European Coal and Steel Community, ECSC, of 1951). These initiatives were based upon calculations that it would be in the national interest to pool resources.

Although Asia is not endowed with the same forms of regional arrangement as Europe, efforts to establish ASEAN in the late 1960s issued from mutual concerns over regional stability. Such integrating moves may also be imbued with ideological commitment; thus, during the cold war membership of the Non-Aligned Movement (NAM), or 'Western Europe' brought inherent responsibilities and directed at least certain aspects of foreign policy orientation. Each of these endeavours is a 'states-led project' whereby national interests recognise the benefits of cooperating in order to reduce transaction costs in the negotiation of specific issues (Gamble and Payne 1996, p. 2; Keohane et al. 1993, p. 175). In other words, regions represent the sum of interests of their constituted members, who themselves utilise regional structures as a means of building cooperative, defensive or aggressive systems (see Hveem 1999, p. 92). Region building in this form, then, is the direct result of political action, and institutions are the concrete outcome of political decisions (Hveem 1999, p. 101). The 'deepening' or 'widening' of those integrative processes may subsequently derive from the closer intentional collaboration of constituent members (Berger and Borer 1997; Hsuing 1993), or from (for example) a scramble for increased recognition in a 'kind of bidding war amongst Europe, Latin America and East Asia to engage US attention and commitment' (Buzan 1998, p. 85). Such developments may also, however, be interpreted – particularly by neoliberal institutionalists – as creating certain habits of collective behaviour, thereby facilitating anticipatory responses and permitting the extension of reciprocal cooperative actions over time (Keohane 1986, p. 2; Risse–Kappen 1996, p. 69). In this interpretation, regional mechanisms come to be viewed as a channel for the collective resolution of common problems (such as investment impediments), or as a socialising framework within which errant members can be brought into line with the dominant rules (Gamble and Payne 1996, p. 2). Some commentators have begun to transcend neorealist and neoliberal interpretations, to focus on how the process of regional interaction itself may in turn transform the nature of constituent members through deeper forms of socialisation. This aspect of development will be examined in the section on inter-regionalism. Both types of approach outlined here retain a focus on state agency, and regard regionalisation as a means of negotiating domestic (intra-state) demands against a background of changing external forces. One further approach places greater emphasis on the effects of those external factors.

'Defensive' Regionalisation

The term 'defensive' regionalisation shares with the two previous categories the understanding that regionalisation is at some level a response to globalisation. While autonomist and integrating forms of regionalisation may be regarded as organic or internal amalgamations of interests, the defensive form of regionalisation is seen to develop explicitly in response to the dynamic changes of the international system, particularly in response to the perceived effects of globalisation. To speak of globalisation is to speak in the vaguest terms about 'multiple levels of analysis: economics, politics, culture, and ideology' (Mittelman 1997, p. 2); and to combine within one portmanteau term a range of interpretations, from the complete dominance of transnational corporations (TNCs) in conjunction with market forces (Ohmae 1990), to an insistence that 'the world economy remains an *inter-national* system' (Hirst and Thompson 1995, p. 408). Nevertheless, these multi-headed approaches to a multi-headed set of phenomena tend to result in the conclusion that there are 'two distinct sets of processes at work in contemporary world politics: globalization and interstate interaction' (Armstrong 1998, p. 461), or indeed, that one has triumphed over the other; for, if globalisation succeeds, the nation state will become extinct, and if the nation state prevails, it will do so by assuming a global mantle (Hirst and Thompson 1995; Friedman 1993). In this framework, regions come to be regarded as a response to, or consequence of, globalising trends (Hettne et al. 1999; Fawcett and Hurrell 1995; Yeung et al. 1999), or as a stepping-stone to global processes, of which they are a 'manifestation' (Mitchell 1996, p. 340). As a result, regionalisation occupies more clearly than ever a mezzanine level between the local and the global: a foil or mediating mechanism for globalisation; or a space in which the tension between territorial-based politics and global economics is contested (Mittelman 1999, p. 34) or harmonised (Hettne et al. 1999, pp. xxi and 16). As Mittelman observes: 'Paradoxically, regionalism both shields domestic society from and integrates it into the global division of labor' (1997, p. 11), thereby offering a form of subsidiarity for new global realities (Falk 1999, p. 241). In these ways, extant scholarship tends to locate globalisation at the apex of a hierarchy of interests which subsumes the region, the state level and substate actors at the lowest level (see Hirst and Thompson 1996; Bhagwati 1992). Buzan's view of the Asia Pacific as 'one element in the emergent structure of the post-Cold War global political economy' (1998, p. 79) is typical of the literature which seeks to locate (implicitly or explicitly) regionalisation as a response to, or outcome of, changing external conditions (see also Gamble and Payne 1996, p. 2; Fawcett and Hurrell 1995). Under global pressures, regionalisation is a process 'drawing states and groups together on the basis of their proximity both because of transport and information cost advantages and because of shared regional interests and ties' (Brook 1998, p. 231). In responding to globalisation, regions can be seen to be addressing specific issues (for example, a security region) or to be acting as a thoroughfare for national and global interaction. The overriding tendency of this approach is to regard it as a direct response to the international (sic) system, of which it will always remain a sub-system (Hettne et al. 1999, p. xv). For some observers, this is a positive development: 'Despite the difficulties that will arise, there is room for optimism that the new regionalism [will] lead to more effective, functional multilateralism leading eventually to rule-based governance of most international and inter-regional transactions' (Mistry 1999, p. 141). It may also be seen to act as a 'building bloc' to similar ends (Woolcock 1996, p. 115). Others are less sanguine, and view the inherent tensions of globalisation as likely to engender global conflict, setting region against region (Mittelman 1997, p. 17). Almost all of the current interest in regions is focused upon their role as a response to, or consequence of, globalising trends, with the result that regionalisation is a 'natural' step in the face of inexorable globalising dynamics or a conscious unit of resistance against its perceived evils (Hettne et al. 1999; Fawcett and Hurrell 1995; Yeung et al. 1999).

On the one hand, regionalisation is regarded as a stepping-stone on the road to addressing the inexorable process of globalisation. In this way, regionalisation offers larger units of resource – from global market competitor (EU, North American Free Trade Agreement (NAFTA), APEC, or the ASEAN Free Trade Area), to political voice (ARF, ASEAN, ASEM) – in the face of global forces against which the nation state can no longer compete alone. In particular, the changes in the system since the ending of the cold war have led some states to 'push for integration as a way of positioning themselves in response to global change' (Grugel and Hout 1999, p. 10). At the same time, external forces (such as the rapid flow of information resulting from globalisation) may quicken the pace of responsive independent processes and give rise to new social and political movements (Woods 2000, p. 3). As the distribution of power is seen to shift, regional coalitions are formed in order to redress or redefine power structures and counterbalance other equivalent regionalising forces. From this perspective, the example of ASEM may be read either as an attempt to balance the role of the US in the region (particularly as a result of the EU's being refused observer status to APEC) or as a structural necessity to develop the 'third side of the [EU–US–Asia] triangle'. This defensive posturing represents an attempt to claw back power in an increasingly diffuse international system. Moreover, by participating as members of larger (regional) units, states coalesce in a defensive attempt to balance their status within a changing international system. The examples of Germany and Japan as important regional forces are instructive in this regard. Similarly, power may reside either within the constituent member states (for example, consider the role of the US in APEC, or that of Germany in the EU), or else it may be held by a power balancer that lies outside the region (such as the shadowy role of the US with regard to

ASEM) (Buzan 1998, p. 72). Within Asia, for example, the regional roles played by Japan and China are often directed by exogenous influences, such as the US or global market conditions, while the role played by them within the regional context can be seen to serve either to stabilise or destabilise the whole regional enterprise. Within Europe, too, power may be held by regional entrepreneurs such as the European Commission, whose role may affect the regional participation of state members (Young 1999). While regionalisation may be regarded as a stepping-stone to globalisation, it may also be a stepping-stone needed to deal with the pot-holes along that road: 'In the absence of satisfactory global structures, the development of regional structures becomes salient' (Higgott 1999, p. 93). In other words, regionalisation fills (temporarily?) the gaps that globalisation has yet to address. In any of these guises, regionalisation may be characterised as a passive response to a changing international system (Keating 1997, p. 24).

On the other hand, regionalisation has also been seen as a challenge to globalisation, rather than merely a pragmatic response to it, and this observation goes some way to allowing us to question the hierarchy of levels imposed by much of the literature. In responding to globalisation, regions may be seen to coalesce as sites of resistance against its dark and pernicious forces: regional participants act collectively either to resist it or merely to survive (Chin and Mittelman 1997). Regional actors may be forced to harmonise trading rules in order to compete in a global market, to derail the inexorable forces of the global market, or to form a 'regional security system' in response to security threats that transcend national boundaries (Wriggins 1992, p. 7). This collective resistance serves to protect group members from becoming swallowed up by the 'ideology of globalization' (Cox 1997, p. 29). Taken further, the idea of regionalisation as a site of resistance enables us to introduce the notion of the 'politics of difference' against the fixing of identities (Calhoun 1998, p. 21; Jessop 1999). Moreover, it establishes the idea that regionalisation occurs as a result of an identification with an external force, or set of forces. In fact, the characteristics of 'region' are only presented in the face of other regions or significant others. These forces do not necessarily imply globalisation, but may also issue from interaction with other regional entities, as will be examined below. Unfortunately, these interpretations of globalisation share a tendency to divide state and global levels, with the effect that all that lies in between them is no more than a mezzanine level of state-global progression. In this way, many scholars omit to investigate the potential impact of regionalisation per se, and leave no room to account for the growth of inter-regionalism. Anyone with a concern with regionalisation, then, will see that it is frequently negated by the globalising process: it is no more than accessory or hindrance.

In the case of Asia–Europe relations, a structural triangular framework offers an even more convincing means of seeing the growth of regions in Asia and Europe as a necessary corollary to globalising trends. Indeed, for some observers, the Asia–Europe relationship '*must* be viewed in the light of the 'triangular' relationship between the EU, the USA and Japan' (Smith, H. 1998, p. 307, italics added; see also Bridges 1999b; Dent 1999a; and Hänggi 1999). In this categorisation, too, regions represent the intermediate level between the supra-structure of globalisation (which incorporates in its structure trilateralism), and the sub-structure of coalescing national forces, thereby hindering further serious debate over the nature of inter-regionalism per se. This chapter contends that regionalisation constitutes more than simply the 'co-hegemony' of trilateralism (Mittelman 1999, p. 46), and therefore disagrees with Mittelman's assertion that regionalisation represents 'but one component of globalization' (Mittelman 1996, p. 189). Rather, in taking a closer look at the level of region-to-region engagement, it is possible to examine how the impact of repeated human actions upon the structure within which they operate comes to affect both actor and structure within that process (Cox 1981). Mitchell has already observed that: 'Conceptualising regions as both being shaped by and, in turn, helping to determine world order allows regions to be incorporated more systematically into recent political economy debates' (Mitchell 1996, p. 341). But what he and others fail to do is to acknowledge the potential impact of having to behave as a region in order to interact with other, seemingly like, regions. Within the globalisation literature, there is a sense that 'globalization involves a social and institutional restructuring that is largely internal to the states in question' (Richards and Kirkpatrick 1999, p. 689), and that examining 'hierarchies of spaces or social relations of production' may be of greater utility than focusing on state–state relations (Mitchell 1996, p. 339). Mitchell concludes as a result that regions are 'co-determined by processes and social forces that operate transnationally and by the organisation of national communities' (1996, p. 340). But by stopping here he neglects to examine fully the role of ideational aspects of region formation, which place a greater emphasis upon the role of social interaction in defining regions. And of particular importance for our focus is the role of social interaction *qua* region with what is perceived as another region. This section has illustrated that regionalisation itself is a contested phenomenon, whose parameters are not always apparent and whose derivation is often regarded to be self-evident. The case of inter-regionalism tends to be neglected, or regarded as a form of 'double regionalisation' or 'supra-regionalisation', locating two similar entities side-by-side or subsuming them within a greater region-like structure. The sections which follow contend that, for regionalisation and inter-regionalism alike, it is important to identify the process of interaction itself as constitutive of the type of arrangement produced.

INTER-REGIONALISM

Asia and Europe are two regions which now meet regularly – as regions – within ASEM, in which they are recognised as equals. Such bold assertions require us to suspend our belief in the evident reality that 'Asia' and 'Europe' are, in fact, distinct and in many respects incomparable notions of collectivity built on different sets of socio-economic and political histories. Ideas of 'Asia' and 'Europe' within the ASEM process are replete with notions of equality and assumed boundaries of regionhood. To date, the focus of interest on ASEM has centred upon identifying a 'cluster of relationships' that derives from indigenous responses to global phenomena (Maull et al. 1998, p. xiv). Growing attention to the inter-regional forum has precipitated confident statements about the nature of 'Asia': 'For the first time in the modern era, Asia is emerging as a *distinct regional state system* – a cluster of strong, prosperous, independent nations dealing intensively and continuously with one another in diplomatic, strategic and economic matters' (Friedberg 2000, p. 147, italics added; see also Mittelman 1996, p. 194). It is a truism to note that inter-regionalism presupposes the existence of regions. Seen as a socio-political construct, however, inter-regionalism may also shape the very nature of its constituent regions, while they, in turn, influence the terms of mutual engagement. Adapting Armstrong's definition, inter-regionalism may be understood as the ongoing reiteration of a 'set of shared cognitive, normative and juridical assumptions among [regions] that emerge from their social interaction' (Armstrong 1998, p. 469). While a habit of cooperation may derive in the first instance from decisions taken by regional representatives to communicate with one another over particular issues (Glarbo 1999, pp. 635–6), the communicative channels and patterns of behaviour established as part of that process may themselves affect one region's view of itself and the other. In concrete terms, then, what is understood by 'region' in the context of Asia–Europe relations will depend to a large extent upon how Asian and European participants view themselves and each other within, and as a result of, the process of interaction. Within this process, typificatory labels will become attributed both to self and other, and over time will be reciprocated (Glarbo 1999, p. 637; Wendt 1992, p. 405). Simply put, Asia and Europe will come to see each other in a particular light through the process of mutual interaction. It would be more appropriate to inscribe inter-regionalism into Calhoun's acknowledgement of a changing global environment, in which different groups of actors have to 'face the modern challenge of deciding how to fit into projects of collective and individual identity that presuppose inscription in a multiplicity of often incommensurable identity schemes' (Calhoun 1998, p. 12). Through inter-regional actions, moreover, each 'region' becomes a reflexive agent that both constitutes and is constituted by, its inter-regional interaction and its ongoing 'externalisation' within this forum (Scholte 1993, pp. 69–70). While inter-regionalism may represent only part of today's complex jigsaw puzzle, it nevertheless remains an important missing piece.

Framing Asia and Europe

If 'what is Europe?' has become a frequently asked question, then 'what is Asia?' is even more problematic, given that part of its nature is formed through how Europe (as a perceived 'developed' region) interacts with it. In this framework, (East) Asian regionalisation continues to be labelled as the 'least well advanced' region, thereby demonstrating the teleological assumptions underpinning accounts of regionalisation as a (successful or failing) transition to the European model. Auguring ill for understanding regionalisation within Asia and Europe alike, this approach de-problematises the competing discourses which vie for dominance within and among their co-existent narratives of region, and de-historicises the universes inhabited by both sets of actors. Unfortunately, the laudable inter-regional efforts of ASEM to date tend to be premised upon both de-historicised notions of interaction and unproblematised conceptions of 'region': to wit, the 'Asia' and 'Europe' of the process and the ways in which it came about have been systematically neglected in order that short-term political expediency might obtain under a veil of natural progression. At the same time, ASEM tends to be examined through state-centric, rational-actor perspectives, which are most keenly articulated in notions of trilateralism, whereby Asia–Europe relations form only the 'weak link' when compared with US–Europe and US–Asia linkages in a global system. Inter-regionalism, in this view, is no more than the sum of state responses to changing global conditions. All of these conventional views deny the role played by inter-regionalism itself in shaping and reshaping the nature of its constituent regions. A continued insistence that Asia and Europe interact only in the context of a triangle, or in reaction to globalisation, leads only to fixed notions of Europe-as-completed-region and Asia-as-imperfect region, and ignores the constant renegotiation of self and other that takes place below this superficial veneer. What is more, the cognitive learning that derives from mutual interaction leads to an ongoing renegotiation of initial assumptions of region. Asia, within ASEM, then, is formed and reformed by post-colonialism, European Community (EC) and EU integration modelling, a desire to keep the US involved in the region in the light of changing global structures and the constant redefinition and reinforcement of 'Asian values', which cumulatively may 'alter preferences, create feelings of shared identity, stimulate the development of norms and encourage cooperative behaviour' (Harris 2000, pp. 500-503).

A focus on the level of inter-regionalism per se is important for a number of reasons. First, rather than comparing forms of regionalisation with inappropriate tools, this study establishes a means of understanding the meta-level of inter-regional interaction, which allows for the continual reshaping and redefinition of both sets of participants, and of their constant reassertion of regionness. After all, the state system is exactly that: one state has an identity in the face of other recognisable 'states'. Second, a focus on interaction between Asia and Europe eradicates the notion that successful Asian region building will necessarily imply emulation of the EU. In practice, the EU may act as a counter region or anti-model. Third, countering observations of inter-regionalism as a stepping-stone between state and global levels of interaction (Higgott 1999, p. 94; Mistry 1999, p. 152; Richards and Kirkpatrick 1999, p. 688), inter-regionalism needs to be confronted as a locale in its own right (cf. Hettne et al. 1999, p. xxii). Fourth, inter-regionalism offers an additional level of interaction on which the notion of region itself is most keenly felt. Thus, despite their very different histories, Asia and Europe come to be known through this process as certain types of regions. One typification may also spill over into other fields of activity. In the case of the EU, the treaties laid down elsewhere by its member states (most recently in Amsterdam in 1997 and Nice in 2000) also form many of the foundations for the ways in which it behaves, as a region, towards Asia. For its part, the process of interacting as a region within ASEM has strengthened calls within Asia for a similarly constituted response to other issues, from a revitalisation of the EAEC to the establishment of a single Asian currency. The notion of the 'Asian Ten' has become important in this regard. At ASEM 1 (in 1996) the flimsy label of 'Asia' was introduced, but by ASEM 2 in 1998 it had become embedded to the extent that it was utilised both to criticise and address the responses to the regional financial crises by its significant (European) other. In so doing, participants from Asia and Europe now bring to their inter-regional encounter 'a set of pre-conceptions from which [they] set out to reconstruct other articulations' (Diez 1999, p. 607). Fifth, the inter-regional framework of ASEM enables each partner to perceive a 'like' region in their mutual conversations. This level of interaction has been largely neglected in the midst of these varied approaches to regionalisation and globalisation, or has been casually dismissed (cf. Hänggi 1998; Richards and Kirkpatrick 1999). Work incorporating the role of inter-regional groupings tends to examine the supra- and sub-structures of globalisation and region building, rather than analyse the potential impact of inter-regionalism itself (Cooper et al. 1993; Haas 1992; Higgott 1993; Young 1991). Moreover, as noted above, inter-regionalism comes to be seen merely as a phase towards globalisation, or the sum of two or more regions interacting; while regions themselves are frequently deployed as tangible and concrete expressions of identity with universal applicability. These approaches ignore the possibility that inter-regionalism can – as a process – contribute to the (re)creation of notions of how 'Asia' and 'Europe' are intended (see Diez 1999, p. 605). Not only is this level important for the development of mutual notions of 'region' which then become political and economic tools for negotiation, but it also serves to inform the options that may be mobilised in building mutual historical experiences into the behaviour of actors which are acting *as* regions. From this vantage point, the debate over globalisation outlined above prevents us from seeing how the discourse of globalisation serves to reinforce notions of region, by generating and sustaining novel intersubjectivities (Rosamond 1999, p. 653). In other words, 'Europe' and 'Asia' are not real, but become embedded as regions within a dominant discourse of contemporary global affairs. Such reification not only distinguishes Asia from Europe (as is clear in the case of human rights, market deregulation and so on, where Asian versus Western values tend to be defined), but also serves to create a sense of 'us' in the face of an identifiable 'them' (for the failings of such dichotomies, see Rodan and Hewison 1996, p. 31), with potentially disastrous consequences (Huntington 1993). The previous sections began to suggest that it is time to move away from regarding inter-regionalism as simply the sum of two regionalising entities facing global conditions. In the case of Asia–Europe relations, accepted interpretations of region-to-region encounters tend to conclude, apparently incontrovertibly, that 'Europe' is an advanced region, while Asia still has a considerable way to go. The consequence of this division is that the EU tends to be proffered as the (highly integrated, Western, legalistic) measure against which other (consensual, Asian) regional projects are (de)valued (Ravenhill 1998, p. 267), so that other pathways to regional identification are neither acceptable nor considered.

THE PROCESS OF INTERACTION

It has been suggested that regionalisation itself is a process: from state recognition of the need and possibility to reduce transaction costs and maximise structural power within the region, to institutional dynamics which create space for cooperation and the means of imposing sanctions for unacceptable conduct, and on to the creation of an intersubjective community derived from a mutually trodden historical, discursive and interactive path. In an inter-regional setting, this process takes place simultaneously with the creation of self and other, through the interaction of one region with a significant 'other'. The process of interaction itself, therefore, needs to be construed as a distinct level of analysis (Wendt 1999, p. 147). Such cognitive interpretations facilitate an assessment of the level of learning achievable through interaction, and are able to account for an actor's own capacity to reshape the structure in which he/she works. This interpretation paves the way for the possibility that the region may become a space in which supplementary loyalties obtain. This (often referred to as a 'constructivist') approach incorporates ideas and interests as factors endogenous to interaction, with the result that people act towards objects according to their understandings of the meaning of those objects. Based on theories of structuration, actors are seen to reproduce normative structures and change them by their very practice (Ruggie 1998, p. 99). Thus, interaction may be understood as 'the stories that social actors tell, and by which, in the process, they come to define themselves or to construct their identities and perceive conditions that promote and/or mitigate the possibility for future change' (Chin and Mittelman 1997, p. 32). Viewed from this perspective, institutions may provide the social forum in which 'individual ideologies develop into shared, intersubjective, community conceptions of normality and deviance, which produce relatively consistent interpretations of the empirical world' (Klotz 1995, p. 32). In the final analysis, this perspective demonstrates how all knowledge – both of self and other – is socially derived. In the case of inter-regionalism, there are two key means for the projection of that knowledge: channels of communication and the perception of an 'other'.

Channelling Communication

The most obvious means of channelling communication among the participants of a region or at the inter-regional level is through institutions. This section explores how these are important but not the sole repositories of mutual cognition, and examines how the very process of interaction itself has the potential to affect both the nature and constituents of that interaction. In these ways, the channels of communication involved refer to both physical and cognitive processes of engagement.

There is much confusion about associating regions with specific institutions. Institutions may represent the hinge upon which regional identity rests; thus, ASEAN may be regarded as the voice of Southeast Asia, and the EU has become increasingly synonymous with the very idea of Europe (to the extent that much of the British press, representatives of a reluctant EU member state, cast aspersions on an evil 'Europe'); while the briefest glance at the list of abbreviations in this book shows the growing proliferation of regional and sub-regional institutions. Institutions are understood here as regularised channels of communication among state representatives acting in accordance with obligations set out in treaties or declarations (such as ASEM, APEC and the ARF) and not necessarily enshrined in physical locations, such as headquarters (like the EU and the United Nations (UN)). Through their structures, regions become politicised and their identities become internalised among constituent members, and are recognised as such even beyond their boundaries. In this way, institutions delineate the borders between insiders and outsiders. At the same time, regional institutions, often unproblematically acknowledged as such, are themselves seen to 'define issues, mobilise resources, provide differential access, mediate interests [and] implement policy' (Keating 1997, p. 35). Furthermore, they may function in a way that mediates 'processes of thought and decision [and] processes of action' (March and Olsen 1989, p. 11). Like regions, themselves, then, institutions are hard to define. They are, nevertheless, important in aiding an understanding of where the locus of regional identification may lie: in the legally binding rules-based system of the EU, the various organs of the Union (especially the European Commission and the European Parliament (EP)) reify a *European* level of identity; at the same time, looser regional associations such as ASEAN or the ARF also co-opt their members to adopt collective patterns of behaviour. Structural constraints alone, however, will not adequately account for institutional development or deficit (Ravenhill 1998, p. 248), since they may also be affected by the discourse in which they are embedded. Ruggie offers three levels of institutionalisation which are useful for our purposes: the cognitive level (where epistemic communities lie); the level of mutual expectation (as embodied in rules and norms); and the level of formal international organisations (Ruggie 1998, p. 55). In other words, participants may recognise that they are part of a framework of mutual exchanges; these may or may not be based upon shared rules; and may or may not be embedded within formally organised structures. The first type may be seen in the EAEC set up by Malaysian Prime Minister Mahathir with a clear 'Asia for the Asians' agenda, thereby drawing on a shared sense of history (in the face of colonisation) and ethnicity (non-white, non-Western), in an attempt to fend off what he (and others in the region) perceive to be the Westernisation (especially Americanisation) of deeply-held Asian values and societal structures. The second type of institution is that represented by ASEAN and the ARF. While their formal institutional frameworks are loose, they nevertheless build up expectations of behaviour among members, to which all are supposed to adhere. Non-interference in domestic issues is a case in point. Finally, the EU and the UN embody the most formal structure of institution, endowed with physical headquarters and founding treaties, whereby membership requires adherence to the rules and non-adherence can lead to sanctions by the rest of the participants. These definitions suggest that, in addition to storing information for future reference and providing a template for interaction (see Higgott 1994, p. 373), institutional forms represent cumulative processes of self-identification in the face of internal dynamics and interaction with the 'outside', rather than simply 'givens'. To different degrees, then, institutions may establish mechanisms for interaction through which participants define and redefine their own identities (Katzenstein 1996, p. 17; Checkel 1999, p. 545). Institutions are more likely to consolidate group feelings when a group feels endangered by a common external threat or challenge. Contemporary debates over the validity of ASEAN, Western/US domination over the resolution of the financial crisis, and European inadequacy during the Balkan conflict can be seen to have precipitated moves to create the ASEAN+3, reassert an EAEC identity and propose a self-contained European defence force, respectively.

As the foregoing section suggests, the role of institutionalisation is to establish channels for mutual comprehension and communication among the actors of a region, by creating sustainable processes through which collective thinking comes to be (re)shaped and reciprocal typifications develop. Not only do institutions embody sets of principles and ideas, they also channel 'behavior in one direction rather than all others that are theoretically or empirically possible' (Ruggie 1998, p. 57). This is an important point; for, in embedding market principles, fundamental human rights and the requirement of reciprocity in its deeply rooted institutions, the EU appears to offer a dominant form of region. It should be remembered, however, that this is the embodiment of a choice from among a number of alternatives, which has been typified through the 'generative grammar' of Europe's own institutions (Ruggie 1998, p. 63). Matching the institutional and discursive parameters becomes an important part of legitimising a region and it therefore comes as no surprise that the European Commission made deliberate attempts after the 'relaunch' of the European Community during the mid-1980s to 'develop and confirm the existence of a European economic space whose territorial reach corresponds with the actual and potential boundaries of the EU' (Rosamond 1997, p. 14). In this way, an institution can be seen to express the 'natural' identity of a region and the normative superiority of one form of discourse over another. Moreover, once embedded in an institution, a region's identity comes to be informed by the public narrative it carries with it and which then speaks over the heads of its constituent individuals (Somers 1994, p. 619). This narrative element will be examined in the next section.

Through processes of interaction, norms of behaviour come to be established. For neorealists, norms codify relations originating in material conditions, and represent the result of decisions taken by rational actors. Neoliberals argue that states develop norms to facilitate cooperation and minimise transaction costs, while for regime theorists norms can cause behaviour that otherwise would have been unlikely. For constructivists, in a context where agent and structure are mutually constitutive, norms may provide structure and help to create identity, by defining the terms of interaction and the actors themselves (Flynn and Farrell 1999, p. 510). Flynn and Farrell go on to suggest that 'enabling' norms allow actions that otherwise would have been impossible, thus considering norms as a means of agency (1999, p. 511). Katzenstein identifies two types of norm: constitutive norms which 'specify actions that will cause relevant others to recognise and validate a particular identity and to respond to it appropriately'; and regulatory norms, which 'operate as standards for the proper enactment or deployment of a defined identity' (Katzenstein 1996, p. 54). While neorealists and neoliberals tend to focus upon the latter, constructivists and social learning theorists of other kinds emphasise in addition the role of the former. For this group, norms may be seen to represent 'shared (thus social) understandings of standards for behavior' (Klotz 1995, p. 14; see also Checkel 1999, p. 548), and collectively 'norms establish expectations about who the actors will be in a particular environment and about how these particular actors will behave' (Jepperson et al. 1996, p. 54). The process of interaction itself, then, leads actors to consider themselves as part of a 'we-group' that is created by, and reflected in, the existence of certain norms. Norms may be created by individuals, but will only be sustained through the process of social learning (Checkel 1999, p. 549). Norms emerge through a process of communication, and become embedded both through institutionalisation (Sikkink 1991, p. 2) and through the discourse in which they arise (Christiansen et al. 1999, p. 532). In this way, moreover, they provide a foundational 'framework of meaning' for participants bound by them (Dessler cited in Doty 1997, p. 376). Certain norms may undergo change, through individual agency or an alteration in structural conditions. For example, in the wake of the Charter of Paris of 1990 which altered the Peace of Westphalian tenet that the internal sovereignty of a state was beyond the reach of others, the norm of collective intervention became embedded increasingly in international and not just Western discourse (Flynn and Farrell 1999, p. 524). In a similar way, the norm of free market principles has become enshrined in the World Trade Organisation (WTO) and has led to some fundamental shifts in the nature of national economies (most notably that of China). What is more, whether opposed to it or not, the norm of 'human rights' has become part of the international dialogue which cannot be overlooked. Once norms become embedded as part of a narrative or dialogue, they act as the frame of reference in which each interlocutor locates his own identity. Thus, in the example of the EU, which has 'come to include shared norms, commonly accepted rules and decision-making procedures', the normative framework at the Union level has also come to influence its constituent states (Christiansen et al. 1999, p. 538). This shows how norms influence the choice of path for social learning, and that issues from both normative and discursive structures may lead to the development of new interests. By participating in an interactive process, a member comes to adopt the norms embedded in that process, even in other contexts if those normative structures are salient. These normative and institutionalised processes serve to enhance and develop social bonds, which come to be defined 'in terms of unity, exclusivity and boundlessness', rather than being 'givens' at the core of inter-regional relations (Devetak and Higgott 1999). Regionalisation, in the same way as globalisation, then, can be regarded as different groups which 'express themselves in a range of collective Imagineries' (Jameson and Masao 1998, p. xii). Moreover, rather than a fixed external structure, globalisation can be taken as a contested political concept (Gills 1997, p. 12; Rosamond 1999, pp. 652–3), or as the 'structural context' for a range of 'interrelated' processes (Jessop 1999, pp. 19 and 23). If we can readjust our sights in this way, to view globalisation as encompassing a wide range of discourses which help to reify Europe and Asia as 'regions', it becomes possible to see power not only as the ability to set agendas, but also to impose the very terms of interaction.

Understanding processes of communication, then, is important for demonstrating how Asia–Europe relations come to represent a contest over what 'regions' are. On the one hand, 'Europe' may occupy a dominant position due to its institutionalised global stature as a region, but on the other 'Asia' may coalesce in the face of such dominance to reinterpret its own regional space and to create an alternative regional discourse (for example, through an assertion of 'Asian values'). Such power structures can only come into being through interaction itself: in the same way as the state is in part defined by its *inter-national* existence (Hirst and Thompson 1995, p. 410), the regions of Asia and Europe will in part be constituted through their *inter-regional* engagement. By analysing the discursive power of regionalisation it becomes clear that, just as states are '"socially constructed" in the course of their international relations' (Armstrong 1998, p. 472), regions, too, are constructed by their own interaction with a similar other, namely a region. Indeed, to use Berger and Luckmann's analogy (1966), if primary socialisation issues from the internationalisation of regionness, its secondary mode derives from the learning and construction of new modalities of regionness (see Armstrong 1998, p. 473). These are addressed below.

SELF AND OTHER

This section examines the very nature and (re)formation of self within the process of interaction with an other. The EU, for example, may come to be regarded as being more than simply an 'intercultural dialogue in which the culturally diverse sovereign citizens of contemporary societies negotiate agreements on their forms of association over time and in accordance with three conventions of mutual recognition, consent and cultural continuity' (Shaw 1999, p. 580). Rather, the very nature of the interacting cultures may themselves change through the process of engaging in inter-cultural dialogue, in which existing rules, identities and interests may be altered (Dunne 1995, p. 372). Scholte's words of warning are useful: 'Identity is always *en route* rather than *rooted*, and it "must be continually assumed and immediately called into question"' (1996, p. 69).

In the case of Asia–Europe relations, an inter-regional dialogue can only take place if the self can identify an other with whom to communicate. On the one hand, self/other analyses can lead to a dichotomy of Asia as the opposite of Europe, and vice versa. In this way, the ASEM discursive framework can be seen to posit an oligarchical Asian self against a capitalist European other. On the other hand, however, the very process of interaction in a bilateral and global context may be seen to shape and reshape the nature of both self and other. This is the more interesting examination to make: why, even if they reject the discourse, do Asian states such as those of ASEAN and China have to negotiate human rights issues with Europe? Why are the states of Asia forced to liberalise their economies? That is not to say that they react solely to a European discourse: the picture is far more complex, and confuses global, regional and national narratives. But the Asia–Europe engagement freezes a moment of that discursive confluence, to demonstrate that we are dealing with more than simply one pre-existing region interacting with another. The Asia–Europe framework sets up a discursive and normative set of boundaries within which a distinguishable and parallel 'other' exists, and which in turn will influence the (re)formation of self. In many ways the views of that 'other' help to define how Asians act within ASEM.

Wendt, in a familiar constructivist refrain, observes that the structure of any social system comprises its material conditions, interests and ideas, which all interpenetrate one another (1999, p. 139). In this way, interaction – unlike in neorealist or neoliberal analyses – exists at a distinct level of analysis between unit and structure, since agent and structure are mutually constituted by that interaction (Kratochwil 2000, p. 82). This underpinning also allows us to examine inter-regional level interaction as a distinct unit of enquiry, and to underscore the impact of self and mutual perception as a result of the process of engagement. The inclusion of ideas in any interpretation of regions enables one also to view the existence of social order 'only as a product of human activity' (Scholte 1993, p. 70), in that the construction of a given reality is the outcome of an actor's view of it (Hewitt 1997, p. 15). At the same time, such ideational structures also delimit the boundaries of the region: 'if social systems are not simply "there" but arise as the result of construction, then one of the interesting questions is that of the boundaries of such systems' (Kratochwil 2000, p. 96).[2] As one bounded entity comes into contact with another, a pool of recognition and knowledge comes into being at the level where the interaction occurs (Wendt 1999, p. 160), with the result that, for example, 'Europe' and 'Asia' come to recognise each other as such in particular forms (the EU and the 'Asian Ten'). Indeed, Scholte demonstrates how identity derives from the 'reciprocal typification of habitualized actions by types of actors' and stresses that the social order is a human product, or, more precisely, an ongoing human production, and that agent and other are mutually constitutive (Scholte 1993, p. 72). This mutual perception derives from both endogenous moments of representation, and from the creation of regional Imaginaries as an alternative or supplemental form of collective identity in the face of what are often regarded as the homogenising processes of globalisation (Scholte 1996, p. 39). Not only, then, does a 'multiplicity of often incommensurable identity schemes' derive from the need for collective and individual identities to contend with contemporary global conditions (Calhoun 1998, p. 12), but, in addition, the comprehension and identification of self is a result of the ways in which such identity schemes are enacted.

By simply locating Asia and Europe side-by-side as like 'regions', there is a tendency among scholars to 'mis-locate the "Other"' (Somers 1994, p. 610), by regarding inter-regionalism merely as either supra-regionalism or a tool for globalisation. The effect of such an interpretation is to see European integration as a 'stronger' form of region, and to conclude that Asia–Europe relations rest on the 'weak side of the triangle', thereby setting up normative frameworks which posit as inferior 'Asian regionalism' and as superior US–Europe and US–Asia relations, respectively. Such unproblematic assertions negate the struggles over 'narrations' which constantly define and redefine identity, as one group of 'normatively valued forms of symbolic representation' come to predominate (Somers 1994, p. 630). If the EU's integration process symbolises 'regionalisation', then Asia will only ever offer an imperfect or incomplete form of region until such a time as it resembles that in Europe. What is more, when such narratives of regionness become embedded in Asia, then it, too, will reflect its own identification through the same lens as a result of these 'representational silences' (Somers 1994, p. 630). In order to explode such silences, it is important to see how discourses embed themselves through the process of interaction, and how the identification of *difference* influences intersubjective understandings at the inter-regional level. The foregoing discussion has already acknowledged implicitly that a fundamental part of one's identity derives from the juxtaposition of self with an other (Chatterjee 1991, p. 522). It is useful first of all to question how ideas and narratives become normatively bound in the first place, because a dominant discourse is one that comes to be adopted from a range of possible discourses and which brings with it the power to produce subject identities (see Diez 1999, p. 603). Part of the role of discourse is to facilitate conversation; thus, 'Asia' and 'Europe' cannot communicate with one another without enabling mutual translatability (Diez 1999, p. 607). This is not a question of languages, but the question of finding a common set of understandings upon which to base a conversation: 'In their common use of language, persons enter a system that already contains the objects one can speak about and the relationships one can invoke' (Shapiro 1981, p. 132). What is more, the adoption (or not) of this language signifies opposition and inclusion, as will become clear below.

Analyses of regions that issue from IR and IPE perspectives rarely take into account the formative role of regions as significant others (Berger and Luckmann 1966, p. 117). Closer scrutiny of identity formation is provided by the work of Anderson and Adler: the former's 'imagined communities' provide us with a useful point of departure, from which to observe that collectivities are artificial or social constructions underpinned by the (trans)formative role of ideas (Anderson 1983); while Adler, for his part, examines how community-building takes place as a process of social construction among individuals, states and international organisations, which collectively create intersubjective knowledge and a shared sense of identity (1997, p. 250). From these beginnings, moreover, 'intersubjective structures' may form at the inter-regional level, and through interaction actors may try to project and sustain images of self. Thus, 'by engaging in cooperative behavior, an actor will gradually change its own beliefs about who it is, helping to internalize a new identity for itself' (Wendt 1994, p. 390).

As part of that interaction, identity is established in relation to difference (Connolly 1991, p. 64). Indeed, the 'need for recognition – to define oneself (or who one wants to become) and to have that identity acknowledged by others – is a first-order preoccupation in social relations' (Scholte 1996, p. 40). Crucial to this project, then, is the delineation of difference, since identity formation involves the creation of '"others"' whose actuality is always subject to the continuous interpretation and re-interpretation of their differences from "us"' (Said 1995, p. 332). In other words, self cannot exist without an other, 'since self-interest presupposes an other' (Wendt 1994, p. 386). Indeed, the definition of region turns on both self recognition and recognition by others, particularly by another perceived region (Calhoun

1998, p. 20). Participants of Region A, by definition, find something in common by distinguishing themselves from members of Region B (Cohen 1985, p. 12). As Taylor notes: 'A self can never be described without reference to those who surround it' (1989, p. 35). As A and B engage over time, A will inadvertently appropriate B's reiterated roles and model his own role-playing (Berger and Luckmann 1966, p. 74). In the case of inter-regionalism, the pertinent 'significant other' is the other region (Searle 1995, p. 127).[3] In Said's words: 'The construction of identity involves establishing opposites and 'others' whose actuality is always subject to the continuous interpretation and re-interpretation of their differences from "us"' (1995, pp. 227 and 332). Such accounts define no pre-existing phenomena, but encapsulate definitions of self and other as taking place through the very act or process of engagement (Kratochwil 1989). Adding to Berger's assertion that social processes engage actors in a constant interaction with each other and particular social conditions in a dialectical social structure (cited in Neumann 1999, p. 13), it is important to probe the ways in which the constituency of self is determined and altered by these social processes. As practices of interaction continue, ideas and understandings of self and other are constantly formed and reformed, to the extent that without the other the self would be incomprehensible, since that other 'clothes us in comprehensibility' (Sampson 1993, p. 106). This passage to comprehensibility, however, is far from smooth; for, in their mutual interaction, regions encounter one another in a 'zone of contestation' in which dominant discourses may be asserted (Rosamond 1999, p. 653). This level of activity supplements the contest over, for example, globalisation in the form of the spread of neoliberal discourse and economic liberalisation, which may result in either a shared knowledge framework for 'both' participants or region-to-region contestation. In addition, such a contest results in the use of cultural values as 'myths' 'to legitimate a certain political order while at the same time portraying others as lacking legitimacy because they do not appear to resonate with certain cultural "givens"' (Lawson 1996, p. 108).

The 'other' may be determined in a number of ways, and Mead's (1934) categories offer a useful point of departure: historical others; real others (with which we are dealing in the present); imagined others (what would other 'regions' do?) and a generalised other (the abstract addressee reflecting our particular group). This section focuses on the latter two categories, as they are embodied in the self as reflection and self as identity-through-interaction, and they represent the significant others which influence the identification of self. First, interaction with an other or others may cause reflected appraisals, or mirroring, by which route the inscription of otherness (for example as foreigner, or inferior) serves to identify the inscriber. In this way, too, notions such as 'enemy' represent an other which does not recognise the right of self to be autonomous; rather, self in this way becomes identified through a process of differentiation with an other. One region may therefore be influenced by the dominant discourse of another region, as exemplified in Western as opposed to Asian, and in 'crony' versus 'legitimate' forms of capitalism: 'the social space of inside/outside is both made possible by and helps constitute a moral space of superior/inferior' (Campbell 1998, p. 73). At the same time, values identified with the other may be appropriated by self, to the point where the self/other nexus may even come to blur distinctions between them. This formulation evokes Said's analysis of the Orient, which, he notes, 'is an integral part of European material civilization and culture' (1995, p. 2). In constructing this self/other nexus, Said brings into question the binary opposition that makes east more east and west more west (1995, p. 46), and enables us instead to see how Orientalism produces the occident as a 'reversed image, looking-glass wonderland' (Lindstrom 1996, p. 34). These interpretations, linking notions of East and West as part of one history, eschew the kind of dichotomous assumption that views the West's past as the rest's present (Sardar et al. 1993, p. 85).

Self and other come to be mutually defined within a routinised boundary, or 'locale' (Giddens 1984, p. 170). As the self-actor engages with the other, this interaction in turn creates a self-receptor, or sense of 'we-ness'. In the case of ASEM, Asia acts as Asia for the purpose of engaging with the EU, and in the process of that interaction is responded to as though its interlocutor is responding to 'Asia', thereby reinforcing a sense of communal identity among a group not previously constituted for any other purpose. These processes strengthen the sense of resistance to any who would then counter it, as can be seen not only in Mahathir's regional proposals, but also in the now frequent calls for regional economic cooperation (see Chapter 3). In this way the region is 'essentialising' its regionness (see Lindstrom 1996, p. 34). As the sense of 'we-ness' increases, moreover, the collectivity may improve its ability to choose which self to project, by developing its own discourse of region. This presupposes an essentialist rendition of self, which posits an internal coherence developed in response to, but existing even in the absence of interaction with, an other. Thus, the EU retains the dominant discursive authority by which to influence the nature of Asian regionalisation. However, if we return to the level of interaction itself, the EU too will (re)define its own sense of we-ness in the context of its inter-regional dialogue with the significant other of 'Asia'. The modus operandi of the ASEM process (based as it is on non-European foundations) suggests that Asia cannot simply be dismissed as the weaker partner. By this interpretation self, in Searle's inimical words, is an institutional rather than brute fact, cocktail party and not mountain. In other words, it cannot exist without being thought or acted into existence. It is then authority over these narratives rather than any essential power, which enables one self to dominate another at a given moment.

The engagement of self with other, then, represents more than an engagement of different symbolic universes (Berger and Luckmann 1967, p. 125); rather, a significant other (re)defines the very notion of self. What is more, once the significant other and self are mutually aligned, the sense of otherness may serve to engender a stronger feeling of 'we-ness' (Berger and Luckmann 1966, p. 117). The mutual interaction of self and other in this way becomes a mechanism for self reinforcement. At the same time, the sense of inter-group distinction may also come to be matched by discursively present notions of intra-group homogeneity. Moreover, within a field of shared relevance the promotion of salient identities can lead to in-group essentialism, thereby imputing in a non-essential entity an essential discourse. Those portrayals may embed inferior we-images vis-à-vis the other, or by the same token the process of interaction may result in more even power ratios, which can then lead to challenges against perceived inequalities (themselves arising from the process of self-other identification). Thus, when 'Asia' encounters 'Europe', it is forced (by Europe's superior discursive power within this bilateral relationship) to confront the burden of European regionness, in the face of which Asia appears weak, or incomplete. In response, Asia may embrace the European discourse and form a mirror image of the European self, or else set itself up in opposition to it. Similarly, the EU responds to the other of APEC, by reinforcing its own boundaries of self. Camroux and Lechervy observe how regions 'serve to structure the evolving nature of other regions' (1996, p. 450). Those identities and interests will not necessarily remain static, but will continue to be influenced by the presence of the other as well as by the growing internal conviction that a collective 'we' in the case of (say) ASEM can become the dominant 'we' for all aspects of external ('Asian') interaction (Wendt 1994, p. 386).

Definitions of self are reinforced by the application of a putative or reinterpreted past: 'We thus encounter the paradox that, although the re-assertion of community is made necessary by contemporary circumstances, it is often accomplished through precisely those idioms which these circumstances threaten with redundancy' (Cohen 1985, p. 99). In this way, tradition is invented to bring gravitas to the legitimacy of the region. Asian 'values', therefore, draw upon a collective response to Europe which is founded on a putative superior past, and which is written into its present collective discourse. At the same time, the constant reiteration of self in the face of an other provides an important regionalising dynamic among a choice of alternative formulations of region. Interaction with a significant other thereby embeds through discourse the most authoritative narrative (see Rosamond 1997, pp. 6 and 11).

DISCOURSES OF INTER-REGIONALISM

The processes of mediating self and other are directed by the interpretation of symbols, which are rooted most potently in language, and conducted through speech acts. Discursive acts of signification constantly recreate the self which is undergoing them, by providing performative utterances ('I declare war'; 'The meeting is adjourned'), which create the very state of affairs they represent. Using Searle's analogy once again, institutional facts can only exist in relation to other facts, and are themselves represented to one another through language, and especially through labels. At the same time, those linguistic forms are partly constitutive of the facts themselves. This represents politics through discourse, not the politics of discourse. In order for language to be transmitted between self and other, a shared relevance field must come into existence, in order to provide the 'public reality' within which regions can talk to one another *qua* regions. The public reality of the cold war, for example, shaped and sustained the language frames, so that according to Anderson, the cold war began the 'imaginery' of Southeast Asia that it continues today (1991, 1998). Globalisation provides a similar function in the post-cold war era. Asia and Europe have a number of relevance fields and are mutually constituted through recourse to globalisation, to trilateralism, to proliferating regionalisation, and to inter-regionalism. These discursive structures not only set up interlocking belief sets and common knowledge, but are also integral to the shaping of self and other.

We do not begin with two distinct discourses of 'Asian' versus 'European' (or 'Western'), since, for example, the very idea of 'Asia' is in part embedded by and in Western discourses. However, bringing together two distinct forms as it does within its institutional boundaries, ASEM necessitates an Asian response to Western questioning, and (to a lesser extent) vice versa. Since the rhetoric and discourse of 'Europe' is embedded within internationally reaching institutions such as the European Commission, and as Europe through the EU becomes increasingly a 'vehicle for the elucidation of reflexive narratives' (Rosamond 1997, p. 15), Europe currently holds a relatively dominant discursive framework. Much of Asia's own discursive activity does, indeed, tend to be set in opposition to that Western discourse which it sees as a threat, although some commentators discern a salience in the discursive power of Asia. While it is inaccurate to speak of 'Asia' as a coherent and clearly definable entity, collective actions have led to the development of a clearer 'Asian' identity over specific issues and towards particular audiences. For example, Higgott notes the emergence of an 'intra-regional mobilizing agent' to represent collective interests to the outside world (1994, p. 368). What Higgott fails to examine, however, is the way in which a discourse of 'Asia' (in his case 'Asia Pacific') is also mobilised through interaction as a region in a global arena. As well as serving to carve out identity, discourse also creates spaces across a range of actors and issues. Lobby groups in the EU, for example, know the value of going to the European Commission and the EP to air their concerns, rather than to member states, since the public that its narrative reaches is so much broader. At the same time, discourses may also captivate several interest areas within one field; so that an Asia–Europe dialogue can take place simultaneously across a range of economic, political and cultural zones and yet all be considered part of the ASEM narrative. As noted above, rival narratives, of globalisation and sub-regionalism for example, are concurrent with this process and serve both to challenge and reinforce dominant discourses. Discourses, then, bring with them the power to define both self and other through mutual typifications (Weldes et al. 1999, p. 18). Examples from Asia and Europe illustrate how 'comforting' notions of Confucian Asia and Christian Europe both legitimise and hinder change (Maull et al. 1998, p. 48). On the 'Asian' side, Mahathir exemplifies such usage: 'We on the Asian side of the Pacific are permanent neighbours. Surely the neighbours themselves should have more right than others to determine how they wish to relate to each other in economic, security and political matters, for now and for the future' (cited in Palmujoki 1997, p. 278). Mahathir embeds through his rhetoric a clearly delineated 'them' versus 'us' agenda. In economic relations, these myths are used even more prominently, particularly through recourse to the idea of Asia–Europe relations as the third side of the triangle of contemporary economic affairs (with the US at its apex). The creation of self perception therefore derives from a dominant sense of 'we-ness' at any given time, drawn from the multiplicity of self. In this way, one discourse gains authority over others. Inter-regionalism, then, is more than an extension of the analysis of regions, and cannot simply be reduced to its core nation-state participants. It represents instead the continual re-negotiation through mutual engagement of self and other in the form of mutual regional recognition. In so doing, it elicits an additional emergent discourse that arises from the rapprochement of entities which come to know themselves mutually as regions. Thus, a region is what a region thinks itself to be within the context of a symbolic set of inter-regional dynamics. It is worth observing, therefore, that 'rival reflexivities' may indeed arise within a given locale (Rosamond 1997, p. 17), that each region has a 'multiperspectival polity' (Kowert 1998, p. 107), and that, therefore, a sense of 'we-ness' can arise for a given locale and may or may not be transferred to other instances of collective response (Adler 1997, p. 255).

Summarising the Debate

This theoretical debate is important for a number of reasons. First, the view that asserts Asian 'success' or 'failure', or measures Asian region building against that of the EU, beguiles the observer into believing that the 'foundations of community building in a globalising world are shifted from exclusionary sameness to inclusionary diversity' (Scholte 1993, p. 70), that regionalisation is simply a response to globalisation (Mittelman 1996), or to changed political preferences (Mattli 1999, pp. 3–7), that the three levels of 'global co-operative processes, regional institutions like the EU, and the traditional national level' are the only channels through which to espy regionalism and, by simple extension, inter-regionalism (Coleman and Underhill 1998, p. 4). In these ways, regions are reified to the extent that the EU offers one ideal model. Second, all causes and origins of regional activity come to be subsumed within a discourse of atomistic self-seeking regionalisation-from-below or imposed regionalisation-from-above as necessitated by globalisation. Finally, looking at Asia–Europe relations in this way moves away from a rather static notion of trilateralism and instead interprets developments within the 'bilateral' relationship itself. In summary, the forces of inter-regional confluence may include not only levels of regional integration (and, indeed, may not even be influenced by these) but also the depth and extent of inter-regional history, and other shared characteristics. In addition, external forces (such as perceived globalisation and trilateralism) may serve as a spur to create either new sites of resistance through collective leverage creation or else as a facilitator of globalising processes with a view to obtaining a (re)distribution of wealth through the pooling of resources designed to tap into global markets. In this respect, globalisation may indeed also offer the normative framework within which inter-regionalism can legitimate itself. But it is not fixed; rather, globalisation is observed to represent a politically contested space within the socially contested and historically open nature of all political economy (Gill 1997, p. 13).

CONCLUSION

Inter-regionalism, then, is considered here to represent more than an intermediary of the state versus the global, in which elements of statehood (territoriality, loyalty, exclusivity, monopoly of legitimate force) come to be pitted against the 'market' (which itself necessitates functional integration, contract and increased interdependence between buyers and sellers, facilitated by autonomous economic agents). In acting as part of an inter-regional engagement, a region denotes itself and its interlocutor as such, and is in turn recognised as a region by that same interlocutor. By simply examining Asia and Europe at a regional level of theory we are destined to conclude that they are – forever – innately different. However, at the level of inter-regionalism their differences become woven into the network of inter-regionalism, and – for the purpose of the inter-regional exchange at least – each participating side *is* a region. In other words, the very perception of one 'region' by another may affect their respective conceptions of both self and other. These perceptions are obtained through the continual processes of interaction, in which each region constantly (re)enacts its regional role. In addition to the valuable insights into the interplay of political and economic activity underlined by the different forms of regionalisation examined above, then, the level of communication and interaction between self and other itself becomes important. The aim of the remaining chapters in this book is to demonstrate that inter-regional channels of communication are not merely the socio-political 'cement that mitigates self-interest and opportunism' (Maull et al. 1998, p. 98), but that they represent the very means by which self-interest and self are in part determined.

The consideration of inter-regionalism as an independent unit of analysis is important for the examination of Asia–Europe relations, for a number of reasons. First, it dissuades the observer from treading what has become an almost ritualistic path towards trilateralism, by investigating more closely the distinct contribution to the relationship made by mutual interaction. Second, it removes the need to compare (unfavourably or artificially) 'Asia' and 'Europe', prior to assessing their region-to-region engagements, so that in fact regionalisation comes to be understood as a part of the inter-regionalism process, and vice versa. Third, on a policy level it is important to find an 'alternative way of conceiving and advancing Europe's Asian policy' (Richards and Kirkpatrick 1999, p. 704), by disentangling ourselves from received notions of what 'Asia' is and how it can – therefore – be expected to behave. Fourth, Asia's responses to Europe cannot simply be determined by the level of integration within the EU itself, because elements of perception through interaction also serve to inform opinion at a regional level. As was illustrated above to be the case with regionalisation, there are a number of ways to approach the study of inter-regionalism: from state-centric neorealism, to a more nuanced form of political economy, to ideational perspectives. The foregoing section advances a combined approach, which enables the observer to locate inter-regional meetings within their historical, intra-regional, systemic and perceptual frames of reference and to regard them as a *process* rather than fixed set of identifying symbols. The chapters that follow adopt this approach to examine the particular aspects of political, economic and cultural activities undertaken by Asia and Europe to date. Prior

Concepts of Inter-Regionalism

to them, the next chapter sketches the ways in which 'Asia' and 'Europe' have been perceived since 1945.

Notes

1. The categories of 'autonomist', 'integrating' and 'defensive' regions are drawn from Keating (1997, p. 24), but do not necessarily conform to his definitions of them.
2. While Wendt retains in his study the key functions of the state, and Onuf signals the importance of rules in creating such ideas (Onuf 1985; and see Kubálková 1998, p. 20), other constructivists depart from state-centred accounts in order to problematise explicitly the constitution of both interests and identities (Rosamond 1997, p. 10).
3. Note that some regard significant others, without defining them (Armstrong 1998, p. 474).

2.   East is East...

'Behold there the degeneracy of the East,' said the doctor, pointing to
Mattu, who was doubling himself up like a caterpillar and uttering grateful
whines. 'Look at the wretchedness of hiss limbs. The calves of hiss legs are
not so thick ass an Englishman's wrists. Look at hiss abjectness and
servility. Look at hiss ignorance – such ignorance ass iss not known in
Europe outside a home for mental defectives. Once I asked Mattu to tell me
hiss age. "Sahib," he said, "I believe that I am ten years old." How can you
pretend, Mr Flory, that you are not the natural superior of such creatures?'.
'Poor old Mattu, the uprush of modern progress seems to have missed him
somehow,' Flory said, throwing another four-anna piece over the rail. 'Go
on, Mattu, spend that on booze. Be as degenerate as you can. It all
postpones Utopia.' (George Orwell, *Burmese Days*)

Since their sixteenth-century forays into 'the East', European missionaries,
traders and colonisers have repeatedly impressed the mark of their own
excellence upon the minds and societal structures of their ignominious
charges. In short, until the postwar era, Asia was available to satisfy a
European yearning for raw materials, markets and power. From a broadly
Asian perspective, white Europeans introduced trading opportunities, but
often at the ultimate price of subjugation. From the middle of the nineteenth
century (and particularly following the Opium War of 1840–42), Europe's
Great Powers were to hold sway over the economic and political lives of
many of the peoples of Asia. Japan saw in their model the only means of
advancement and emulated their economic developments and territorial
expansion, in an attempt to avoid the possibility that it, too, would be
colonised. Gross stereotypes issue from the disparate engagements which
were to follow: during the twentieth century Europe became the locus of
industrialising greatness and global territorial embrace, the home of
distinguished and despised colonial masters, the headquarters of the victors of
a protracted war across two continents, and the site of an integrating
community of huge economic proportions and international political
pretensions; Asia, as is often noted, entertains no such region-wide identity,
but its name evokes a spread of colonised lands, of national and sub-regional

tensions, of the collective 'flying geese' momentum towards unprecedented and rapid economic change, and of a 1997 financial crisis whose severity has been compared to the Wall Street Crash of 1929. Even in a post-cold war era, attempts at Asia–Europe engagement continue to implicate many of the fragile myths of bygone colonial days. This chapter aims to examine how contemporary modes of exchange among representatives of Asia and Europe build upon these experiences of the recent past, constantly to refine and redefine mutual images of region-hood. It seeks not to provide a history of relations (for that, see Lach 1965), but rather to identify the roots of mutual recognition today, and to illustrate the complex nature of region-to-region relations at the start of the twenty-first century.

Chapter 1 illustrated how notions of 'Asia' and 'Europe' are no more or less than creations adapted to the needs of the political leader, the traveller, the historian or the observer. For, notwithstanding geographical, political and economic boundaries, reified as they might be in treaties, constitutions or agreements, how a region is defined will always be historically contingent and politically contestable. This chapter examines some of the changing ideas that have supported the labels 'Europe' and 'Asia' during the past 150 years. Specifically, it analyses the development of colonial and post-colonial identities, the growth of inter-continental engagements during the 1960s and 1970s, and the new and identifiable discursive universe of ASEM, which frames interactions between the legally bound region of the EU and the recognisable 'other' of the so-called 'Asian Ten'. This rendition of Europe–Asia relations, as will be demonstrated, delimits the boundaries of intra- and extra-regional dynamics by invoking elaborate and often mythical memories of a shared (colonial) past. In the light of the distinction made between 'self' and 'other' in Chapter 1, this chapter offers a brief survey of the ways in which ideas of 'region' within both Asia and Europe have been developed, consolidated and challenged since the end of World War Two, before examining how mutual exchanges have contributed to regional identification, a theme which will be examined in greater detail in the chapters that follow.

COLONIAL FOOTPRINTS ACROSS ASIA

Colonialism is a label attributed to a panoply of Western government and business interventions into a region comprising different forms of states, and represents a phenomenon which gained salience during the latter half of the nineteenth century and continued beyond the end of World War Two. The 'varied and changing nature of the processes that operated' within the mantle of colonialism makes it undesirable to draw rigid conclusions about its forms and effects (Dixon 1991, p. 57), but that it left an overall significant impact is undeniable. Indeed, in several instances, for example, the colonisers themselves drew the very boundaries of the Asian modern state, such that the term 'Southeast Asia' itself originated under Lord Mountbatten's command (SarDesai 1997, p. 3). The internal dynamics and constitution of such labels may well have changed during the past half century, in parallel to the changing arrangement of 'Europe', but the legacies of the colonial interlude continue to weigh upon contemporary engagements among Asians and Europeans.

Before the most recent colonial period in Southeast Asia, trade within the region already involved a vast network of people and a wide variety of sought-after goods, especially spices such as pepper, ginger, cloves and nutmeg (Dixon 1991, p. 57). Indeed, it was these same spices which would lead the European powers (particularly the Dutch, British and French) more deeply into the region, as they sought to satisfy the need for territorial expansion to accommodate burgeoning trading interests. Reinforcing self and mutual justificatory schemas through recourse to 'Civilising Missions', 'Manifest Destiny' or 'the White Man's Burden', the Western colonial powers sought to gain taxes, and to impose legal, educational and local authority structures in line with their own national interests, in order to open up these countries and, among other things, 'to trade and plunder in the region' (Maull et al. 1998, p. 4). Following Spain and Portugal into the Asian region, but replacing missionary zeal with trade imperatives, Britain, the Netherlands and France came to divide the region up largely among themselves, and in so doing also set the terms of local negotiations. The British extended their interests – often through the East India Company – from India, China and Singapore into Burma, and took a much greater interest in Malaya when the Straits Settlement was transferred to the Colonial Office in 1867. For its part, the Dutch East India Company focused on coffee and other plantations on the Indonesian archipelago. Meanwhile, the French began their territorial conquests in the second half of the nineteenth century and came to occupy increasingly large tracts of Indochina, with their annexation of Cochinchina (namely, South Vietnam) in 1862, and the imposition of sovereignty over Cambodia and eventually over the whole of Vietnam between 1884 and 1885 (Colbert 1992). The Philippines, which had been conquered by the Spanish in 1521, were subsequently seized by the Americans and annexed in 1899. This transformation from traders to colonisers 'was both a reflection and part of the development of international capitalism, stimulated in particular by a British desire to gain access to the "backdoor of South-West China" and by the competition engendered by such ambitions' (Dixon 1991, p. 69). Japan was not colonised, but after 1854 opened its own borders to external traders in the form of the so-called 'unequal treaties' with the US, Great Britain, France and Russia, a precedent which had been established by the British with their victory over the Qing dynasty in China during the Opium War of 1840–42. They provided for the Western powers tariff, trading and extra-territorial concessions, left little negotiating strategy on the Asian side, and were replicated in the Anglo-Thai Treaty of 1855, the 1862 and 1867 treaties between Great Britain and Myanmar, and the 1962 treaty between France and Cochinchina. The changes wrought upon the local populations by these Western impositions should not be underestimated. While the production of luxury products continued, a growing trend towards lower-value products occurred, which included teak and tin, coconuts and rice, alongside new products such as oil and rubber (Dixon 1991, p. 85). In order to fulfill the capitalist aspirations of the colonial powers in the region, many of the local infrastructures also had to be changed, and the region came to be incorporated into the world economy, an experience that 'altered the pattern of development, created deep divisions between territories and markedly uneven development at all levels' (Dixon 1991, p. 121).

Japan's position was anomalous within the region, but was to have significant repercussions for post-colonial movements. At the end of the nineteenth century, the revocation of the unequal treaties with Japan gave succour to Tokyo's own colonial pretensions. By its victory over China in 1895, Japan gained, inter alia, the island of Formosa (later known as Taiwan), while Korea became a Japanese protectorate in 1905 and was fully annexed in 1910. Although it was ultimately to prove futile, Japan's invasion and occupation of huge tracts of East Asia and the Pacific from 1941, conducted in the name of regaining 'Asia for the Asiatics' and in order to create a 'Greater East Asia Co-Prosperity Sphere', bequeathed a legacy of Asian defiance in the face of returning European colonial powers. In this way, Japan fostered an (albeit imperfect and self-seeking) recognition of an 'Asian' level of interest in the face of European colonialism: the 'enemy' without provided a powerful stimulus to a growing sense of identification within. As a result, returning Western powers after 1945 were faced with the choice of conceding independence (as the US did to the Philippines in 1946) or sustaining long and bloody wars which they would not win (as the French did in Vietnam and the Dutch did in Indonesia). Japan's own colonial practices served to fuel this sentiment in two ways: by training military and intellectual élites to resist European domination and thereby to destroy the myth of European invincibility (Bridges 1999b, p. 13); and by prompting a collective anti-Japanese movement within and among those countries being treated most harshly. Modern nationalist movements in Asia were formulated and implemented under these two mutually reinforcing influences of resistance to colonial powers and growing sense of self identity, stimulated by indigenous nationalist movements. On the one hand, European colonialism had been vanquished by an Asian power, a fact that set the scene for the fracturing of European universalistic reasoning. On the other, departing masters had left in many places modern education, economic and legal systems, efficient infrastructures, and even the European philosophical ideas which were to contribute to the basis of nationalist reasoning in much of Asia. The effects of such legacies were not invariably positive; for example, the British system in Malay segregated Malays from Chinese and Indians in school and thereby precipitated the rise of localised forms of nationalism after the war; the colonisers left the region as a group of sealed units with poor (if any) infrastructure and communications among one another; and the disparities in wealth creation from region to region grew where, as in Java, colonial policies 'locked' the majority of the rural population into the highly subsistent rice sector (Dixon 1991, p. 130).

POSTWAR NATIONALISMS

Following the Japanese surrender on 14 August 1945, the US military occupied Japanese soil; Korea was divided; Cambodia and Laos were left in search of alliances with great powers; fighting would still continue between nationalists and communists in China and between the Vietminh and the French in Vietnam; and the very formation of Indonesia and Malaysia was still to occur. Although taking radically different trajectories, they all, nevertheless, had to contend with finding a route to development and national identity creation or reinforcement, an experience which ensured that between 1946 and 1958 'the formal colonial structure in South East Asia was effectively dismantled' (Dixon 1991, p. 138). The creation or re-emphasis of nationalism is not, of course, a uniform process that is easy to pinpoint. Representing as it does 'complex webs of culture, economic necessity, political choice, experience and expectations' (Farrands 1996, p. 6), the trend towards nationalism revealed 'essentially a collective concept which addresses the ways in which those individuals can be understood to be identified with, or to identify themselves with, a national entity' (Youngs 1996, p. 25). This process of collective identification issued from a confluence of domestically, regionally and internationally generated factors that hindered or facilitated the development of an 'Asian' response to external power, as well as to internal tensions and cooperation.

Domestic Concerns

The bilingually instructed élites within the region's colonies all had to contend with 'models of nation, nation-ness, and nationalism distilled from the turbulent, chaotic experiences of more than a century of American and European history' (Anderson 1991, p. 140). These foreign structures served to shape many of the economic and political infrastructures of nascent nationalism, while many of the rifts between party political, ideological or ethnic standpoints issued from the colonial experience itself. As Godement observes: 'the relative balance between the nationalists and the communists was often determined, or unwittingly influenced by the uncertainty of the British, Dutch and French colonial polices' (1997, p. 86). For example, the departure of the Japanese from the Dutch East Indies left behind a potent mix of communist, Islamic and nationalist forces which ensured that Sukarno and Hatta's nationalist proclamation of an Indonesian Republic in September 1945 would not go uncontested. Similarly, a British attempt to promote independence in Malaya through a proposed Malayan Union in 1946 was rejected by the ethnic Malays (particularly the newly formed United Malays National Organisation, UMNO), so long as equal citizenship was proffered to the Chinese and Indian communities. The ensuing armed struggle led the British to declare in the new Federation of Malaya a state of emergency in 1948 (which officially lasted until 1960), and the way was finally paved towards municipal elections and subsequent independence in 1957 only when the Malayan Chinese Association, comprising non-communist Chinese, allied with UMNO. Even once the majority Chinese Singaporeans had left the new Malaysian union in 1965, continued discrimination by the dominant Malays (*bumiputras* or 'sons of the soil') against the Chinese and Indian minorities within Malaysia led to racial riots during the following years. In Singapore, the socialist David Marshall, who managed the city-state's transition towards independence after 1955, was ultimately defeated in the 1959 election by Lee Kuan Yew's new Political Action Party (PAP) which had united with pro-communist forces and trade unions. In Burma, a formal transfer of power and the creation of the Republic of the Union of Burma with the adoption of formal independence in January 1948 came at the cost of the assassination of Aung San and six of his colleagues in July 1947. In China, nationalists and communists famously struggled against each other until 1949, when Mao Zedong took power on the mainland and nationalist leader Chiang Kai-shek fled to Taiwan. These developments had to be negotiated at an internal domestic level, while mutual recognition came through a cadre of leaders who shared similar backgrounds in their respective struggles towards post-colonialism.

Many of these domestic battles for power raged around a core group of strong and charismatic leaders, who were able to incarnate ideas of national identity. The leaders who had fought against, or even collaborated with, their colonial masters during the war were an important asset to the birth and re-establishment of nationalist movements. For the most part, they instituted a variety of forms of authoritarian rule. In Indonesia, President Sukarno's 'Guided Democracy' gave way to the growing authoritarianism of Suharto's New Order. Lee Kuan Yew in Singapore retained power through his terms in office, so that even following his replacement as prime minister by Goh Chok Tong in November 1990, he remained in the influential position of 'senior minister'. Lee's strong personality clashed between 1963 and 1965 with the equally towering figure of Malaysian leader Tunku Abdul Rahman, with the result that Singapore's presence within Malaysia could no longer be sustained. The Malaysian leader himself suppressed communist insurrection and outlawed the Communist Party, increasing his authoritarian grip as UMNO continued to dominate the Barisan Nasional (National Front) umbrella party. The party's leadership was taken over by Dr Mahathir bin Mohamad in July 1981, who in turn became a dominant voice, both for Malaysia and for the region. In China, Mao's authoritarianism led to mass campaigns of control of the individual and to the suppression of opposition voices of all kinds. His Hundred Flowers Campaign between April and June 1957 ostensibly welcomed the articulation of dissenting voices but ultimately used the exposure to crush them. The death toll from his 1958–61 Great Leap Forward, a massive but misguided plan for industrial and agricultural transformation, was to be much greater, when between 13 and 30 million people died as a result of famine and poor harvests caused by Mao's planning (Godement 1997, p. 123). Equally confusing, and bringing with it a death toll of approximately one million people, Mao's Cultural Revolution between 1966 and 1971 was a similar exercise in misplaced authoritarian power. His era only ended with his death in September 1976, when Deng Xiaoping began (especially after 1979) to instigate major reforms. Kim Il Sung's power in North Korea (1945–94) was spurred by Chinese nationalist example and based on a brutal strategy of eliminating all rivals through violence. In Vietnam, while Diem's nepotistic corruption and growing alienation from his own people contributed to his downfall, Ho Chi Minh endured by sheer hero cult in the North, in spite of the harsh conditions borne by the people he governed. Meanwhile, the small country of Cambodia kept its neighbours at bay in part through the charismatic and energetic diplomacy of Prince Sihanouk. And the rather gentle autocracy of oil-wealthy Brunei, which would only regain full independence from the British in 1984, continued and continues to eschew political rights in favour of a high standard of living and welfare. Although the Philippines began after the war with a form of democracy, they too were to be overwhelmed by a powerful, centralising and greedy leader in the person of President Ferdinand Marcos, who imposed martial law between September 1972 and January 1981, and whose political opponent, Benigno Aquino, was assassinated on 21 August 1983. Only when Aquino's wife (Corazon) took over and fought elections against Marcos in

1986, did the latter finally flee to the US. Drawing on experiences of Western education – in Europe, the US and Russia – by staging their national struggles these leaders launched a simultaneous, if not consciously collective, attack on everything that colonialism had represented.

Although rarely presenting their individual struggles in the name of an Asian consciousness, these leaders created two important impressions: from a Western perspective they were regarded as a group that needed collectively to be steered clear of the path of communism; and among their number voices gathered to articulate an alternative voice, as occurred at the Bandung conference (Indonesia) in 1955. As an attempt to reject association with ideological or economic Western modes of development and to avoid being locked into the cold war framework, Bandung offered a collective neutral stance. China pledged progressive neutrality, while the Indonesian host and his Burmese counterpart advocated non-alignment within the region. The spread of ideas from Japanese colonialism, Chinese communism and alternative paths such as that of neutralism as set by Nehru, all suggested that Asia, too, could present a united regional front in the face of continuing cold war tensions. In reality, however, continued bilateral links to the superpowers and different ideological positions among their own number ensured that within Asia there did not exist one clear alternative path to development. More pressing international matters were to consume domestic and regional attention, as will be illustrated below.

The path of development taken by each country during the postwar era depended to a large extent initially upon the remnants left in the wake of colonialism. Thailand, which had not been physically occupied, integrated itself into the international community immediately, promoted regional cooperation and sealed its fate through close alliance with the US. Japan, occupied only after the war by American Allied forces, was set upon a rapid economic development trajectory and locked into a defense alliance with the Western superpower. The Philippines, too, were dependent both economically as well as militarily on the US, which provided preferential tariffs on the export of a number of agricultural products. The Philippines Trade Act, passed by the US in 1946, provided reciprocal free trade until 1954, and the peso was tied to the US dollar for the same period. Since the 1960s, Singapore's phenomenal economic growth has ensured its transformation to a major manufacturing and financial and banking centre, and by the mid-1990s it had become (according to per capita income) one of the ten richest countries. This, too, was facilitated by US assistance and later by close economic ties with Malaysia. Thus, while the ending of the European colonial moment was to see a break with much of the political dependence of Asian nations, it was neither possible nor desirable to curtail economic involvement (Maull et al. 1998, p. 5). Some countries, such as

China, North Korea and Vietnam, followed (successfully for a time at least) Soviet models of economic planning. Mao stabilised China's economy and set to work on an industrialisation programme, while in 1954 Kim Il Sung introduced his own *juche* (self sufficiency) policy. In North Korea, the first five-year plan lasted from 1953 to 1957, and transformed the countryside by increasing the standard of living and through the rapid collectivisation of agriculture from 1955. South Korea, although still playing catch-up with the North during the 1960s, was to outstrip its counterpart once it started to follow Japan's economic model closely. Following a coup in Indonesia in 1965, Suharto replaced Sukarno and introduced his New Order, which focused on economic development and the end of the resource-wasteful *konfrontasi* against Malaysia. The ending of this campaign also brought to the fore the regional role of Malaysia, as it sought to develop closer ties to Indonesia and moved towards alignment within ASEAN (Yahuda 1997, pp. 70–71). These bilateral links with the superpowers made it difficult and undesirable to follow a specifically 'Asian' path towards development. Indeed, interest in Asian economic development was to be stimulated much later, as a result of the opening of the Chinese economy to Western capitalism from 1979, Soviet premier Gorbachev's *perestroika*, massive investment into Vietnam after 1987, the trend towards normalising relations with the West (for example, between the US and Vietnam in 1995), and the deepening of collective ASEAN policy making. The removal of cold war bonds and the staggering economic growth within Asia precipitated external interest in the phenomenon of the 'East Asian miracle'. The effects of such economic developments upon relations with Europe will be examined in Chapter 3.

In addition to strong leadership and tangible infrastructural legacies from the colonial period, the different nations of the region espoused their own unique brand of national identity, built not only upon the immediate past of colonialism, but also upon mythical historical foundations of nationhood and Asianness in particular forms. Enshrined in its 1945 constitution, Indonesia's *Pancasila* was founded on: a belief in one god, humanitarianism, national unity, consensual democracy and social justice, and came gradually to be linked with the 'traditional' values of the country. In Thailand after 1948, the military regime gained a unifying legitimacy in the semi-divine 'Lord of Life' figure of the king, who has been used consistently as a symbol of 'national unity' (SarDesai 1997, pp. 253–4 and 275). In Myanmar, U Nu tried to revive Buddhism as a cohesive force in the face of divided minorities which had been excluded by the British, along with his 1952 plan of transforming his country into a *pyidawtha*, or 'land of happiness'. The failure of this attempt was to lead to the imposition of military government after 1962 (under Ne Win and his Burma Socialist Program Party) and the official path of the 'Burmese Way of Socialism'. These examples demonstrate the importance of embedding a 'history' even into the new states of the region. These rhetorical commitments to the nation accompanied almost all attempts at change and development, and demonstrate that nationalism (like regionalisation) is in many ways dependent upon the social practices of actors *behaving as if* they were doing so in the 'national interest', and being recognised by other similar units as such. In this way, external nations were important in providing a mirror or counter in the face of which to create and hold up images of the 'self': 'Nationhood has thus generally involved complementary assertions and suppressions of identities, whereby the elevation of one construction of the self has entailed the marginalisation and silencing of others' (Scholte 1996, p. 43). In this process of recognising oneself among others, moreover, the growing idea of the 'region' also has a part to play, since 'forms of identity are not simply the result of a social process, they also contribute to social processes' (Farrands 1996, p. 17). Actors such as Mahathir with his 'Look East' policy, for an inclusive, non-Western, Asian community, draw upon imagined regional commonalities. It is not the purpose of this book to examine the role of the various nationalisms that took root in Asia in the postwar period, but it is important to recall that the turmoil over national identity continues to be played out alongside simultaneous regionalising trends.

Regional Concerns

During the early postwar decades, there was no great overarching Asian project to match the ECSC of the 1950s, and mutual support within the region arose only sporadically, and over a number of specific issues. When Sukarno sought to remove the Dutch from West Irian in the early 1960s, for example, he was supported by almost all Asian countries (excluding Taiwan but including China). However, this achievement spurred him to try and prevent the formation of the Federation of Malaysia, and he instigated a *konfrontasi* against Malaysia from 1963–6, moves which would not ensure popularity for Indonesia within its own region (Yahuda 1997, p. 33). As a result, Indonesia's dependency upon the Soviet Union grew. Other examples replicate this pattern of confrontation and dispute rather than cooperation, and are highlighted most acutely in the tortuous negotiations over the establishment of Malaysia. By 1960, there were discussions with the British (then negotiating independence for Singapore) concerning Malaya's possible merger with Singapore, Sarawak and Borneo (then not independent) within a Federation of Malaysia. This was duly established on 31 August 1963, and included an uneasy mix of Malay and Chinese populations. This combination fragmented further after Singapore was expelled from the Union in 1965 and became an independent state. As for Malaysia, the new government of Abdul

Razak (1970–76) marked a break with the British, through the promotion of non-alignment and the signature of a range of bilateral defence arrangements in November 1971, with Britain, but also with Australia, New Zealand and Singapore. Malaysia, under Abdul Rahman and later Mahathir, has in fact shown itself favourable to regional cooperation, in an attempt to reduce dependence upon external powers. Its government has consistently promoted the ending of alliances with external powers in conjunction with a treaty of non-aggression and the declaration of a policy of non-intervention, which was to become a key principle within ASEAN, too (SarDesai 1997, p. 288). From his 'Look East' policy – calling for a rejection of Western influences in favour of Japanese and South Korean examples for development – to his proposal for an East Asian Economic Grouping (EAEG, later the EAEC), Mahathir has been especially vociferous in encouraging an Asian network in the face of collective Western criticism, and in championing 'Asian values' (Chan 1998; Mahathir 1999; Milner 2000). Within other parts of Asia, cooperation has progressed through bilateral exchanges and interest, such as the good relations developed between Singapore and China, particularly since the introduction of Deng Xiaoping's open door policies at the end of the 1970s. For its part, at the end of the war Thailand promised the return of territories to Burma and Malaya, and, later, gave up territories to Vietnam and Laos. Thailand also participated in the Manila Pact with the US in 1954 and Bangkok became the headquarters of the Southeast Asian Treaty Organisation (SEATO) when it was set up in 1954. In this way, Thailand, too, was quickly integrated into regional activities. At the same time, however, territorial disputes ensured that suspicion continued to dog attempts at cooperation: most notably, events in Vietnam in 1975 affected regional stability and left China chary of Vietnam's intentions towards Laos and Cambodia. Cambodia and Laos, for their part, had little to contribute to any development of Asian regionalism, concerned as they were not to become embroiled in other countries' territorial disputes and not to be absorbed territorially themselves. Once it seemed clear that the NLF (National Liberation Front) would triumph in Vietnam, Sihanouk made relations with China and Vietnam's communists the central plank of his foreign policy, but as the North's guerilla group, the Khmer Rouge, moved further into Cambodia itself, Sihanouk moved back towards the US. The US, however, was to precipitate a civil war in the country during Sihanouk's exile (1970–75), by invading Cambodia in order to attack Vietnamese communists based there. Subsequently, the Khmer Rouge would not end their fighting and instead brought down the Cambodian regime and renamed the country the Democratic Republic of Kampuchea in 1975. When Hanoi joined COMECON and agreed to a friendship treaty with Moscow, an emboldened Vietnam invaded and occupied Cambodia in December 1978 and renamed it the People's Republic of Kampuchea, further exacerbating tensions on the China-Vietnam borders and provoking a futile Chinese attack into North Vietnam in February 1980 (Yahuda 1997, p. 89). Laos was also drawn into regional conflict, when it was used as part of the Ho Chi Minh trail during the second Indo-China war.

If these are the 'local' difficulties faced by regional states, there were also attempts at greater regional cooperation through institutional initiatives such as SEATO in 1954, although in fact this organisation (which included US membership) represented a clear attempt to promote American military strategy in the region. The most important institution in terms of promoting regional identity was and remains ASEAN. This will be dealt with in more detail in Chapters 3 and 4, but it should be noted here that its establishment drew together a number of different national interests. In Indonesia, Suharto took seriously preparations for joining the organisation, while for Malaysia (also a founder member) it is within this process that it ended its dispute over Sabah with the Philippines in 1977. Singapore has also been a committed member of ASEAN, which gives it regional leverage, and Brunei was admitted to ASEAN as its sixth member in 1984. Brunei holds great store by this membership, which it regards as a way of resolving potential disputes with its large neighbours, especially Malaysia and Indonesia (SarDesai 1997, p. 309). In political terms, closer ASEAN cooperation was sought following the communist victory in Indochina in April 1975 and subsequent concerns over the potential military might of Vietnam. Fears of communist uprisings in Thailand and Malaysia led to the Declaration of ASEAN Concord and Treaty of Amity and Concord at the Bali summit of 1976. In this case, intra-regional differences were subordinated as a result of the need for unity, and ASEAN joint positions within international meetings became commonplace, and even military cooperation was pursued (Colbert 1992, pp. 250–51).

In 1971, members of ASEAN decided to establish a Zone of Peace, Freedom and Neutrality (ZOPFAN) in Southeast Asia, following the idea raised by Prime Minister Tunku Abdul Rahman of Malaysia a year earlier. This zone pledged efforts to exclude external influence and advance peace and stability in Southeast Asia, and served as a useful means of identifying ASEAN with the NAM. Such cooperative measures would also form the basis for other initiatives, such as the establishment of the ASEAN Post-Ministerial Conference (PMC), the ARF (see Chapter 4) and the December 1995 signature of the treaty creating a Southeast Asia Nuclear Weapons Free Zone (SEANWFZ), designed to prohibit the manufacture, possession and use of nuclear weapons in the region. Such proliferating moves towards peaceful cooperation sit uneasily alongside a rapidly burgeoning arms trade in the region. In the economic field, too, ASEAN often acts as a bloc, and is involved in attracting investment from the US, Europe and Japan, while consolidating regional economic arrangements through the 1992 proposal for the ASEAN Free Trade Area (AFTA, see below). In this way, its engagement in economic issues now accompanies its political role. This has been precipitated by the changing international system in which the Asian region functions, as will be examined in the chapters that follow.

International Concerns

The principal arena for the origins of the cold war was Europe. Nevertheless, many of the countries of Asia would be implicated either directly or indirectly in this bipolar confrontation, with the result that neutralism as an option could for most of them be no more than a chimera (see below). Indirect effects on Asia include the de facto involvement of one or other of the superpowers in the economic and political developments of certain Asian countries after 1945. Having lost the chance to secure China as an ally in the region, the US pinned its anti-communist hopes on Japan. Prime Minister Yoshida's 'doctrine' of an economics-first policy ensured that the 1951 security treaty with the United States locked Japan into the defence strategy of the US for the whole of the cold war period, and that Japan (like Germany) after 1947 would become a key part of Washington's regional strategy. In addition, until its revision in 1960, US forces could even be used to quell disturbances within Japan itself, and thereby 'prevent the election of an anti-American government in mainland Japan' (Hook et al. 2001, p. 137). For Japan's neighbours, this relationship has also had the effect of keeping Japan from re-igniting its militarist past (Drifte 1998a; Iokibe 1998). Other countries, too, were locked into the American side by their earlier association with Washington. The Philippines were granted independence on 4 July 1946, but continued to rely on funds and assistance for the development of their democratic structures, and hosted several US bases on their islands until the US closed their final base at Subic Bay in 1991. Thailand was also dependent on the US, being headed initially by a former minister to Washington and sending a contingent of troops to help the US in the Korean War. The US also used their influence against the Dutch, and persuaded them to leave the Dutch East Indies, lest frustrated nationalism should turn to rampant communism in that country. International negotiations towards a settlement culminated in the formation of the Republic of the United States of Indonesia (initially under the auspices of the United Nations) in December 1949. President Eisenhower, fearing that his 'domino theory' (downfall of one government to communism would trigger others) would prevail in the region, locked the US into a number of strategic arrangements: with the Philippines in August 1951; Australia, New Zealand and Japan in September 1951; Korea in October 1953; and Taiwan in December 1954.

Stalin ruled until his death in 1953, and, like his American counterparts, was concerned mainly with Europe. Nevertheless, Russia was party to the Potsdam declaration of 26 July 1945, calling for Japanese surrender (in spite of the April 1941 Japanese-Russian neutrality pact) and on 8 August declared war on Japan. Agreements elsewhere ensured that Lon Nol in Cambodia was backed by the Soviets until their representatives were driven out by the Khmer Rouge in 1975, while Vietnam was pushed more closely towards ASEAN only after the collapse of the USSR in 1991 meant the loss of Soviet support there. Not only was the presence in the region of Soviet troops or Soviet-sponsored troops important, but the spread of communism served to unite a number of ideological and political positions (Godement 1997, p. 114). China, North Korea, North Vietnam (and later the whole of Vietnam), and after 1975 Cambodia and Laos all saw the rise of communism within their borders, albeit with particular national adaptations. At first, these disparate forms of communism were acceptable to the Soviet Union, and indeed the conference at Bandung in 1955 was in many ways an expression of the harmony of those differences, all shaded beneath the umbrella of neutralism. But the rift between China and the Soviet Union after 1956 was to have profound effects on Asian collectivity. This period, in which rapid economic success gave China the confidence to live without the tutelage of the Soviet Union, itself undergoing unwanted changes by Khrushchev, saw Mao take more and more decisions independently of Moscow. Within the region, the model of a united communist front presented by the 1950 Sino-Soviet Friendship Treaty was replaced by a search for new forms of Marxism and a tendency towards China's growing independent (and nuclear) position away from the USSR. The most direct involvement of the two superpowers in Asia came in the Korean and Indochina wars.

In North Korea Stalin soon established the People's Democratic Republic of Korea (created in November 1948) as a Soviet satellite state, and it was indeed Stalin's Far East Strategy that would lead to the Korean War from June 1950. Supported (even in the planning) by Stalin, and encouraged by Mao, Kim Il Sung's attack on the South on 25 June 1950 led the US to fear an Asian communist pandemic (Godement 1997, p. 108). In response, the US – under a UN flag – launched a successful counter-attack, but its decision to continue into the North prompted the Chinese to join the war in October 1950 (Yahuda 1997, p. 27). Not only did this war bring the large powers in a head-to-head situation in Korea, it also saw the loss of 54 000 American lives, 400 000 South Koreans, 600 000 North Koreans and one million Chinese between 1950 and 1953 (SarDesai 1997, p. 111).

The first Indochina war, which saw the Vietnamese (Vietminh) defeat the French at Dien Bien Phu in 1954, left a country divided along the 17th parallel between a communist north and anti-communist south. When the

NLF was established in South Vietnam in 1956, the US believed that, rather than a reaction to Diem's oppression, Hanoi's communist forces had infiltrated the South. On 2 August 1964 the North Vietnamese attack on the USS Maddox (engaged in espionage) in the name of breaking the twelve mile maritime boundary was all the excuse needed by President Lyndon Johnson (in search of re-election) to attack the north. Eventually, the prolonged US attack and the Tet Offensive by the NLF in the South in January 1968 engendered a debate in the US as to how to disengage from Vietnam. Even after the signature of the Paris Peace Accords in January 1973, however, a final offensive by the North in March 1975 (against which a post-Watergate US was unwilling and unable to respond) saw the taking of the south by Ho Chi Minh's troops and the launching in December that year of the reunification process. During this period, there was not tremendous regional support for the US, although the Philippines supplied bases and the Japanese, for similar reasons, largely supported their major US ally.

The 1978 Vietnamese invasion of Cambodia was to be aided by Russia in direct opposition against the Chinese. Pol Pot's genocidal Khmer Rouge had since 1975 begun to enter Vietnamese territory and Hanoi cut off diplomatic relations in December 1977. One year later, Vietnamese troops took Cambodia by force, and the failure of Chinese attempts to mobilise troops against them further emboldened the Vietnamese (Godement 1997, p. 260). Soviet aid for Vietnam continued to sustain the underdeveloped region until Gorbachev came to power in 1985, and only once it was forced to fend for itself did Vietnam, according to Godement, 'adopt pragmatic measures in order to save the economy' (1997, p. 263). Many years of diplomatic wrangling, confusion and procrastination finally ended in the Paris peace settlement of 1991: rapid and drastic economic transformations occurred and Vietnam became a rice exporter; Sino-Vietnamese relations improved somewhat; relations with ASEAN improved to the extent that Vietnam was admitted as a full member in 1995; and diplomatic relations with the US resumed (Godement 1997, p. 265). Within Cambodia, taken under the wing of the UN after 1991, Pol Pot continued to threaten to seize back control. Only as a result of the UN-monitored 1993 elections, to which the Cambodian rural populations turned out in spite of Khmer Rouge intimidation, was the regime given popular sanction to rule as a constitutional monarchy. Despite shaky foundations, closer relations with its neighbours and eventual membership of ASEAN in 1999 have brought Cambodia much closer into an Asian political and economic network, and, along with the demise of communism and the weakening of the Khmer Rouge, have engendered a stability that was previously unthinkable.

These 'hot' wars of Korea and Vietnam demonstrate Asia's increasing importance as an arena in which the US and USSR would play out many of their bipolar struggles. With the collapse of US-backed regimes in Indochina in 1975 communism peaked, a regional arms race intensified and the Soviet presence deepened as US land forces withdrew. Indeed, Godement notes that 1975 marked the apogee of Asian communism 'albeit amid total disunity' (1997, p. 115). It was only the sustaining presence of the Soviet Union that would enable the troubles in Cambodia to continue, and the ending of the cold war changed the whole regional map.

AN ASIAN IDENTITY?

Collectively recognised and often mutually inspired attempts at liberation from colonial dominance did not, then, herald the birth of an Asian community. Nationalist movements themselves served to set up dominant local political discourses and acted as political tools within each national boundary, while providing a sense of belonging for groups of people undergoing social upheaval. Although many of these movements, such as Japan's designs on Korea and Manchuria, the 'Go East!' movement in Vietnam and 'Look East!' policy of Malaysia, were based upon ideas of pan-Asianism and used as rhetoric for the justification of national projects, none was designed with regional cohesion in mind. Even within the Bandung framework, a neutral position could not be sustained within the region, as a result of the political and military realities of the cold war.

There have been many changes to the economies of East and Southeast Asia in recent decades, which have been well illustrated and examined elsewhere (see Barlow 1999; Dixon 1991; Ravenhill 1995). In 1965 the Asian Ten represented 9 per cent of world gross domestic product (GDP), while in 1996 that figure had reached 25 per cent. As Godement notes, the 'Asian developmental state has risen to the fundamental challenge of the marketplace by enhancing market mechanisms and responding to the demands of international institutions and foreign governments' (1999, p. 102). In other words, the international role of Asian economies has become far more prominent and they have adopted, to an ever larger extent, a rules-based market philosophy set down elsewhere. At the same time, in opening their economies to these external forces, they can also better protect their vested interests. Development in Asia overtook that in Latin America and the Caribbean in the 1980s, and between 1988 and 1993 developing Asia's stock of foreign direct investment (FDI) doubled and investment flows to Asia reached approximately US$59 billion in 1994 (compared with US$32 billion in 1992). The principal sources of FDI stock in descending order are Japan, the US and the EU, which together contribute about 50 per cent of the total. Between 1965 and 1993, the newly industrialising economies of Asia (NIEs) grew at an average annual rate of over 8 per cent, experiencing particularly a boom in investment, production and trade growth (World Bank 1995, p. 65). The populations of ASEAN member states range from 300 000 people in Brunei to the 202 million inhabitants of Indonesia. These figures demonstrate the proven importance of the region in economic terms, but other institutional and perceptual stimuli have pushed this process further.

At the level of economic development there gradually arose a sense of Asian collective identity, particularly from American and European eyes, which witnessed the sudden flooding of their markets by cheap Asian products between the 1960s and 1980s. Rapid urban and industrial development throughout Southeast Asia benefited from an influx of foreign (especially US) capital, especially in those countries which demonstrated greatest political stability. Industrial development through protective tariffs and subsidies was undertaken in order, in general, to reduce national dependence upon imported products (Dixon 1991, p. 152). The inefficiencies of this protective system were, by the mid-1960s, to elicit domestic and international calls for the development of export markets.

The most tangible manifestation of an 'Asian' identity during the post-war period has been the development and continued existence of ASEAN. Initially established as an anti-communist grouping, it adopted from its inception a pragmatic approach to the promotion of regional stability and created the ZOPFAN in 1971. Nixon's decision to recognise the People's Republic of China (PRC) in 1971 reduced Southeast Asia's risk of antagonising the US by approaches to China, and facilitated the improvement of the region's ties with Beijing (SarDesai 1997, p. 358). Throughout the Vietnam and Cambodian crises, ASEAN was used as a forum to encourage agreement among member states whose interests did not always converge over these issues. For example, Thailand and Singapore were suspicious of Vietnam's long-term territorial intentions, while Indonesia and Malaysia focused their concerns on China's regional pretensions (SarDesai 1997, p. 359). Divergent interests were, nevertheless, reconciled in preparation for the 1991 peace settlement, while the collapse of the Soviet Union completely reconfigured intra-regional concerns. This period also corresponded with the growth of ASEAN as a major economic zone to rival that of North America and the EC, as will be discussed in the following section. Questions arose about the future of ASEAN in the light of changes within the regional and international environment after 1989 (see Chapter 4), but since the mid-1980s the participants of ASEAN have strengthened the economic component of the Association, culminating in the proposed AFTA in 1992 (Yeung et al. 1999, p. 46). During that period, competition from other regional bodies such as

NAFTA, the EU and APEC made it clear that ASEAN had to strengthen its own hand.

Japan, China and South Korea are now regarded as the economic powerhouses of the Asian region. Japan's rapid rise to economic supremacy from the 1950s to 1970s is well documented (Calder 1993; Inoguchi and Okimoto 1988; Morris 1991). It set the path for the so-called 'flying geese' formation, creating a development pattern for those economies to 'catch up' later and come after it (Kim, J. 1999, p. 135). Japan's particular form of development, often termed the 'neo-mercantilist' or the 'developmental state', highlighted the role of state involvement in economic development (Maswood 1998, p. 58). China opened up its economy at the end of the 1970s with liberalisation and export policies that would lead to rapid development (Maswood 1998, p. 59). Some argue that, in fact, the role of the Chinese diaspora within Asia is becoming more important than Japan's economic input in the region (see Buzan 1998, p. 82). China's reach is indeed expanding, and its participation in regional, inter-regional and international fora – from APEC to the WTO – demonstrates a growing attention to the international economic structure and a recognition of the need to keep external actors (especially the US) committed to free trade (see Chapter 3). In the wake of Japanese economic successes, the so-called 'Asian Tigers' (Hong Kong, Taiwan, Singapore and South Korea) followed a similar developmental trajectory, with Singapore's transformation to participation in the world economy and a strong state-business network making it the most impressive economic giant in Southeast Asia. By the late 1970s it was clear that Singapore had to become a centre of more capital-intensive production in order to cope with growing competition from within the region. Global recession between 1984 and 1986 hit the open economy of Singapore hard, and since that time policies of privatisation, labour cost reduction, the enhancement of the electronics sector and new areas of promotion have been attempted, but Singapore remains vulnerable to global trends. In Thailand, investment and export promotion activities only took off after the global economic slowdown at the end of the 1960s, and were further encouraged by international institutions during the early 1970s, whose presence was to become dominant by the early 1980s. Thailand did, nevertheless, benefit from its relatively stable political structure to encourage foreign investment and an increased presence of multinational firms, but poor infrastructure and skill shortages prevented its greater development by the end of the 1980s. Inter-racial tension and the New Economic Policy goal of prioritising *bumiputras* ('sons of the soil') in Malaysia have ensured strong state intervention in the economy and over social behaviour, as also occurred in other states of the region such as Singapore, Indonesia and Myanmar. For its part, Indonesia's strongly protectionist and state-led Guided Democracy under Sukarno after 1957 bred inefficiencies not tackled until Suharto's pro-Western policies after 1966 saw the integration of Indonesia into the global economic structure, principally through International Monetary Fund (IMF) and International Bank for Reconstruction and Development (IBRD) assistance (Dixon 1991, p. 193). The nature of Indonesian geography has left rural development well behind that of urbanised Java, Bali and Lombok, and the government instituted a number of policies – including transmigration – in an attempt to address this disparity. Oil revenues sustained development until prices dropped in the 1980s, when international conditions required a reluctant government to reform tax, subsidies and other industrial policies, but without removing its fundamental 'economic nationalism' (Dixon 1991, p. 200). The Philippines were from their independence closely linked to the US economy, whose capital they needed for reconstruction and which permitted a number of foreign exchange and import controls. At the beginning of the twenty-first century, however, they remain encumbered by poor infrastructure and continuing political instability. The poorest states in the region are Vietnam, Cambodia and Laos, which have attempt to reintegrate their economies into the international economy since the withdrawal of Vietnam from Cambodia in 1989. The lesser developed economies of the Asian Ten are also making an impact domestically and within the region. All remain heavily dependent on subsistence farming and continue to function with very poor infrastructures. The changing of the name of Myanmar's regime from SLORC (State Law and Order Restoration Council) to the State Peace and Developmental Council in November 1997 has not removed this country from its economic 'timewarp' and sanction-imposed status. Brunei, for its part, is oil rich and sparsely populated and protects its national wealth. This brief overview demonstrates that each Asian nation experienced its own form of post-independence transition, and followed a different path towards economic recovery and growth. A number of factors determined their trajectory. These include: the experience of colonialism and the nature of relations with the colonial power in the immediate aftermath of the war; the level of indigenous nationalism and maturity of their independence movements; and their own involvement in the cold war. Across the continent, independence movements were often led by Western-trained élites, who had only limited experience of government experience and who exacerbated deep town versus countryside divisions and domestic political and ethnic differences. In addition, all Asian countries had to deal with economic development and with regional territorial disputes, as well as with the local realities of the cold war. Only recently have these national trends coalesced around more formal attempts to institutionalise aspects of intra-Asian cooperation.

TOWARDS ECONOMIC REGIONALISATION

In January 1992 ASEAN decided to move towards the creation of AFTA, and in September 1994 an Economic Ministers' Meeting followed by a summit meeting in Bangkok in December 1995 accelerated that process. In spite of member states' differing views over economic management, agreement could be reached around the idea of AFTA, for a number of reasons, which included the effects of the 1985–6 recession caused by low commodity prices, and the increased standard of living afforded by the relocation to Southeast Asia of Japanese exporters after the Plaza Accord of 1985 (Stubbs 2000, pp. 301–3). AFTA's aim was to reduce tariffs on intra-ASEAN trade of manufactured goods and processed agricultural products, as well as capital goods, to 0–5 per cent within 15 years from January 1993. In addition, member states would seek to remove all non-tariff barriers (NTBs) between them, and, at the core of the agreement, create a Common Effective Preferential Tariff (CEPT) which places 15 products on a fast track, alongside a normal track and an exclusion list. AFTA was also prompted by the establishment of the Single European Market (SEM) in 1992 and NAFTA in January 1994. Within the Asian region itself, the rise of China as a source of manufactured low-cost goods and as an increasingly important target for FDI also stimulated AFTA proposals (Stubbs 2000, p. 310). By 1995 implementation of AFTA requirements had begun, and in Kuala Lumpur at an ASEAN summit in 1997 and in Hanoi in 1998, leaders agreed that intra-ASEAN trade would help to address the financial crisis (Stubbs 2000, p. 311). In Hanoi, they issued a Statement of Bold Measures and the original six member states agreed to move AFTA's deadline from 2003 to 2002, by which time all items on the inclusion list would have a tariff of less than 5 per cent. The ASEAN Industrial Cooperation Scheme and Investment Area was also introduced to increase FDI and allow firms more products within ASEAN at 0–5 per cent tariffs. However, there was some concern during the financial crisis that such pledges were too difficult to uphold (see Chapter 3).

Apart from formal contacts, a web of relations has been established in recent years, as new leaders have come to the fore across Asia. Examples of growing interest and cooperation are numerous, and include: the summit meeting between Japanese Prime Minister Keizo Obuchi and South Korean President Kim Dae Jung in March 1999, where both leaders affirmed the steady implementation of the Joint Declaration-New Partnership between Japan and the Republic of Korea towards the 21st Century and its annexed action plan, and announced the Japan-Republic of Korea Economic Agenda 21, in order to further their mutual economic relations; and Chinese President Jiang Zemin's visit to Japan in November 1998 and the reciprocal visit by Prime Minister Obuchi in March 1999, where they conferred with regard to the terms of Chinese accession to the WTO and agreed 33 other specific areas for cooperation in addition to the 'Obuchi Fund' for assistance in afforestation and greenification initiatives. The latter initiatives are underpinned by a total bilateral trade valued in 1999 at over 7.5 trillion yen, and by the fact that China is now Japan's second largest trading partner, while Japan is China's largest trading partner. The Japanese government has also courted ASEAN member states since 1999, in the hope of forging alliances to stave off any future crises (see below). These growing partnerships are fundamental for cementing intra-regional linkages, particularly in the face of increasing exposure to a range of external influences.

In 1991, Japan's gross domestic product was more than twice that of all other East Asian economies combined, and it continued as an important model for Asian economic development (Maswood 1998, p. 63). Japan, at the top of the chain, supplied FDI and capital goods, as well as increasingly acting as a market for regional products (Kim, J. 1999, p. 139). In addition, Japan is the key provider of official development assistance (ODA) to Southeast Asia and China. The catch-up countries themselves subsequently became exporters and investors. The 1985 Plaza Accord (by which Japan revalued the yen in the face of an appreciating US dollar) was to precipitate a flow of direct Japanese investment to other Southeast Asian countries, in order to offset any loss of competitiveness, and integrated Japanese economic structures even more closely into the region. At the same time, China's domestic economy has become ever more internationalised, and power is shifting gradually from the state to markets, where the increasingly autonomous role of the local actors is being reinforced by the decentralisation of administration and the rise of economic entrepreneurs (Breslin 1999, p. 96). American, European and Asian interest in investment and joint ventures in China continues to provide an external incentive for the much-needed internal down-sizing and closure of many state-owned enterprises (SOEs).

Yoshida et al. note that East Asia's share of world trade between 1985 and 1992 grew from 20.1 per cent to 23.6 per cent, while its quota of world imports grew from 16.8 per cent to 20.6 per cent (1994, p. 61). In addition, the region witnessed huge inflows of FDI from the mid-1980s, with Japan as its key supplier. This growing phenomenon increased the interdependence of the regional economies, since each had to adjust its domestic economic structures (such as tax, foreign capital laws and procedural simplification) to facilitate and accommodate FDI (Yoshida et al. 1994, p. 86). Furthermore, an important change occurred from the mid-1970s, when industrialisation facilitated across the region an increased share of manufactured goods as a percentage of total exports (Yoshida et al. 1994, p. 81). In these ways, the Asia Pacific states collectively came to be viewed as a 'design shop' for 'the latest and most sophisticated instruments of managed trade' (Higgott et al. 1993, p. 2). During the 1990s, these ten Asian economies have come to be seen as an integral part of the 'Asia Pacific' system, institutionalised most notably within APEC (see Weiss 1999). These developments suggest a gradual movement within Asia from disparate economic motivations and actions, towards a limited regional agenda and an increasingly notable perception that a 'regional' economic function is in operation. As the region increases its profile as an economic unit, collective economic policies adopted within the framework of ASEAN continue to form the core of this growing Asian contingent (Soesastro 1997, p. 176).

Imagining 'Asia' Anew

During the early 1990s, then, it was noted that 'new imaginings about the region have redrawn the boundaries of East Asia and what is increasingly termed the Asia–Pacific' (Berger and Borer 1997, p. 292). Underpinned by the notion of 'open regionalism' (whereby benefits accruing to members of the given region must also be applied to third, that is, non-member, countries) this form of regionalisation came to be associated with a new kind of response to globalising trends, particularly in the context of APEC. What is more, this 'open' form of regionalisation legitimises the informal nature of Asian economic cooperation and distinguishes it from (often undesirable) Western alternatives. This form of cooperation was ensured through, inter alia, the 1990 so-called Kuching Consensus which stated that APEC 'should not lead to the adoption of mandatory directives for any participants to undertake or implement' (cited in Soesastro 1997, p. 174). According to one observer, such intangible region building suggests that the region is 'almost in denial about its regionness', a status that is reinforced by its position within a US-driven 'super-regional' order, which itself has employed regionalism only as a form of leverage for greater global gains (Buzan 1998, pp. 83–5). ASEAN reticence over APEC, moreover, is driven in part by a fear of dilution of the smaller institutional arrangement within a larger forum in which a North-South divide is not unthinkable (Soesastro 1997, p. 177). Nevertheless, the rhetoric of intra-regional cooperation – embedded within APEC – is important in engendering a sense of *need* for cooperation, due to spurious historical, geographical, political, or economic ties. As Buzan remarks: 'The existence of APEC and all of its accompanying Asia–Pacific talk suggests that whatever the realities or shortcomings of trans-Pacific interaction, there is no problem about the Asia–Pacific being *perceived* as a region', which, he goes on to note, creates 'the danger of the perception of the region outrunning its rather modest reality' (1998, p. 78). As will be seen in later chapters, the potential for that region to collaborate in the name of a perceived sense of mutual identification is raised at times when 'outsiders' (most notably the US and international financial institutions) are seen to threaten the intra-regional status quo. In particular, the changing role and position of the US have been instrumental in defining and re-defining a sense of 'regionness' within Asia. This same Asia Pacific, once associated with phenomenal growth and dynamism, also became the target for criticism of 'crony capitalist' policies following the 1997 financial crises (see Chapter 3). The greater institutionalisation and association of the idea of 'Asia' within these seemingly fixed economic structures has prompted much prognosticating by scholars of how 'Asia' can and should redress its economic deficiencies. A further point to note is that, increasingly, such reifications of 'Asia' have meant that states such as Australia have been forced to (re)negotiate their own cultural and national identity within a variously defined Asia Pacific enclave. The 'Asianisation' of Asia thereby reinforces both internally and externally derived ideas of the region.

Proliferating views of Asia as an economic bloc have been further reinforced and problematised by changing international conditions: 'Economic interdependence appears to have increased, the economic pre-eminence of the United States has diminished, and the widespread commitment to multilateralism, at other than the rhetorical level, is problematic' (Higgott et al. 1993, p. 5). In particular, the contest over the definition of 'globalisation' has prompted references to an economic Asian region that stands alongside Europe and North America as one of three pillars of the new global economy. Most recent changes – such as the intensifying dialogue between North and South Korea through South Korean President Kim Dae Jung's 'sunshine policy', China's accession to the WTO, Chen Shui-bian's victory for the Democratic Progressive Party against the long-running Kuomintang (KMT) in Taiwan and multiple problems from mass poverty to secessionist demands in Indonesia – underline a greater need for both intra- and extra-regional cooperation. The apparent decline of the role of the US in the region (and potentially inflammatory behaviour by President George W. Bush towards it), and the growing international voice of Asia (through Japan within the G8, through AFTA and through increasing dissatisfaction with Western prescriptions for Asian ills) give further cause to consolidate Asian identity at the start of the twenty-first century (Pelkmans and Balaoing 1996). In these ways, 'Asia' as a unit is coming to gain recognition across a number of fora. Furthermore, ideas of Asia have come to be linked inextricably with notions of Asian values, a debate that is caught up in discussions over the very 'future direction and development' of Asian societies (Kausikan 1998, p. 24). This debate has also come to define a sense of 'Asianness', for example in terms of human rights, in the face of what some perceive as attempts at Western domination: 'Asian states have become increasingly critical of the political ideologies and practices of the West; yet most of their own political vocabularies, constitutional and legal language and structures, and even individual laws were inherited from the West, particularly from their former colonial masters' (Chan 1998, p. 34). This debate, then, goes to the heart of questions of Asian identity, but also demonstrates that ideas of 'Asia' themselves derive from multiple sources.

EUROPEAN INTEGRATION

These, then, were the events that dominated the Asian region, pushing and pulling it towards the sense of Asianness it was later to utilise and develop more explicitly. It is worth contrasting those disparate events briefly with the closer integrative moves towards regionalisation in Europe during the 1950s. Today's definition of Europe emanates from the effects of rebuilding a continent after 1945. The division of the continent by an 'iron curtain' that separated east from West in both physical and ideological terms, soon made it clear that rehabilitating Europe would not be a smooth process. Although Russia was lost from the European fold, the legacy of resistance movements, the need to integrate vanquished countries and extensive discussions about the collective future of Europe brought together leaders from France, Britain, the Netherlands, Belgium, Germany, Italy and others at the Congress of Europe at The Hague in May 1948. Following this encounter, several groupings were established which included the Organisation for European Economic Cooperation (OEEC), and which culminated in the plans by Robert Schuman and Jean Monnet to develop the ECSC (Nicoll and Salmon 1994, Chapter 1). It was their ideas and work which contributed to the development in 1957 of the Treaty of Rome (amended most recently by the Treaties of Maastricht in 1992, Amsterdam in 1997 and Nice in 2000), which established the European Economic Community (EEC, and which became the European Communities, or EC, with the merging of a number of agreements in 1967).

The Treaty of Rome was designed to engender closer union and the free circulation of goods, services and people within the frontiers of the six member states (Belgium, France, Germany, Italy, Luxembourg and the Netherlands). Its institutions included the Commission (the executive), the Council of Ministers (legislative), the Assembly (consultative body, which later became the European Parliament), the Court of Justice and the Economic and Social Committee (a consultative organ). The EEC from its inception aimed to facilitate the development of a single market for its member states. Consuming almost 30 per cent of the GDP of all the OECD states, today the EU is second only to the US. In 1970 the Werner Plan proposed economic and monetary union in three steps with a single currency, but this was not to succeed until it was revivified in a new form during the 1980s, because of currency volatility during the early 1970s and a lack of monetary policy cooperation (Dinan 1994, pp. 417–25). In 1979, the European Monetary System (EMS) was founded, and all countries except for the UK participated in the Exchange Rate Mechanism (ERM) with fixed but adjustable exchange rates.

This initial period of European integration attempted to deal with the necessities of rebuilding political and socio-economic frameworks destroyed by war. It, nevertheless, saw the establishment of a number of criteria by which to deal with external countries and bodies. Community competence in dealing with such 'third countries' (non EEC-member states) was set down in Article 113 of the Rome Treaty, namely the Common Commercial Policy (CCP). The European Commission, as a result, was mandated to make recommendations to the Council, which would then issue a 'directive' adopted by qualified majority voting (Nicoll and Salmon 1994, p. 119). While economic agreements were to be conducted in this way, recognising Community competence over that of national competence, there was no such provision for foreign policy decisions after the proposed European Political Community (EPC) collapsed alongside the failure of the European Defence Community (EDC) in 1954 until the start of European Political Cooperation (EPC) resulting from the Hague Summit of 1969. This was not, however, part of the overall Community framework, until it was formally integrated into the structure of the European Union as a result of the Maastricht Treaty of 1992. Moreover, this newer form of EPC formed the basis for inter-governmental dialogue, designed to be channelled through foreign ministerial meetings at least twice a year, which would be served by a Political Committee comprising the heads of political departments of member state foreign ministries. Every decision was to be agreed by consensus. This was supplemented by the creation of the European Council in 1974, in order to bring together the heads of state of the EC member state to discuss EC and EPC matters in tandem.

While this mode of dialogue evolved alongside EC structures, it did not deepen a sense of European identity. The British attempt to take Europe down a different (inter-governmental) track, furore over British applications for admission to the Community in 1961 and 1967 (resolved only after the resignation of de Gaulle in April 1969), and the Luxembourg Crisis of 1966 demonstrated early on that it would be difficult to achieve consensus among the then nine members (Nicoll and Salmon 1994, p. 36). Nevertheless, these increasingly formalised and codified structures gradually engendered a process of European integration, which had (and continues to exert) a transformative impact on the European state system (Christiansen et al. 1999, p. 529). The EU wears an external façade today despite its internal discussions which witness divisions of seemingly insurmountable proportions between, for example, the UK and the rest over the euro, or Spain and the UK over fishing rights, or different approaches to the development of the proposed European Security and Defence Forces (ESDF) and the Rapid Reaction Facility (RRF). To the outside, however, joint actions or common positions (Articles J.2 and J.3 of the Treaty on European Union) often appear simply to emanate from Union-level decisions.

In 1986 the Single European Act (SEA) adopted a path towards the SEM (Lee 1999, p. 54). The EU is the world's biggest trading power with about 20 per cent of global exports and imports, and a market of over 370 million consumers. In December 1991 heads of state of the then EC decided to create Economic and Monetary Union (EMU) by 1999 at the latest. The 1993 Treaty on European Union (by which the EC became the EU) set the goal of EMU within treaty terms with legal and institutional foundations. The European Monetary Institute (EMI) was established with the commencement of stage 2 of EMU on 1 January 1994, which was subsequently replaced by the European Central Bank (ECB) in order to direct stability-oriented policies and an open economy. In May 1998 convergence criteria were measured and eleven countries were deemed ready and willing to be locked into irrevocable exchange rates on 31 December 1998. Stage 3 began on 1 January 1999 with complete monetary union. The new currency became fully available in note and coin form on 1 January 2002, and July 2002 saw the complete removal of national currencies of participating countries. The project has been looked upon warily by some observers, notably the British government, which regards it on the whole as far more than an economic endeavour. EMU is, in fact, clearly politically driven, despite the fiscal control retained by national governments (Lee 1999, p. 56). The EU now acts as an economic bloc in a growing range of fora, such as the GATT/WTO system. Under Articles 131–134, 300 and 301 of the Treaty of Amsterdam, the European Commission represents the Union for matters pertaining to the CCP. Proposals are initiated by the European Commission, which then negotiates the form of the proposal based upon Council mandates accorded after a qualified majority vote. The proposal is then concluded by the Council, again according to qualified majority voting. Because the CCP does not deal with all aspects of economic policy, some areas (such as Intellectual Property Rights, IPR) are dealt with by 'mixed competence', shared by the EU and its member states. Member states can also reject European Commission proposals when their national interests are at stake. Article 133 deals with agreements with third countries or international organisations, and Article 300 sets out the procedures for negotiations with them. Article 301 promotes consistency between these economic articles and the Common Foreign and Security Policy (CFSP), which ensures a core role for the inter-governmental level of EU activity, through the Council. This also makes sure that political and economic issues are inter-linked; thus, following the NATO bombing of the Chinese embassy in Belgrade in May 1999 a delay occurred in the formal meetings of EU–China WTO negotiations and the EU–China summit. However, while the EU's CCP shows the Union's 'collective exercise of power against third country partners' (Dent 1999a, p. 27), even in European monetary policy there is seemingly 'nobody in charge' (*Financial Times* 22 June 1998). In addition, EU external affairs are dealt with at a range of levels within the Union. Since the restructuring of the European Commission in 1999, primary responsibility for dealing with the countries of Asia lies with the External Relations Directorate-General (they are no longer numbered). Within this structure, most of Asia – excluding Japan and South Korea – is dealt with in one directorate divided into different groups of countries (for example, China is grouped with Hong Kong, Taiwan and Macao). Japan and South Korea come under the directorate (C), which also deals with the US. While this allows both a thematic and institutional approach to organising the EU's external relations, there continues to be a range of actors involved in addressing specific areas of concern related to Asia.

From an external perspective, the EU is often regarded as a protectionist bloc. In employing anti-dumping mechanisms and 'voluntary' export restraint agreements (VERs), many of its actions to date can hardly be said to be worthy of the 'free trade' label. The pursuit since the mid-1980s of the SEM, launched in January 1993, resulted in a spate of mergers and acquisitions (M&As) and internal investment. This market was intended to enhance the international competitiveness of the European economies and to eliminate exchange rate uncertainties. With a population of over 375 million people in 1999, this zone represents a significant international market. Nearly two thirds of the FDI by EU countries in 1992 was concentrated within the EU itself (UNCTAD and European Commission 1996, p. 54), compared with only 31 per cent between 1985 and 1987. This process also encouraged intra-EU investment, promising a large market and economies of scale. In addition, prospective EU member states also became attractive loci of investment and trade when the EU signed European Agreements with them, in order to prepare them for full membership of the Union. This mixed policy process requires coordination at a number of levels and has precipitated the creation of networks of interest groups which lobby national and EU-level bodies (Spell 2000). The role of the 'EU' itself is rather complex, and within the European Commission alone there tend to be differences between different directorates general. For example, during the Uruguay Round Directorate-General 1 (DG1, External economic relations) and DGIV (Agriculture) disputed over which should lead on the negotiations, with the result that the European Commission itself was weakened. As will be shown below, the

European Commission tends to have more technical knowledge than member states, but the latter have different (colonial) histories with different Asian countries. While the Amsterdam Treaty took several measures to address this issue, by enabling certain services and IPR issues to be considered within the scope of the CCP (following Council unanimity), which in practice gives further scope for the European Commission to negotiate on member states' behalf, there nevertheless continues to be confusion at the level of third countries as to which part of the EU is responsible for what. A key manifestation of the European economic dimension is the European currency, the euro, which is currently adopted by twelve of the fifteen member states. The euro was launched on 1 January 1999 and offers an alternative currency for invoicing and foreign reserves, and from 2002 a Europe-wide currency of notes and coins replaced the national currencies of all participating members. Some observers regard the introduction of the euro as a significant event: 'The euro will contribute to the emergence of a bi-polar monetary regime, in which the dollar and the euro will jointly dominate global markets' (Lee 1999, p. 61). However, in the short time since its introduction, it has been largely dwarfed by the impact of the Asian crisis, to which it was unable to respond effectively in the way that the US dollar could. Moreover, inflated initial expectations of its prospects have resulted in disappointing assessments of its success to date. Its slow progress notwithstanding, high-level figures such as French Finance Minister Laurent Fabius have continued to insist that the euro can achieve parity with the dollar, and that its existence has increased European resistance to external shocks. One of the problems with the euro, particularly from a non-European perspective, is that (unlike, for example, the US Treasury) there is no clear point of reference. The lack of political weight of the euro was highlighted when the US propped up the yen in 1998, but any such intervention would surpass the remit of the ECB. Critics of the euro questioned how the member states could deal with events such as a financial crisis without such central authority. In the case of the euro, the finance ministers of all participating countries – Euro-X – would have to have an emergency session, or else all fifteen finance ministers would have to meet. In spite of this rather convoluted decision-making structure, the euro's existence has acted as a spur to leaders in Asia who are trying to advance their own visions of regional economic integration, and in this way provides a potential model or counter model for them (see Chapter 3).

Alongside its economic developments, the EU has also been trying to address its security structures as part of its political pillar, particularly in the light of the military failures of the EU during the Kosovo crisis of 1999. New attempts towards the development of a European Security and Defence Policy (ESDP) suggest a growing confidence within the structures of the EU towards assuming part of the mantle previously worn by NATO. At the same time, the EU per se has assumed a much more significant international role: during its Presidency between July and December 2000, for example, the French government placed on its agenda, inter alia, EU–India, EU–China, EU–Korea relations, alongside ASEM, the G7, NATO, the WTO and the UN. This is certainly not to suggest that the EU represents either a legally binding or emotional attachment by its people to a pan-European superstructure. There remain many disagreements about the deepening and widening prospects of the Union, especially in light of imminent enlargement to a host of Central and Eastern European states. Nevertheless, in contrast to Asian regional cooperation, the European project is able to portray a clear external façade to outsiders. Today, the EU represents the single largest market for goods and services, and is the largest host region for FDI. In its legally embedded framework, it 'embodies deep regional integration including harmonization of social welfare, environmental and other policies, as well as legal rules and standards' (Yeung et al. 1999, p. 38). Many of these standards are brought as a matter of course and necessity to the ASEM table.

ASIA–EUROPE MEETING (ASEM)

In the postwar era, links between Asia and Europe developed only slowly and were frequently subsumed by cold war structures and hindered by respective intra-regional developments. Gradually, economic integration in its different forms became a reality for both regions, which continued to renegotiate notions of regionhood within their own particular historical boundaries (Desthieux and Saucier 1999, p. 111). Trade between Europe and Asia tripled (to US$310 billion) between 1980 and 1993, surpassing that of Europe–US trade (US$251 billion) (Yeung et al. 1999, p. 72), and opening new channels for inter-regional opportunities. Against this increasingly positive background, proposals for ASEM 1 were endorsed by the EU's General Affairs Council in March 1995 and agreed upon at the ASEAN-EU Senior Officials' Meeting (SOM) in May. The origins of ASEM will not be rehearsed here (see Preface; Pelkmans and Shinkai 1997), but suffice to note that, from its inception, ASEM was designed to facilitate an informal armchair dialogue which incorporated a number of existing channels of Asia–Europe interaction. These included the EU–ASEAN summit, various bilateral agreements by the EU with individual countries such as Japan and South Korea, as well as confidence-building activities within the ARF, to which all member states of ASEM belong. At the same time, it also countenanced its inter-regional dimension by acting as a counterbalance to the regional role of APEC, which was seen to undergird one of the two 'strong' sides of the Asia–US–Europe triangle. The triangular setting was perhaps the greatest reinforcement of this need for region-to-region relations and this abstract notion has become the concrete rationale for Asia–Europe developments, underpinned by the need to strengthen the 'weak link in the triadic chain of economic relationships between Asia, North America and Europe' (Yeung et al. 1999, p. 45). This can be seen in explicit attempts to carve out an alternative modus operandi from that which each maintains with the US, as EU Commissioner Manuel Marín noted: 'We don't operate like the Americans. In our search for compromise, we work almost like the Asians' (cited in Ton 1998).

ASEM's three-pillared activities are crowned by the biennial summit meetings of heads of state, but populated by a plethora of government and private-level encounters between them. In the first pillar of the economic field, these include meetings of finance and economics ministers, informal Senior Officials Meetings on Trade and Investment (SOMTI), an environmental technology centre, an Asia–Europe Business Forum (AEBF) and regular business conferences. The second pillar houses political dialogue, which includes encounters of foreign ministry officials and SOMs, and which discusses global affairs that even involve some elements of security, but which largely avoid the more contentious issues such as human rights. Finally, the third pillar loosely assembles cultural and other activities, which include events held by the Singapore-based Asia–Europe Foundation (ASEF), an Asia–Europe university programme, and youth exchange programmes. In addition, 'track two' activities include the People's Forum gathering of non-governmental organisations from all over Asia and Europe, which shadows the summit meetings, as well as the Council for Asia–Europe Cooperation (see Chapter 5). The ASEM process has been much maligned and overly praised at the same time for inaugurating a new inter-regional agenda. On the one hand, it has been described as a 'talk shop' of the 'politically wobbly', while simultaneously fears over greater 'institutionalisation' have been voiced from both groups of participants. On the face of it, this meeting appears to contribute very little to world affairs: internal Asian disagreements over trade opening measures and the pitting of Asian versus Western norms on the subject of human rights leave only a hollow resonance. Its most frequent iteration includes the assertion that 'consensus is more important than breakthrough, camaraderie than formality and process than substance'. But what, exactly, is it, and what does it tell us about both the level of interaction between Asia and Europe and the nature of their mutual comprehension as regions today? ASEM in fact raises several interesting questions about the nature and purpose of inter-regional relations and needs to be examined in its own right. It conducts its affairs as an explicitly region-to-region grouping, while at the same time (to date, at least) dispensing an 'Asian way with Western agenda', thus accommodating within its own framework apparently contradictory modes of decision-making and failing to problematise the difficult issues which the discussion of such modes of behaviour should provoke. The tone of all three meetings to date is captured in the Chair's final statement in Seoul in October 2000:

> Leaders shared the view that a rapidly changing world represents formidable challenges to the whole international community. In this regard, they expressed their commitment to ASEM playing a constructive role in promoting increased multilateral dialogue and cooperation, based on equal partnership, mutual respect and mutual benefit, and in building a new international political and economic order in light of the growing interdependence of Asia and Europe and the changing international environment. (Chair's Statement, October 2000)

The following chapters will examine the different dimensions of ASEM, but two important points are worth making here. The first pertains to the role of the United States as a constantly whirring background noise to the ASEM process. On the one hand, as illustrated above, ASEM participants are attempting to establish their own means of negotiation through facilitatory dialogue rather than sanction-led US-style conduct. On the other, however, the position of the US to date has been an important factor in the decision-making capacity of ASEM member states: at present ASEM is 'almost unnoticed' in the US (Preeg 1998, p. 82); Japan's very willingness to join the process, apparent EU incapacity during the financial crisis; and China's chary attitude to human rights all resonate with echoes of responses to US policy. While this book focuses upon the Asia–Europe dimension of international affairs, therefore, it is in no way suggesting that in the present environment of international relations it can replace – or has aspirations to replace – respective relations with the US. Rather, ASEM acts as a supplementary point of communication for its members. Its format will shape ASEM affairs, either by belittling its significance or by giving member states the opportunity to explore new avenues for cooperation, unhindered by US prescription. The US may be either facilitator or constrainer within this process. In this regard, the US presence also influences the discourse of ASEM, which finds itself in a tripolar straitjacket as the 'tripolarisation' of the global economy becomes the mantra of ASEM's advancement, with the resulting reasoning that if ASEM did not exist, it would have to be invented (Gilson 2001). The inherent contradictions in this label, however, mean that, on the one hand tripolarity serves as the definitive legitimation of Asia–Europe communication, while on the other it also causes Asian and European interaction to be seen inevitably as the 'weak side of the triangle'. The very model for much of ASEM activity has been APEC, while that which has been eschewed (a secretariat and various formal decision-making mechanisms) is framed within the counter models offered by both APEC and the EU. The second point to bear in mind relates to the question of exclusion and inclusion, which underpins the whole premise of this work, and of the ASEM process itself: 'Left to decide who should represent 'Asia', ASEAN stirred controversy by excluding Australia, despite intense lobbying on its behalf by Japan and others' (*Asian Wall Street Journal* 23 February 1996). The Asian veto, especially that of Malaysia, influences the ways in which self and other are shaped through institutional patterning. The exclusion not only of Australia and New Zealand, but also of indubitably 'Asian' states such as India and Pakistan, demonstrates the development of a certain kind of Asia: economically developed for the most part or institutionalised within a framework of development (ASEAN), it defines itself in the face of an unmistakable 'Europe' as an 'Asia for the Asiatics' in the style of the EAEC. Similarly, acting as an international interlocutor in this forum for economic, political and cultural relations, the EU's sense of self, too, is reinforced through interaction with an other in the form of Asia. This forum, too, continues to sharpen the sense that 'Europe' and the 'EU' are, in fact, one entity. Exclusion from either side, therefore, becomes costly in terms of economic advantage and political voice (Scholte 1996, p. 43).

CONCLUSION

During the 1980s and especially the 1990s, regional trade agreements, as opposed to global ones, became 'more politically desirable and feasible due to increased familiarity and comparable cultures, business practices and legal systems' (Yeung et al. 1999, p. 20). These have a number of values, as illustrated by the different forms of collective behaviour within Asia and within Europe. They may provide side payments, such as concessions to poorer areas in exchange for a state's participation, or else act as a 'safe haven' for smaller states unable to muster political or economic clout by themselves (see Yeung et al. 1999, p. 21). They also offer strength in numbers in the face of external challenges such as that posed by globalisation, and may be spurred into life by the lobbying activities of private economic actors promoting regional or trans-regional cooperation. Inter-regional cooperation at the economic level has also come to be matched by a degree of political cooperation and cultural dialogue, through which representatives of each region have come to identify key areas where cooperation is likely to enhance intra-regional interests, in the face of a rapidly changing global environment. These arenas of activity will be addressed in the following chapters. The most important question for this book is to examine how ASEM contributes to the identification of two regions interacting with one another. Central to the whole idea of ASEM, despite British attempts to make it an APEC-like grouping of individual representatives and in spite of regular assertions to the contrary, is the concept of region-to-region engagement. This application of inter-regional dialogue within ASEM serves both functional and, perhaps less obviously, cognitive purposes, by presenting a new kind of partnership between novel kinds of partners. Its purpose, as the European Commission restated in April 2000, is to 'establish a new relationship between the two regions' and 'build a comprehensive partnership among equal partners'. The whole notion of equality, given the colonial heritage upon which Asian and European actors cast back their collective glance, is problematic and informs the way in which Asia and Europe do business. It should be noted here, however, that the discussion is not merely one of multilateralism (that is, the multiplication of national interests or institutional approach) nor of a double regionalism. Rather, if treated on its own level, inter-regionalism can expand our understanding of how mutual identity formation takes place, and is able to reconfigure the idea of reciprocity and offer a different kind of leverage system.

In many ways, ASEM has been victim to, or reactive agent of, changing international political and economic conditions: the Bangkok meeting was praised simply for bringing together Asia and Europe; the second summit was mired in the troubles of the Asian crises; and the third meeting was simultaneously overshadowed and influenced by the rapprochement of the two Koreas and the receipt of the Nobel peace prize by South Korean President Kim Dae Jung. Superficial analyses of these nodal moments tend to dispense the conclusion that ASEM contributes no 'value-added' quality to existing forms of international relations. However, while one may question whether resources are well deployed in sending state leaders across the world every two years, it is also important to examine relations between Asia and Europe from a different set of viewpoints. It is time, therefore, to focus on the following: how can Asia–Europe relations be comprehended on their 'own' terms (that is, not within the triangle)?; how are regions conceived within this process and what is the potential significance of certain kinds of regional interpretation and identification?; and what is the value of inter-regionalism per se as a level of interaction in international and world affairs of the twenty-first century? These questions take us beyond a mere duel over the veracity of 'Asian' versus 'Western' values and recourse to cultural relativism. Rather, they seek to demonstrate how the imposition of region-to-region discourse can serve to create (not reflect) an Asian model to deflect Western liberalism and demonstrate by its own existence that Western values (such as those regarding human rights) cannot be universal. The practice of everyday economic and political exchange, is of course far more nuanced: Western diatribes against Asian human rights' abuses are offset by the pursuit by Western economic interests of Asian markets and resources, which often leads to de facto accommodation with authoritarian regimes by the same 'West' (Robison 1996, pp. 4–7). Such conflicting demands set West (business communities) against West (governments) and leave Asians (governments) adopting harsh stands in the face of Asian opposition (from NGOs and anti-governmental movements).

It is clear that the process of the Asia–Europe Meeting was never designed to match like with like; for, while the EU is neither supra-state nor straightforward interstate forum, notions of 'Asia' are still more difficult to pin down. Nevertheless, within the boundary of an explicitly inter-regional framework, 'Asia' and 'Europe' can indeed act as two interlocutors. Not only in practical, but also in cognitive terms, the concretised idea of 'Asia' can create a sense of identity among a group which previously had no such group formation. Drawing on the fact that the membership of the EAEC is also embedded within ASEM, references to the 'Asian way' of decision-making within ASEM are also used to distinguish Asian from non-Asian (European) modes of behaviour. Such group identities may or may not cause the same collectivity to form in other circumstances, but they are important, nevertheless, in consolidating one form of 'Asianness' in the face of a verifiable external 'other'. ASEM's discursive patterns have also come to de-problematise the identity of the regions per se by embedding the notion of region-to-region dialogue. Thus, instances of 'regional problems', 'regional crises', 'regional meetings' and 'regional networks' are evoked interchangeably, and within that dialogue the growing notions of both 'Europe' and 'Asia' continue to flourish, while the networks created between them are premised on existing discourses to locate a dialogue of equals between Asia and Europe. In addition, within the ASEM process itself participation has become associated with a three-pillared structure of political dialogue, the reinforcement of economic cooperation and the promotion of cooperation in a range of other issue areas, particularly in the socio-cultural domain. In these ways, and supported by the foundations established at Bangkok, ASEM is already beginning to carve out its own cognitive route-map. As such, it offers a means of locking participants into a particular inter-regional discourse and creating a new understanding of interests and identities. This will be examined throughout the following chapters, and the Conclusion will examine the importance of inter-regionalism – as opposed to regionalism – in instilling new modes of behaviour.

3.   Economic Exchanges

The previous chapter examined how historical mutual experiences and the onset of the cold war led to a clear separation of Asian and European interests and a growing focus upon their respective forms of intra-regional development, both politically and economically. This chapter examines how, since the 1980s, inter-regional negotiations have become superimposed upon bilateral and sub-regional exchanges, to turn 'Asia' and 'Europe' into mutually identifiable economic entities. In so doing, this chapter aims to transcend comparative regional economic assessments, in order to look at the nature of Asia–Europe inter-regionalism itself. The first part of the chapter addresses the renaissance of Asia–Europe economic relations from the 1980s, with particular emphasis on the convergence of different bilateral sets of interests. The second part discusses how the EU has come to view 'Asia' increasingly as an economic region and part three examines, in contrast, changing Asian perspectives towards an ever-integrating Europe. The concluding section examines the impact of inter-regionalism on these processes.

According to United Nations Conference on Trade and Development (UNCTAD) figures, in 1995 Asia accounted for 23.2 per cent of the EU's external trade, compared with 17.4 per cent the previous year, having been part of a growing Asia–Europe trade pattern that outstripped the EU's trade with Eastern Europe between 1988 and 1994. Indeed, 'Asia' became an increasingly attractive market for European trade and investment during the 1980s and 1990s (despite the financial troubles of 1997), representing a rapidly expanding and dynamic arena for M&As, joint ventures and investment, and a place where the rise in per capita GDP and disposable income offered and continues to offer new opportunities for European manufacturers. Notwithstanding phenomenal economic success within Asia, however, the region has consistently failed to become a priority area for the EU and the trade policies of its member states. In 1996, for example, only 15 per cent of all Asian imports came from Europe (compared with 25 per cent in 1970), and only one per cent of EU investment was directed towards Asia in the mid-1990s (*The Economist* 2 March 1996). What is more, FDI has been unevenly distributed by Europeans in Asia: for example, while the EU's share of FDI in South Korea has grown, the figure in China has declined. At the same time, European businesses on the whole have been slow to seize opportunities in Asia, and have focused for the most part on new enterprises in Central and Eastern Europe. Reasons for this neglect include continuing problems with Asian tariff and non-tariff barriers (NTBs), structural differences in economic organisation and the dominant presence of American investors and traders. From an Asian vantage point, the growing 'fortress' of Europe with its punitive measures often directed at particular Asian economies, as well as the imminent enlargement of the Union to incorporate several Central and Eastern European economies, led a number of firms, especially from Japan and South Korea, to hasten investment and production in the EU during the 1980s and 1990s. Until the mid-1990s, there was little attempt to address these problems from a collective Asian standpoint, while the Europeans retained their own national trading interests and continued to do business with specific Asian national and sub-regional units. It was, nevertheless, upon the cumulative sets of these relations that ASEM would come to be based in the mid-1990s. A detailed explanation of the historical development of these channels of dialogue will not be presented here (see Bridges 1999b; and Dent 1999a and 1999b). Rather, the following section aims to illustrate how these disparate relationships gradually coalesced to establish the basis of the broader Asia–Europe partnership that began to form in the mid-1990s.

EU–ASEAN ECONOMIC LINKS

The cold war ensured for the most part that relations between the countries of ASEAN and Europe were filtered through the designs of Moscow and Washington, and in many ways remained frozen within the colonial status quo, so that even in the first decade of the twenty-first century, mutual relations continue to be enveloped by a 'tradition' of colonialism and links with a common historical legacy (see Chapter 2). Indeed, during the cold war it was the threat of ending such ties that inspired most resistance to the deepening of European economic integration. Thus, in 1973 when the EC was enlarged to include the UK (along with Ireland and Denmark) both Malaysia and Singapore feared (correctly) that they would lose many of those preferential trading benefits accorded by the UK to Commonwealth states. ASEAN as a whole also expressed concern that other regional groupings, most notably the African, Caribbean and Pacific (ACP) states, would make relative gains with Europe, to ASEAN's detriment. In the 1990s concern shifted towards the EU's intensifying focus on the countries of Central and

Eastern Europe. This uneven relationship between ASEAN and the EC/EU was to prevail even after the establishment of formal institutional relations.

Several attempts were made to deepen ties between ASEAN and the EC during the 1970s. In 1972 the EC recognised ASEAN as its first formal dialogue partner and ASEAN set up a Special Coordinating Committee to establish informal relations with Europe. An ASEAN–EC Joint Study Group was then formed in 1975, with the remit of examining how mutual relations might be strengthened. Following the first EC–ASEAN Ministerial Meeting in Brussels in November 1978, a Cooperation Agreement was signed in 1980. This agreement provided for mutual most-favoured nation (MFN) status, joint trade promotion and investment activities and collective research into how trade barriers might be reduced. It also pledged to intensify European aid to ASEAN, and to deal jointly with issues pertaining to the environment and poverty, as part of a broader dialogue. Further initiatives to stimulate greater mutual trade issued from this pledge to deepen relations, and included the establishment of an ASEAN–EU Business Council in 1983, as well as the setting up of joint ASEAN–EU investment committees in each ASEAN capital from 1987. At the same time, the European Investment Bank (EIB) gradually increased its operations within the ASEAN region, and, following the first EC–ASEAN Economic Ministers' Meeting in Bangkok in 1985, an Economic Agreement was signed between the two groupings, to be directed in particular at enhancing the presence of Europe's small and medium-sized enterprises (SMEs) in the ASEAN region. While ASEAN–EC trading figures did increase during this period for traditional as well as manufactured products, ASEAN's contribution to the EU's total trade remained at around three per cent. In practice, their relations continued to be based upon mutual neglect and ignorance, while trade increases were due in large measure to the national economic development enjoyed by many ASEAN member states. What is more, relations between the EC and ASEAN tended to be framed within the terms of a donor-recipient arrangement, and were perpetuated by the nature and structures of ODA (see Dent 1999a, pp. 36–75).

Aid and Assistance

Although the European region as a whole represents the largest source of ODA (for example, reaching 43.3 per cent of total world ODA in 1990), that figure drops by approximately three quarters (to 11.8 per cent for the same year) if only EU-level aid, and not that of specific member states, is taken into account. Most European aid is destined for the ACP countries, and ASEAN countries have seen their status decline on the list of development aid recipients since the early 1980s. Since the 1970s, over one billion ECU has been spent by the EU on development aid for ASEAN, with additional funding (23 billion ECU) for humanitarian assistance, including the settlement of refugees, the promotion of human rights and aid in the wake of natural disasters. The Philippines, which have been receiving aid since 1976, gain the lion's share of EU ODA for the region (an average of 37.7 million ECU per year by the mid-1990s), and over 75 per cent of that aid is directed towards poverty alleviation and rural development, principally through financial and technical assistance. The next largest beneficiary is Indonesia (receiving 30 million ECU per year by the mid-1990s), which underwent a shift in focus after 1992, from rural development and irrigation projects to forestry development and protection. A similar amount is spent on Vietnam, while Thailand, Cambodia, Laos and Burma have also benefited from EU ODA disbursements. Recent ODA allowances have continued to focus on poverty alleviation, rural development, social programmes and environmental protection, but have also broadened in scope to include the fight against AIDS and drugs problems in the region. As Asian economies have grown in international stature, ODA has gradually been replaced by cooperation programmes in fields such as science and technology and information technology. The Commission's DG1B responsible for the region works with ECHO (European Communities' Humanitarian Office) to liaise more closely not only with governmental agencies, but increasingly with non-governmental bodies in each recipient country. These and national efforts ensure that the EU remains the second largest ODA donor to ASEAN after Japan.

In addition to ODA, the Generalised System of Preferences (GSP) has been another distinguishing characteristic of EU–ASEAN relations. Introduced by the EC in 1971, it was designed as a means of allowing imports from developing countries to enter the EU market either duty-free or at preferential or reduced rates of duty, and provided concessions for those countries not eligible to benefit through the Lomé Convention. In the 1990s, a contentious 'graduation mechanism' was introduced into the GSP, whereby those countries deemed to have become more advanced (initially including Malaysia and Thailand) would lose their 'developing country' status and their GSP benefits, and be forced to extend reciprocity. This affected particular sectors, such as the fishery products sector in Thailand, and a number of sectors in Indonesia. The gradual elimination of these forms of aid and benefit illustrates both the changing and static nature of EU–ASEAN relations. On the one hand, they exemplify a growing European recognition of 'Asian' development (see below), but, on the other, threaten directly the survival of particular sectors of the Asian economy. The GSP has also been used as a political tool, when, for example, it was suspended against Myanmar in 1996, following further domestic political problems there. These tensions between developing and developed status for Asia have been locked into the ASEM process, as will be shown below.

EU–ASEAN in the 1990s

EU economic agreements during the 1990s came to be infused with demands for the linking of other issues. In November 1991 the EU passed a resolution to insert a human rights clause into the text of economic cooperation agreements with third parties. At an ASEAN–EU ministerial meeting that year, ASEAN participants voiced concern over this plan, believing it to be an imposition of Western values. The issue was complicated further in 1992 by Portuguese attempts to link the question of East Timor to ASEAN–EC agreements, and new cooperation agreements were vetoed until that was settled. Without resolution, both sides agreed to disagree in 1994, but calls for Indonesia to improve its human rights record in East Timor were maintained, a move which incited ASEAN leaders to reprimand Portugal at their own informal summit. The whole linkage of the human rights clause with membership of the ASEAN–EU dialogue grew more and more tense with the negotiations to admit Vietnam, Laos, Cambodia and Myanmar to ASEAN. While EU agreements with Vietnam (in 1995) and Laos and Cambodia (in 1997) did indeed include human rights clauses, disputes over Myanmar raged on, particularly once the latter had gained observer status to ASEAN in July 1996, and full membership in July 1997.

In the midst of these difficulties, there were attempts in Europe in the mid-1990s to revivify slumbering relations with Asia, most notably through the EU's 'New Asia Strategy' of 1994 (see below) and subsequently the launch at the Singapore Ministerial Meeting in February 1997 of the EU's 'New Dynamic' in EU–ASEAN relations. This latter initiative pledged deeper political dialogue and closer international cooperation (see Chapter 4), as well as a strengthening of economic ties. In order to fulfil this aim, a Work Programme for the Implementation of the New Dynamic was convened, to focus on specific trade issues, including discussions over a range of topics, such as protocols on customs cooperation and certification, and how to facilitate the liberalisation of trade in services. A number of agreements were signed to this end (see www.europa.eu.int).

A key factor in re-engaging European interest in ASEAN was the decision in 1992 to establish an ASEAN Free Trade Area (AFTA) by 2003 (with extensions for Vietnam, Myanmar and Laos). This project aims, principally through its Common Effective Preferential Tariff (CEPT), to liberalise intra-regional trade and reduce intra-regional tariffs, as well as to eliminate NTBs and establish cooperation in customs procedures. Even though some observers question the certainty of AFTA's future (Stubbs 2000, p. 312), growing economies of scale in this fourth largest trading area of 400 million people, continue to make it an attractive target for trade and investment. If European introspection contributed to ensuring that Asia remained low on the list of European priorities throughout the 1990s, new activities brought Asia into greater relief. These included the launch of ASEM in 1996, as well as an EU–ASEAN Managers Exchange Programme in November 1996 and, paradoxically, the financial crisis from 1997 that saw a 40 per cent decrease in EC exports to the region, but which precipitated a number of initiatives between the EU and ASEAN. EU–ASEAN relations were established a long time before ASEM, and for many issues provide a template to be used by the newer forum. It was clear by the mid-1990s, however, that not only was ASEAN wrestling with its own raison d'être, but that relations with Europe had reached an impasse over questions of human rights and the admission of Myanmar to ASEAN. By locating itself at the forefront of ASEM negotiations, the ASEAN grouping has enjoyed some success in playing a distinctly 'Asian' role within an inter-regional context. Moreover, what it has not been able to muster in a region-to-region relationship on European terms within the EU–ASEAN forum, it is now renegotiating as part of a larger 'region' in the ASEM framework.

EU–JAPAN ECONOMIC LINKS

In 1999, at 6.9 per cent of the EU's total, Japan was the third largest combined import/export partner for the EU (after the US and Switzerland taking 22.3 and 7.5 per cent respectively), according to Eurostat figures. Following Japan's phenomenally rapid economic rise by the end of the 1960s and beginning of the 1970s, the EC and its member states joined their American counterparts to call for voluntary as well as formal restraints in those sectors where Japanese products were seen to be flooding European markets. Since that time, European attempts to address what has been perceived as an over-penetration of the continent by Japanese firms have included in the 1980s a European 'request' for VERs, as well as anti-dumping and local content requirements (Rothacher 1983; Gilson 2000). In the 1990s these were supplemented by a formal statistical monitoring mechanism known as the Trade Assessment Mechanism (TAM), and Mutual Recognition Agreements (MRAs) in testing and certification for sectors such as telecommunication equipment and electrical appliances (COM(2000) 25 final, 9 February 2001). These actions have not, however, redressed the imbalance in Japanese and EU exports, since by 1998 the value of EU imports from Japan represented over double the value of exports (Eurostat 2000). Having peaked at US$34 billion in 1992, the EU's trade deficit with

Japan fell to US$17 billion in 1996 before creeping back up to US$34 billion in 1998. Much of this deficit (74 per cent in 1998) could be accounted for by vehicles and machinery (Eurostat 2000).

Financial and economic woes in Japan from the mid-1990s, exacerbated by the Asian financial crisis, have also seen Japan trying to export its way out of trouble at the same time as consumer demand for (often luxury) European products has declined. In 1997, for example, Japan's total exports rose 2.5 per cent year on year to US$422.9 billion, while imports dropped 2.9 per cent to US$340.4 billion. As a result, the European Commission in particular has instituted a number of actions to supplement trade negotiations with 'cultural' approaches in order to reduce trade barriers. These range from the ongoing Executive Training Programme (ETP) that began in 1979, to export promotions such as 'Gateway Japan', initiatives implemented through specific centres such as the EU–Japan Centre for Industrial Cooperation, and the promotion of business-to-business dialogue. In addition, the mid-1980s saw the EC launch a broader dialogue with the Japanese government, within which to subsume trade tensions and by which to begin to carve out a non-US style of negotiation. There followed an increasing institutionalisation of these bilateral relations, through the establishment of regular ministerial meetings in 1983 (which were, in fact, to prove rather irregular for a time) and through the creation in 1991 of an annual Japan–EC summit and attendant processes under the guise of the EC–Japan Joint Declaration at The Hague (Gilson 2000).

Global changes – particularly the ending of the cold war and the increasing globalisation of trade – stimulated further debate over the value of Japan-EU relations, by placing them as key poles of the global economic structure. In international fora, representatives from Japan and the EU have worked together over a number of issues. One important priority has become the promotion of a new round of WTO trade negotiations: Japan and the EC co-hosted an informal meeting in Geneva on 27 March 2001, for example, where they encouraged other countries to commit themselves to a new round by the time of the fourth WTO ministerial meeting in Qatar in November 2001. Both sides have an interest in preventing a return to bilateralism, although for different reasons: Japan is keen, among other issues, to address the contentious subject of anti-dumping; and the EU wishes to strengthen multilateral trade rules as part of its overall external economic strategy. The international dimension of their relationship has always been important, and since the start of the Trilateral Commission (TC) in the early 1970s, Japan–EU economic relations have been viewed as a support for a trilateral economic world order. Interestingly, the Japanese pole of that triangle has increasingly come to be replaced by 'Asia' or 'Asian ASEM', leaving general notions of trilateralism firmly intact but applied to new subjects (Dent 1999a, p. 96). From a Japanese perspective, this newer triangular setting allows Japan to claim to be acting on behalf of its region and therefore to gain more leverage vis-à-vis the larger EU and US partners in the triad. At the same time, this re-positioning of trilateralism continues to ensure the position of the US at its apex.

The role of the United States (US), never far from Asia–Europe relations, looms large in the case of Japan's economic relations with Europe, not least because of Japan's close alliance with Washington throughout the postwar period (Hook et al. 2001). More recently, the US–EU Transatlantic Declaration of 1990 and New Transatlantic Declaration of 1995 (which foresaw a New Transatlantic Marketplace to eradicate progressively barriers to trade and investment, see Dent 1999b, p. 374) have provided models not only for EU-Japan relations, but also for ASEM. Japanese reticence to participate initially in the ASEM process, financial responses to American criticisms during the Asian crises, and close cooperation between Japan and the US over the Korean peninsula all testify to the fact that the US remains an important shadow for these bilateral relations. The placing of Japanese insurance, construction and flat glass sectors on the so-called 'Watch List' of the Super 301 procedures of the US, Japan's initiation of WTO dispute settlement procedures against US anti-dumping measures on hot-rolled steel in late 2000 and the dogmatic position adopted by new US President George W. Bush over international environmental agreements (notably the Kyoto Protocol) in March 2001 may make the ride somewhat bumpy, but fundamentally the bilateral relationship continues to occupy the centre-stage of Japan's foreign policy. Thus, as relations with Europe continue to grow, they fail singularly to become a priority for the Japanese government. This factor has been long recognised and is built into the format of ASEM.

EU-Japan relations have offered a template for the EU's economic policy making responses to the other countries of the region, whose trade deficits with the European continent have caused similar concern. As a result, subsequent problems faced with regard to other Asian countries have often been treated with the same prescriptions. China, too, is now viewed from Europe through a lens designed for Japan (see below). In addition, the longevity and institutionalisation of these relations have also facilitated Japan's role as a bridge between Europe and the rest of Asia. Given its close connections to the rest of Asia and the role of Japan as a model for regional economic development, Japanese behaviour offers useful insights for its European counterparts into the nature of Asian development. In this respect, ASEM elicits both inter- and intra-regional commitments from Japan (Gilson 1999).

EU–CHINA ECONOMIC LINKS

Unlike Japan, China has been a relatively recent economic partner for Europe, largely due to the closed nature of its economy and its political distance. The first EC–China agreement was concluded in 1978, followed by an EC–China trade and economic cooperation agreement in 1985, both of which were important for increasing trade relations between the two. This timing mirrored the opening of China's economy under the tutelage of Deng Xiaoping, and the early 1980s revival of the EC. For the Europeans, the opening of China ushered in a range of market opportunities, while China for its part recognised the growing status of the European region as an external market (Zhang 1997, p. 196). Since 1978 EU–China trade has seen more than a 20-fold increase. With a cumulative total of 70 billion euro in 1999 and year-on-year growth rate of 16 per cent in the first nine months of 2000 (www.europa.eu.int), excluding trade with Hong Kong, the EU is the third largest export market for China (after the US and Japan) and second largest source of imports after Japan (Eurostat). In addition, in 2000 the EU represented the largest provider of FDI in China (after Hong Kong), and China remains the principal beneficiary of the EU's GSP, taking a share of more than 30 per cent of all preferential imports under this system. That China is an important market for Europe is clear from the rapidity with which economic relations were resumed following the Tiananmen Square massacre of June 1989. Only three years later, relations were re-ignited: 'One after another, Western governments have thus abandoned their human rights policies towards China and instead begun to engage in mutual competition for contracts' (Godement 1997, p. 278). At the same time, the Chinese administration has recognised the need to deepen its involvement in regional and international fora for economic interests linked to the Asia Pacific, where new challenges 'are forcing Chinese leaders to face the challenge of market liberalization in a rapid and comprehensive manner' (Zhang 1997, p. 201).

In the 1990s, a number of issues came to preoccupy EU–China interlocutors, and were expressed in the EU's 1995 strategy paper on China covering key issues such as trade liberalisation and industrial policy reform (see Bridges 1999a). In addition, Bridges explains how EU policies towards China had come to be linked more closely to issues of human resources, economic and social reform, business and industrial reform and environmental issues (1999b, p. 100). Following in the footsteps of Europe's channels for economic dialogue with Japan, a number of initiatives have been used to enhance trade, and include the China–Europe Business Forum and Shanghai's China–Europe International Business Schools, as well as high-level visits by European heads of state. The European Commission communication on 'Building a Comprehensive Partnership with China' of 1998 offered a framework for talks on China's WTO accession, and in that year the first EU–China summit occurred (see Chapter 4).

The issue of China's GATT/WTO membership has been a central part of EC/EU–China discussions since March 1987, following China's formal application to GATT in 1986. EU businesses still face market barriers in China, but multilaterally the EU, having lifted in 1998 the label of China as a non-market economy, has actively supported China's admission to the WTO, most vocally in the person of EU Commissioner Sir Leon Brittan. For the European Commission, China's accession to the WTO would enhance the transparency and predictability of dealing with Beijing, as well as reduce levels of tariffs and non-tariff barriers (NTBs) incurred by doing business with China. The EU signed an agreement on China's entry to the WTO in Beijing in May 2000 (following the US–China agreement of November 1999), in which it included demands for about 50 per cent of foreign ownership in joint ventures of telecommunication services, compared with the 49 per cent negotiated by the US with China; as well as greater market access for the telecommunications and insurance industries (*Financial Times* 17 May 2000 and 15 May 2000). Their package deal also included the pledge that both sides would remove their respective quotas by 2005.

China–EU relations may represent a small part of the ASEM structure but they show how the inter-regional forum has been used to enhance, rather than replace, bilateral linkages. The broader framework also provides a less controversial framework in which to deal with potentially explosive issues such as human rights and pollution as they relate to trade. ASEM is useful for both China and the EU in their bilateral relations, but for different reasons; while ASEM gives the EU a chance to confront Chinese trading barriers along with those of the rest of Asia, China regards ASEM as a means of promoting inward investment. For these reasons, their bilateral relations continue to be pursued in this broader forum.

EU–SOUTH KOREA ECONOMIC LINKS

In 1999 Eurostat figures rated South Korea the eighth largest import partner for the EU (at 2.3 per cent) and the 18th largest destination for exports (at 1.5 per cent of the total). The EU's relations with South Korea have followed a similar, but delayed, trajectory to those with Japan. South Korea, however, offers not only an important site for trade and investment, but also presents the potential both for opportunities and dangers from any reunification with the North. Like Japanese firms, South Korean ones have also penetrated many areas of Europe, after loosening FDI restrictions in the 1980s and realising that the market size, infrastructure and investment incentives offered within the EU made it an increasingly important target for Korean investment (Bridges 1999b, p. 67). Many aspects of relations between Korea and the EU echo those of the EU with Japan, in terms of the implementation of VERs and anti-dumping measures, and the role of broadening dialogue through a joint agreement in 1996. The EU–South Korean axis also raises a number of points for inter-regionalism, by opening broader channels for promoting inward investment to South Korea, and providing Europeans with a collective grouping with which to discuss various market opening measures.

INTER-REGIONAL INITIATIVES

ASEM, as noted in the Preface, is the newest and most comprehensive channel for Asia–Europe economic cooperation. Its first pillar deals with economic and trade cooperation and covers a wide variety of government-to-government and business interaction. Indeed, this pillar was the driving force of Asian interest in the origins of the ASEM process, and representatives were particularly keen to deal collectively with specific concerns, such as the removal of EU anti-dumping duties, and further to stimulate European investment in Asia. In addition, the transfer of research and development and technological advances was also important for Asia, and it is no coincidence that the Chinese government offered to host the ASEM Science and Technology Ministers' Meeting (STMM) in Beijing in October 1999. ASEM has also provided technical assistance through its Trust Fund (see below), and there it has been suggested that a dialogue be established between authorities in Asia and Europe to formulate and oversee supervisory and regulatory standards. Cooperation over information technology and e-commerce has also been pursued. For example, Korea has proposed that the EU's TEN-155 and South Korea's KOREN system be aligned as part of a Trans-Eurasia Information Network, which would ultimately link with other national and regional systems, in a way similar to the Asia Pacific Information Infrastructure Network set up in 1995. In addition, ASEM deals with important issues that cover regional boundaries, such as water and waste treatment. A workshop on Asia INTERPRISE Water Treatment and Water Processing Technology was held in May 2000 to promote direct contacts between Asia and Europe, and to draw on the existing alliances within the region (such as the Société Générale des Eaux, Eaux Lyonnaises and Thames Water in Malaysia). Thus, the larger forum once again provides a useful additional channel to pursue bilateral interests.

A number of projects have been launched under the ASEM umbrella. First, in addition to the biannual summits, the establishment of regular high-level meetings by Economic Ministers, Finance Ministers, Customs representatives and the SOMTI provides a government-level framework for action. While SOMTI meetings consider issues such as (in Brussels in July 1996) the role of the WTO (including the implementation of Uruguay Round agreements, trade and investment and trade and development), as well as the possible facilitation of trade and investment, it was proposed at ASEM 1 that SOMs be established to provide coordination and economic cooperation. SOMTI V in Brussels in July 1999 discussed preparations for the second Economic Ministers' Meeting (EMM II) to be held in October 1999 in Berlin, as well as the ASEM III agenda and WTO issues. In reviewing the different priority areas of the Trade Facilitation Action Plan (TFAP), the meeting also focused on the need to address concrete measures towards the step-by-step removal of trade barriers, especially NTBs. In addition, it adopted a list of national investment promotion and policy initiatives found to have been effective in promoting inward investment. The first Economic Ministers' Meeting in September 1997 in Japan was opened by Prime Minister Ryutaro Hashimoto as part of the 'new comprehensive Asia–Europe Partnership for Greater Growth' proposed at the first summit. This meeting was attended by all national economic ministers, and the Luxembourg minister of economy also acted as Presidency of the Council of the European Union, while the European Commission was represented by one of its vice presidents. Subsequently, a discussion paper on ASEM economic cooperation was prepared by Japan and ASEAN, and proposed the promotion of open, non-discriminatory trade, interaction with business and free trade and investment. Since that time, a regular ASEM Trade and Investment Week has also been proposed, to start from 2002. The first meeting of high-level officials discussed the ASEM Finance Ministers' Meeting in October 1996 in Washington DC (in conjunction with the World Bank/IMF meeting), which it agreed would be hosted by Thailand in September 1997 before the World Bank/IMF meeting in Hong Kong. The role of finance ministers is twofold: to discuss the macro-economic situation, as well as developments in foreign exchange markets and in EMU; and to find means of cooperating in financial regulation, customs and administration. The first customs' meeting was held in Shenzhen in June 1996 and included issues such as increasing cooperation against drugs traffickers and smuggling operations, the increased exchange of information on illicit trade and the relevant training of officials. It also considered an agreement for the control of chemical precursors, action against money laundering, and the harmonisation of the World Customs' Organisation (WCO). Its recommendations were to feed into the SOMTI. In addition, the ASEM Customs' Director-Generals/Commissioners meet regularly, and working groups on customs enforcement and procedures meet once a year. A representative example is the third meeting of the DGs and Commissioners in Brussels, which discussed illicit drugs trafficking in five areas: a general framework for cooperation; joint seminars for ASEM membership; cooperation between regional Intelligence liaison officers; risk assessment; and uses of modern technology. There are also important customs elements in the TFAP, with the aim of harmonising and simplifying the procedures of customs operations within ASEM and beyond.

ASEM also promotes private-sector activities, such as the AEBF, that has been hosted by France, Thailand, the UK and South Korea, and is designed to promote business partnerships through dialogues and exchanges. Working groups and ad hoc meetings address specific issues and may exchange opinions with the SOMTI. The AEBF's steering committee comprises the present chairman, the two most recent chairmen and representative of the country of the next forum, and it incorporates private sector representatives from coordinator countries and European coordinators, as well as one representative from an AEBF sponsoring economic organisation of the host of the next ASEM summit, the chair of the AEBF ad hoc groups and other experts where necessary. The first AEBF was held in Paris in October 1996, where it set out aims to promote business-to-business and business–government dialogue, within a non-discriminatory framework, and alongside specific recommendations relating to infrastructure, SMEs, financial services, the Europe–Asia Infrastructure Fund and the promotion of SME partnerships. The report on this forum was forwarded to the Foreign Ministers' Meeting and the Economic Ministers' Meeting. The AEBF IV was divided into six working groups. The Trade Working Group was created to examine ways of simplifying customs procedures and harmonising regulations and related systems among ASEM Member States, and recommended an increase in the use of MRAs. It also proposed ways to simplify and standardise the administration of Intellectual Property Rights (IPR). The Investment Working Group operates on the premise that FDI stabilises economies, and has a number of priority areas, which include economic and political stability, investment promotion, the creation of a liberal regulatory environment, developing an open administrative system (as defined in GATS for the enforcement of non-discriminatory laws), increasing the transparency and efficiency of national administration, and improving the general economic environment and infrastructural developments. The Financial Services Working Group aims to strengthen Asia's banking system (it recommended the adoption of the Basle Core Principles for Effective Banking Supervision) and to involve the private sector in the resolution of corporate debt problems. In addition to the working groups, the AEBF has established two task forces to examine trade facilitation and investment promotion.

The promotion of business-to-business relations is an important element of ASEM, and places particular emphasis on SMEs. By way of indication, business in Japan, Indonesia, the Philippines and Thailand is constituted by over 97 per cent SMEs, which 'contribute significantly to employment creation, to foreign exchange generation, and to more equitable income distribution' (Peña 1997, p. 9). Most of them are export oriented and therefore provide an important source of foreign exchange. Concurrently, the role of SMEs remains crucial in Europe, too, where for example Germany's SMEs now represent 98 per cent of all companies. In both regions, increased competition through globalisation threatens the sustainability of SMEs and this sector has thus become an important target of inter-regional negotiations. ASEM serves more than an élite purpose in this regard (cf. Rüland 1996), since its remit is integrally tied to the role of SMEs. Specific areas for concern include the need to establish a broad investor base for fixed income investment, promote tax incentives for corporate debt issuance and establish rating agencies and efficient custody mechanisms. Some European export credit agencies have made available credit lines to government-owned banks, in order to support the import of key raw materials, while local banks are able to provide intermediate export credits for SMEs. With regard to SMEs themselves, local development or commercial banks have been encouraged to channel long-term funds from European governments and multilateral financial institutions to SMEs, while assistance for them has also been proposed, in order to enable them to be better qualified to gain access to financial resources. A working group on SMEs has also been charged with facilitating conferences and exchanges, such as the Conference on States and Markets in Copenhagen in March 1999. This examined the role of public authorities and private actors in the promotion of economic and social progress, and examined market opportunities and ways to correct inequalities generated by market forces. SME profiles in Asia vary widely, according to the level of development of their host country (Peña 1997, p. 7), but there is now an effort underway within ASEM to establish a Cooperation Centre for SMEs to exchange information and expertise, support market access initiatives and promote cooperation in priority areas.

The most concrete manifestations of ASEM economic cooperation are the Trade Facilitation Action Plan (TFAP) and the Investment Promotion Action Plan (IPAP). The establishment of TFAP was agreed at the SOMTI I in July 1996 in Brussels, endorsed by the Economic Ministers' Meeting in Japan in September 1997, and adopted by leaders at ASEM 2 in 1998. The proposal for TFAP's priorities, system and timetables was drawn up by four 'shepherds' (representatives of the Union Presidency, the European Commission, the Philippines and Korea). Its aims are to reduce NTBs and barriers relating to the fields of customs, tests, standards, certification, accreditation, technical regulations, procurement, quarantine, SPS (sanitary-phytosanitary standards) procedures, IPR and the mobility of business people. It is, however, not a forum for negotiation. It has also held thematic meetings, such as one on standards, accreditation, certification, testing and technical regulations in September 1998. At ASEM 3, TFAP was praised for making 'good use of the non-confrontational, non-binding, voluntary and informal nature of the ASEM process', and an annex was added to the plan, in order to set a concrete timeframe for a number of goals to be reached by 2002. The IPAP was proposed at ASEM 1 and designed to generate greater investment flows. Its preliminary structure was prepared by Thailand and fed into a government and private sector working group meeting in Bangkok in 1996. It was adopted at ASEM 2 and divided into two pillars: Pillar One is responsible for investment promotion, and Pillar Two for investment policies and regulations. Both encourage government–business cooperation and an Investment Experts Group (IEG) was endorsed at ASEM 2 to coordinate the IPAP. The IEG group explores avenues for best practice in the fields of transparency, non-discrimination and national treatment, privatisation, investment incentives (tax/regime breaks), performance requirements, dispute settlement, IPR, investors' behaviour and the entry of key personnel, and IEG 2 presented the results of these studies to the Economic Ministers' Meeting in October 1999 and to ASEM 3. To date, most work has been done on the investment promotion side of IPAP. At the second IPAP IEG meeting in February 1999 a draft IPAP homepage (Virtual Information Exchange, VIE) was presented and this channel of information is now functioning (www.asem.vie.net/). These initiatives demonstrate some of the activities that function under the banner of 'ASEM', in order to develop concrete steps towards addressing and resolving where possible certain specific and generic concerns among European and Asian governments and businesses in the fields of trade and investment and the sectors affected by them. However, the framework of ASEM by which they are subsumed retains no legal basis to bind participants to these commitments, with the effect, according to Lee, that IPAP is unlikely to increase inter-regional investment flows (Lee 1998, p. 27). At the same time, ASEM's loose framework imposes no strict regime of accountability, with the result that an evaluation and measurement of these projects has not been rigorously undertaken (interview with NGO representative, December 2000).

Many of the projects undertaken as part of ASEM represent the continuation or acceleration of existing national or sub-regional projects, such as the Mekong Basin Development. The ASEAN secretariat provides an inventory of projects undertaken bilaterally and sub-regionally, which include the Mekong River Commission for water management, the Asian Development Bank (ADB)-initiated Greater Mekong Sub-region forum for development and planning and the Inter-Ministerial Conference on Mekong Basin Development initiated by ASEAN, which inter alia, looked at the Malaysian proposal for a railway from Singapore to Kunming in China. The proposed trans-Asian railway network would ultimately, it has been proposed, develop into a rail link between Asia and Europe. In this way, ASEM structures finance and support existing channels for project initiatives, secretarial support and implementation. ASEM, then, has served as vehicle not only to bring together a number of disparate initiatives, but also to consolidate into one communal history the different strings of relations enjoyed by the EU and various components of what has increasingly come to be recognised as 'Asia'. The following section examines in greater detail how Europe has come to 'imagine' Asia in this context, and to suggest some of the potential implications of such imaginings.

THE EU IMAGINES ASIA

The previous sections demonstrated a growing set of links between Asia and the EU, which served to raise the status within Europe of 'Asia' per se by the 1990s. The formative relations of the EU with ASEAN, Japan, China and South Korea, each following similar patterns and lending themselves to increasingly familiar declarations and institutional formats, strengthened the separation of this East Asian contingent from its Southern and Western neighbours. By the 1990s, then, the 'Asian miracle' combined with historical linkages to set in the European consciousness an idea of 'Asia'. The kinds of thinking that such an image of economically advanced Asia provoked, however, were rarely positive: 'European countries tend to have a one-dimensional and rather cynical view of Asia. They know it presents huge business opportunities ... The problem is that most European countries have not balanced their interest in commerce with a serious approach to Asia's political and security problems. The leitmotif of the European approach to Asia has been a kind of cynical opportunism' (*The Economist* 2 March 1996). A joint UNCTAD/European Commission report explained this deficit further:

> The benign neglect of Asia by European Union TNCs was encouraged by regional integration in Europe. Successive enlargements of the Community, removal of internal trade and investment barriers, monetary arrangements to reduce exchange-rate volatility, free trade agreements with non-member European countries and 'Europe agreements' with Central and Eastern European countries all tended to nourish an inward focus of European Union TNCs. (1996, p. 55)

European investors and traders seem to have realised Asian potential much later than did Japan and the US and, as a result, European TNCs cannot compete with their established Japanese and US counterparts in Asia, and lack, in addition, a familiarity with Asian business practices and distribution systems. In addition, Japan enjoys a competitive advantage due to its geographical placement and intra-Asian networking, while US firms also have a longer tradition of links with Asia and better access to information about Asian markets, particularly through the Japan External Trade Organisation (JETRO) and the US Department of Commerce. The EU per se has no investment promotion agency, but since the 1980s has operated a number of promotional instruments in order partially to rectify these imbalances. The following tables illustrate the growing significance of these relations in spite of such apparent neglect, and show, more interestingly still, how 'Asian ASEM' has become a recognised regional grouping for the purposes of analysing EU trade flows.

Table 3.1 Geopolitical Groupings: Imports (1999)

Rank	Partners	Value (mio euro)	%
	WORLD*	772.086	100
a)	**NAFTA**	**176.833**	**22.9**
b)	AMLAT	36.391	4.7
c)	CEEC	92.261	11.9
d)	CIS	31.893	4.1
e)	MED	47.076	6.1
f)	**A.ASEM**	**191.299**	**24.8**

Table 3.2 Geopolitical Groupings: Exports (1999)

Rank	Partners	Value (mio euro)	%
	WORLD*	753.342	100
a)	**NAFTA**	**209.521**	**27.6**
b)	AMLAT	45.583	6.0
c)	CEEC	118.094	15.6
d)	CIS	20.844	2.8
e)	MED	69.053	9.1
f)	**A.ASEM**	**96.8**	**12.8**

Table 3.3 Geopolitical Groupings: Imports and Exports (1999)

Rank	Partners	Value (mio euro)	%
	WORLD*	1.530.428	100
a)	**NAFTA**	**386.354**	**25.2**
b)	AMLAT	81.974	5.4
c)	CEEC	210.356	13.7
d)	CIS	52.777	3.4
e)	MED	116.129	7.6
f)	**A.ASEM**	**288.099**	**18.8**

Notes:
a) USA, Canada, Mexico
b) 20 countries of Latin America
c) Bulgaria, Cyprus, Czech Republic, Estonia, Hungary, Latvia, Lithuania, Malta, Poland, Romania, Slovakia, Slovenia, Turkey
d) Armenia, Azerbaijan, Belarus, Georgia, Kazakhstan, Kyrgyzstan, Moldova, Russia, Tajikistan, Turkmenistan, Ukraine, Uzbekistan
e) Algeria, Cyprus, Egypt, Gaza and Jericho, Israel, Jordan, Lebanon, Malta, Morocco, Syria, Tunisia, Turkey
f) Brunei, China, Indonesia, Japan, Laos, Malaysia, Myanmar, Philippines, Singapore, South Korea, Thailand, Vietnam
*World excludes intra-EU flows

Source: Eurostat

Table 3.4 Share of World Trade (1998 as % total)*

	Commercial Services	Goods
EU*	24.9	18.9
Asian ASEM	19.4	21.0
US	20.1	18.9

Note:
*Excludes intra-EU trade

Source: Eurostat

Table 3.5 Foreign Direct Investment (FDI) (1998 as % total)

	Inflows	Outflows
EU*	19.4	45.0
Asian ASEM	14.4	8.0
US	37.4	28.0

Source: Eurostat

Asian overtures to international trade and investment, combined with the rapid growth of key Asian economies during the 1980s and 1990s, made European governments and industry sit up and take notice of the potential rivals and partners of the Asian region and of the 'Asian dynamism' which accompanied it. As Asian economic strength grew, moreover, European views of the Asian region came increasingly to regard its constituent states as a collective group which could, more and more, be dealt with as such. In a growing Europe whose diplomatic and personnel capacities were being ever stretched, this consolidation of Asia made political and economic sense. While the phenomenal growth of Asia's NIEs provided a number of investment opportunities for Europeans in Asia, TNCs from the EU provided Asia with a share of only two to three per cent of both EU FDI outflows and outward stock during the 1980s and 1990s. These values rose during the 1990s when the importance of Asian natural resources became part of FDI strategies, and as a result Asia represented a larger concentration in the primary sector than is the case for EU FDI elsewhere. Similarly, Europeans do not look to Asia as a manufacturing base in the same way that Japan does, even though investment in the manufacturing sector equals the European commitment to this sector in other parts of the world. Rather, EU FDI in Asia is concentrated in chemicals, petroleum, other services and financial services (in that order). These amounted to about 70 per cent of EU FDI in developing Asia in 1993 (UNCTAD and European Commission 1996, p. 22). The EU's share of FDI in services is below that for EU FDI elsewhere, while EU firms, unlike their Japanese and American counterparts, are virtually absent from transport equipment FDI in Asia. Nevertheless, an increasingly complex and sophisticated Asian market, combined with R&D programmes, facilitate the development of closer relations with European firms and thus help to diversify investment. This has also been accompanied by a concerted Asian attempt to attract inward investment and European technological know-how, supported by a wave of liberalisation of outward FDI flows. Despite these attempts and in spite of continued investment in Asia after the financial crisis, European businesses continue to be reluctant to invest in Asia, viewing it as an area lacking in transparency, harmonised laws, protection and enforcement, IPR provisions and control over business enterprise in general (Lee, C. 1998, p. 21).

The use of 'Asian ASEM' as a label gives more concrete expression to European ideas of the region. Supported not only by the vague notion of 'Asian development', but also by the joint participation of the Asian ASEM members in other fora such as APEC, the ARF and the ASEAN+3, the relative institutionalisation of Asia in this form has given rise to external benefits for, and assumptions about, the nature of Asia (Smith, M. 1998, p. 295). For example, previously excluded countries such as Vietnam became more economically interesting to Europe and the West once their likely membership of ASEAN appeared evident and Western European firms were incentivised to develop business ties with Vietnam. This institutionalisation derives from a number of factors. First, as mentioned above, it issues from increased collective participation of the Asian ASEM states in international economic institutions. Second, it is supported by a growing web of intra-regional Asian linkages. One particularly good example concerns the most populous country of Southeast Asia, namely Indonesia, whose threatened instability holds potential repercussions for the whole regional balance. When President Abdurrahman Wahid took over in October 1999, he made a point of working closely with Japan, as well as the other member states of ASEAN, in order to garner regional support for Indonesian economic development. Third, this limited form of institutionalisation issues from a growing dissatisfaction (most notable during the financial crisis, see below) at the blanket restrictive measures being heaped upon Asia by the West (Fodella 1997). Moreover, Asian grievances have been supported by authoritative voices: Joseph Stiglitz, formerly chief economist at the World Bank, became one of the most ardent critics of IMF and US Treasury Department orthodoxy, while renowned American economist Jeffrey Sachs criticised every single IMF initiative since the start of the crisis in July 1997.

Specific sectoral developments also herald the growing recognition of an 'Asian' identity, and include the arms trade. While Western European spending on arms declined by 3.8 per cent during the 1993–7 period, East Asia saw a 5.1 per cent increase for the same period (US Department of State 2000, p. 1). For East Asia, this represents an increase from nine to 21 per cent of world spending in arms between 1987 and 1997, compared with a change from 29 to 34 per cent for North America and from 16 to 22 per cent for Western Europe (US Department of State 2000, p. 1). As a result, of the world's top ten military spenders in 1997, three were in East Asia and three in the European Union, as shown in Table 3.6. While the top Asian spenders in 1997 were China and Japan, the level of military expenditure for economically less developed countries such as Indonesia, Singapore and Vietnam is extremely high and rising rapidly. In arms transfers, too, East Asia's share more than doubled, to reach 30 per cent of the global total in 1997 and imports increased by 19 per cent in the same year. Although the financial crisis curbed some (but not Chinese) military spending and training (Acharya 1999b, p. 13), ongoing and revitalised modernisation and defense strategies ensure that it has picked up once again. These impressive figures offer important opportunities to European firms, although many arms sales continue to rely on long-established relationships.

Table 3.6 Top Ten Military Spenders in 1997 (US$ bn)

United States	276
China	75*
Russia	42*
France	42
Japan	41
UK	35
Germany	33
Italy	23
Saudi Arabia	22
South Korea	15

Note:
*Estimates

Source: US Department of State

For example, although its principal market is the Middle East, the UK also sells to Indonesia and Malaysia, France's most important sales are to Taiwan and Germany sells mostly to South Korea and Thailand. China continues to purchase heavily from Russia, rather than EU states (US Department of State 2000, p. 13). This regional industry is of increasing interest to Europeans as a whole, and is built largely upon a *lack* of Asian institutionalised cooperation and depends rather upon intra-regional suspicions. These suspicions engender a regional 'Asian' arms race that provides rich opportunities for external suppliers (Mak 1998, p. 94). With an estimated Chinese capacity, according to the editor of Jane's fighting ships, to dispatch 11 000 troops and 250 main battle tanks by sea, and the regional concern which that build up evokes, the regional arms race is being taken seriously (*Financial Times* 29/30 July 2000). However, results of the NGO-sponsored Europe–Asia Hague Peace Appeal in May 1999 demonstrated that, while the arms trade is an important issue for both Asian and European activists, it is seldom analysed in the context of security relations. Indeed, the first ASEM NGO in 1996 (see Chapter 5) had called for the ARF to be transformed into a Multilateral Security and Disarmament Conference for the Asia Pacific region involving all regional military powers, in order to prevent an Asian arms race. This issue represents, however, a key point of intra and inter-regional competition, as European suppliers compete with one another and collectively face the challenge of US influence in this industrial sector. The implications of this particular form of economic competition, nevertheless, are significant for the security field, as a military build-up in Asia and the ensuing increase of arms sales on the part of Europeans and Americans shape and challenge the current balance of power in and beyond the Asian region. In addition, economic interests in this area inevitably colour Western approaches to Asian human rights' abuses, as in the case of Indonesia (see Chapter 4). This sector, then, illustrates how a growing perception of a regional arms race within Asia motivates European firms to face the dominant challenge of the US in that region, with the result that the Asian entity is reaffirmed and economic issues spill over into the security realm. What is more, the National and Theatre Missile Defense (NMD/TMD) programmes under development by the US have the potential seriously to undermine Asian regional stability, most notably by drawing Japan into a new type of alliance with the US that is directly aimed at China and likely to raise hackles in Beijing (Mak 1998, p. 96). All of these issues complicate the economic rationale of selling arms to the region.

A number of documents issued by the EU track the changes in approach towards the Asian region. At the core of these remains the important, but bland 'New Strategy Toward Asia' of 1994 and its 2001 revision (see Chapter 4). As Pelkmans and Balaoing conclude, however, while this document 'may have been the fruit of a most-useful process of changing the ways of thinking on Asia and EU–Asia relations ... it adds up to little more' (1996, p. 1). As they go on to note, somewhat ironically, this document would suggest that the EU had an 'old' strategy in the first place (1996, p. 2). Several innovations did nevertheless result from the strategy paper, and include the Asia-Invest programme to promote two-way trade and investment flows, especially through information and coordination and with the active participation of industry. This scheme includes a Business Priming Fund to assist projects such as marketplace monitoring, language and business acculturation and technical assistance. In addition an annual Asia-Invest Conference, Asia-Invest Membership Scheme and Asia-Invest Inforoute were also introduced. These were complemented by Asia-Invest Support Activities (such as six-monthly Asia Branch Network meetings), the extension of a Business Cooperation Network (BC-NET) and Bureau de rapprochement des Entreprises (BREs) and EU-Information Centre links with Asia, and an SME-directed European Community Investment Partners scheme (ECIP) that ended in 1999. By the end of 1998, China was receiving 16 per cent of the ECIP benefit, from which over 60 joint ventures resulted. These various methods enable European businesses to identify potential partners and conduct feasibility studies. In 1994 a Communication on Industrial Competitiveness and an action programme were also set up and included seminars, an increase in scientific and technical cooperation, training and the dissemination of technology. All of these undertakings were rocked by the Asian financial crisis, which had serious – negative and positive – repercussions on European views of Asia. The 1994 Strategy paper was updated in September 2001, with the publication of a new communication from the Commission, entitled 'Europe and Asia: A Strategic Framework for Enhanced Partnerships'. This paper reflects upon, inter alia, the principal developments in economic relations among the states of ASEM, with particular emphasis on the effects of the Asian financial crisis, the imminent enlargement of the EU, the development of the World Trade Organisation (WTO) and a 1998 ASEM 'trade and investment pledge'. A number of concrete initiatives ('action points') include ongoing pledges to reduce technical barriers to trade, to promote transparency and to strengthen private sector cooperation between Europe and Asia, as well as encouraging Asia to take advantage of European 'experience in regional cooperation on economic and financial policy' and to make the most of the 'new possibilities offered by the euro' (COM (2001) 469 final, 4 September 2001). These pledges were set out alongside the development of a poverty reduction programme and expanded dialogue on social policy, targeting the poorest countries of the broad Asian region represented in this document.

FINANCIAL CRISIS OF 1997

In many ways, the financial crisis demonstrated both the weaknesses and potential of the European understanding of, and approach to, Asia. When over-borrowing by Thai financial institutions, especially of 'hot money' (Beeson and Robison 1997, p. 6), combined with a slowdown in growth and a stock market slump, speculators fled and the Thai government was forced to float its currency, the baht, on 2 July 1997. Thus, there began a train of events that would come to be known as the 'Asian crisis' or 'contagion' (Garnaut 1998, p. 14). Between early July 1997 and January 1998, Indonesia's stock market lost about 75 per cent of its value, Thailand 63 per cent and South Korea subsequently lost 67 per cent (Godement 1999, p. 79). Initially, the crisis split the region: some governments (namely, Thailand, Indonesia and South Korea) accepted strict IMF rescue packages; while others (most notably Malaysia, which in April 1998 refused IMF assistance after Mahathir lambasted foreign speculators) implemented their own recovery plans. The IMF, for its part, targeted the weak banking sector and large amount of unhedged short-term foreign debt by the corporate sector in Indonesia, while in Korea excessive government interference in the economy, close bank–conglomerate links and inadequate regulation were the principal foci of concern (International Monetary Fund 1999, p. 30). The crisis saw the flow of investment to Asia drop by half from 1997 to mid-1998. In spite of their common problems, Asian countries did not cooperate initially in their responses, as Ramos, Chuan and Mahathir all pointed fingers at their neighbours' own performances (Godement 1999, p. 63). Not only were they domestically oriented, but, even where expressions of solidarity were conveyed, there was no regional mechanism through which to channel a collective response and therefore expectations of one were somewhat unreal. What is more, although ASEAN was seen by some to have 'failed' in the crisis, the informal pragmatism that underpins the grouping and its AFTA aspirations were never designed for this kind of crisis management. Meanwhile Japan, overcome by its own financial problems, failed in its one attempt to offer a regional solution through its Asian Monetary Fund (AMF) proposal of 1997 (Hook et al. 2001; see also Leifer 2000). For their part, member states of the EU barely acknowledged the extent of the crisis until 21 November 1997, when the South Korean government called in the IMF, having failed to defend its falling currency, the won, and its suffering banks, by spending huge amounts of its reserves (Smith, H. 1998, p. 78).

Interestingly, Asian representatives did voice regional concerns against the attitude of the US-led IMF approach and the apparent inefficacy of the European response. One common criticism from within the region and beyond was directed at the harshness and inappropriate application of traditional IMF tight monetary and fiscal strategies (Vines 1999, p. 154). Its programmes focused on financial sector restructuring, the closure of non-viable financial institutions, intervention in the weakest banks, the establishment of new frameworks of monetary policy and an increase in efficiency in financial structures. However, these, according to Vines and others, were responses to excessive domestic spending and served to make matters worse, while freeing international banks from bearing the costs of recovery (Vines 1999, p. 154). Joseph Stiglitz said the institution's policy of conditionality was flawed and he condemned the so-called 'Washington consensus' (bastion of neoliberalism embodied by the collective representation of the US Treasury, World Bank and IMF), for imposing rapid trade and capital account liberalisation and the privatisation of state-owned enterprises (*Financial Times* 29 November 1999). The crisis showed ASEAN vulnerability to the global market, as well as the limitations of APEC, giving rise to new doubts 'about the benign nature of "open regionalism"' (Acharya 1999b, p. 15). Discussions over recovery prescriptions were also infused with human rights requirements, causing further disquiet about the appropriateness of international responses to regional problems. Moreover, the resentment evoked by prescriptive IMF intervention, dominated as it clearly was by US interests, recalled for many in Asia the colonial period of domination and drew participants closer in mutual antipathy for the international body and its underwriters. Not only that, but those very prescriptions were often given for the wrong diagnosis and, as a result, the IMF's public criticism of regional governments and economic policies also depressed demand further and worsened the crisis. In some cases, the body even had to backtrack and renegotiate its agreements (Godement 1999, pp. 73 and 78).

At first the EU scarcely seemed to register the Asian financial earthquake, and at the Finance Ministers' Meeting in September 1997 only three of the fifteen European representatives attended, since most were too busy dealing with the effects of the euro. In contrast, almost all Asian representatives were there (Godement 1999, p. 65). European moves to reassure Asians resembled those undertaken in 1989 when faced with accusations of fortress Europe: they were only partially successful and were regarded with suspicion. There was much criticism of Europe's reaction to Asian ills, and it was observed that 'Western powers are remarkably uninterested in the region's power balance' (Godement 1999, p. 18). Most serious, however, was Europe's lack of *visibility* (*Far Eastern Economic Review* 19 March 1998): typical was the fact that the idea of sending an EU envoy was dropped, on account of its not being part of EU competence. For some critics, the crisis represented the 'end of the beginning', for the following reason: 'Where it had seemed that interregional dialogue would teach Europe lessons from East Asia, it now appears that it will become a conduit for the imposition of a reformulated Western orthodoxy on the east' (Cammack and Richards 1999, p. 704). ASEM leaders may indeed to have been mistaken even in their initial optimism. To suggest that Europeans generally received less criticism than the US during the crisis (Bridges 1999a, p. 464), then, is a misreading: they received less attention generally and when they were confronted it was for their feebleness. The words of EU Commissioner Thibault de Silguy, responsible for the launch of the euro, have been trumpeted for their promises to protect the launch of the euro in spite of the Asian crisis. Less well reported is the fact that he also made clear that the EU, through the euro, would be in a better position to coordinate help for such crises (Thibault de Silguy 1998). In January 1998, Jacques Santer made a speech in Singapore, which finally demonstrated that Europe had noticed the crisis, that Europeans were contributing 30 per cent of the IMF quota (compared with the US' 18 per cent) and keeping their markets open. It could not, however, dim the US dynamo. According to the BIS (Bank for International Settlements), in June 1997 European banks held 40 per cent of Asian debt and 50 per cent of debts contracted through Hong Kong and Singapore, but this tended to be overlooked (Godement 1999, p. 66). European banks also brokered IMF agreements to avoid default by debtor countries, and some European governments were softer than the US in their response to Asian resistance to IMF conditionality (Godement 1999, p. 67). There was also a flurry of visits from Kohl to Suharto, Delors to Suharto and Derek Fatchett of the British Foreign and Commonwealth Office (FCO) on a tour of the region (Godement

1999, p. 67). At the end of the day, however, European interests in Asian problems were vague and largely unnoticed.

The crisis dampened EU exports to Asia (matched by a fall in Asian FDI into Europe), but resulted in an increase of imports as Asia tried to export its way out of trouble. Intensifying exporting strategies have increased links with Europe and extended the web of complex links between them (Dent 1999b, p. 382). For example, sales of Korean cars to the EU grew by 38 per cent compared to the previous year in the first eight months of 1998 (Bridges 1999a, p. 460). By 1998, there was a growing realisation in Europe that ASEM could be used as one vehicle to push collectively for better access to Asian markets as a whole (Yeung et al. 1999, p. 74). By 1999 most Asian countries had earned new record inflows of investment. A belief in long-term prospects combined with new opportunities and some fairly strong fundamental structures, despite the 'crony capitalist' legacies, led to increased European demand. M&As from Europe have increased since the crisis, in the wake of attractive falling asset prices (Bridges 1999a, p. 461). Following the crisis, brand names and financial houses have been snapped up by the US, and there has been limited European activity in the region. For example, ABN Amro of the Netherlands has taken over the Bank of Asia (Thailand's number 11), the Société Générale bought the marketing and research branches of Peregrine in Hong Kong, BASF bought several Korean firms and Volvo bought Samsung's construction equipment unit (Godement 1999, p. 198). However, most European banks have had to scale back their operations in Asia, so that Europe can hardly be said to have stamped an indelible presence there. Governmental attempts were made to address the longer term problems resulting from the crisis. At the Economic Ministers' Meeting in Berlin in October 1999, the Chair's statement noted that Asian export levels to Europe during the crisis had been maintained, and that although European exports to Asian had declined there were signs of recovery. In addition, the EU also pledged bilaterally US$5.9 billion to the Republic of Korea's second line of defence (compared with US$10 billion from Japan and $5 billion from the US), in addition to the bilateral technical assistance offered by some EU member states. Meanwhile, private European banks also rolled over some of their short-term credits. On one side, Asian participants recognised the need for European investment and funds to help redress the economic chaos and to keep European markets open to Asian goods, especially with the threat of increased US protectionism in its own market. On the other, the EU recognised long-term benefits in aiding the Asian recovery. Since Asian borrowers were still paying off the estimated US$365 billion they owed to European banks (as of June 1997, and compared with US$275 billion for Japan and US$45 billion for the US), there was a need to recoup European investment. The following viewpoint was articulated by the *chef de cabinet* of European Commission President Santer: 'Asem is a long-term investment. The financial crisis in Asia has made it even more important' (*Far Eastern Economic Review* 19 March 1998).

The most concrete attempt to do something about the crisis was the ASEM Trade and Investment Pledge made at ASEM 2 and the Trust Fund at the World Bank from June 1998. Although 'neither impressive nor very original' (Godement 2000, p. 125), they provided the seven countries most affected by the crisis with money for technical assistance, advice on restructuring their financial sectors and measures to deal with the growing social problems caused by the crisis, at an estimated cost of more than US$45 million (42 million ecu). In addition, a European Financial Expertise (EFEX) Network was established to provide assistance to Asian economic representatives, in order to help them gain access to European expertise in reforming their financial sector and to bring European and Asian experts together. An extension of the Trust Fund to Phase 2 was approved at ASEM 3 and its modalities determined in Kobe in January 2001. Specific issues such as the importance of indirect regulation and the need to address problems in Offshore Financial Centres were also pinpointed, as was the need to act in conjunction with private creditors. Throughout the period of the crisis, there were regular contacts between Asian and European representatives, such as through the Japan–EU summit, ASEM and the SOMs, which provided opportunities for the mutual exchange of experiences. In the wake of that crisis, moreover, the need to consult mutually over other crisis situations has been recognised: 'Brazil invades Europe–Asia Summit Agenda' read the *International Herald Tribune* headline of 16 January 1999, referring to the Foreign Ministers' meeting in Frankfurt. The turmoil of the Brazilian currency could not be ignored by ASEM, and Japan and Germany even declared themselves in favour of an exchange rate regime involving key inter-regional currencies. However, the US, as ASEM member states are aware, remains hostile to any new financial architecture.

In the wake of the regional crisis and in the face of external influences, a number of intra-regional initiatives have been proposed, giving further succour to the idea of Asian regionalisation. These include: Thai Foreign Minister Surin Pitsuwan's call for 'flexible engagement' (or 'intrusive regionalism'), as a result of hindsight suggesting that Thailand should not have been left alone to deal with its troubles (Acharya 1999b, p. 19); and leaders of the ASEAN+3 (Japan, China and South Korea) meeting in Manila in November 1999 adopted the 'Joint Statement on East Asia Cooperation', by which they resolved to promote cooperation in a wide range of areas encompassing monetary and financial cooperation, social and human resources development, scientific and technical development, the cultural and information area, development cooperation, political-security and transnational issues. Some observers and practitioners have called for an Asian variation on European monetary integration, most notably the creation of some sort of currency union, like or unlike the euro. An international currency is, like a domestic one, applicable as a medium of exchange, a unit of account and a store of value. It can be used to settle international trade and financial transactions and for invoicing, as well as to express exchange rate relations and behave as an investment asset, including foreign exchange reserves (Kwan 1994, pp. 158-9). The US dollar remains the currency anchor in Asia, and although Asian currencies no longer fix their exchange rates against it, most Asian current account transactions continue to be conducted in dollar denominations. In addition, the proportion of Japanese imports from Southeast Asia denominated in yen and external debts of the Asian countries denominated in yen has increased (Kwan 1994, p. 160). Concrete suggestions for the development of an Asian currency include the January 1998 suggestion by the Minister of Trade and Industry of the Philippines to move to regionally pegged currencies to displace the dollar (Godement 1999, p. 190), an idea that was taken by Malaysian Prime Minister Mahathir in February 1998 to Indonesia, Thailand, Singapore and back to the Philippines. At the same time, Japan's Vice Minister of Finance for International Affairs, Eisake Sakakibara, promised an increase in the use of the yen in Japan-ASEAN trade, and by April 1998 the idea of a monetary union and a financial early warning and surveillance agreement was entrusted to the ADB. Lee Kuan Yew has also noted that such a union may 'be to the advantage of Southeast Asia because much of the intra-ASEAN, intra-East Asian trade can be done in yen' (*Far Eastern Economic Review* 8 June 2000). In concrete terms, Japan has helped shape, but been assiduous not to lead, a proposal to set up a web of bilateral pacts to swap and repurchase central bank reserves among ASEAN, Japan, South Korea and China, as agreed at the ADB meeting in Thailand on 6 May 2000. Known as the Chiang Mai Initiative, this project represented for some practitioners the 'Asian Monetary Fund Reborn' (*Far Eastern Economic Review* 18 May 2000). As the *Review* emphasised: 'the Chiang Mai accord does give Southeast Asia and Northeast Asia a structure and excuse to keep talking about regional economic issues in concrete terms' (8 May 2000). This model has been stimulated by the system of EMU in Europe, but framed within non-Western norms. The idea of currency union, however, is still vague, and vacillates from the idea of Japan as a centre of economic gravity within the Western Pacific to the use of the yen as a regional currency peg (Kwan 1994, p. 158). The possibility of a 'yen bloc' has therefore been voiced, and although it is frequently discounted, brings greater salience to the idea of 'a grouping of countries which use the yen as an international currency and maintain stable exchange rates against the yen' (Kwan 1994, pp. 6 and 8). If they move from a loose pegging to the dollar to becoming gradually pegged to the yen (or to a basket of currencies with the yen at its core) more Asians importers and exporters would invoice in yen and borrowers would hold portfolios in yen-denominated assets. However, to date, the volatility of Asian currencies against yen has restrained its use in Asia as an international currency. For example, Japan mooted its support for an East Asian Common Market in Manila in November 1999, and supported the Thai Minister of Commerce's candidacy for the head of the WTO, against Washington's favourite, New Zealand's Michael Moore. It seems that the Japanese government wants to capitalise on Asian discontent with the US, while at the same time trying to counterbalance the economic role of China in the region, and has, for example, increased its foreign aid to Cambodia by 50 per cent. In addition, Japan is 'flirting with a slightly less deferential approach to the US' (*Financial Times* 16 January 2001), notably through advocates such as Sakakibara who, in December 1999, promoted the introduction of an Asian currency (*The Korea Times* 4 December 1999). He said that one of the causes of the crisis was excessive dependence on the US dollar: 'the Japanese government is trying to contribute to an increasing Asian influence over international financial institutions' (*The Korea Times* 4 December 1999). He attacked both US and European dominance of international financial institutions: 'The day is over when Europe and the US can dominate the policy process of the IMF and World Bank – that is quite archaic' (*Financial Times* 24 March 2000). The Chief Executive of Hong Kong's Monetary Authority, Joseph Yam, said the yen was not a regional currency, and declared himself in favour of an Asian currency, the Asian currency unit (*Financial Times* 6 January 1999). Joseph Estrada of the Philippines at Manila in July 1998 also espied prospects for a single currency (*Financial Times* 25/26 July 1998). These proposals may represent continuing reactions from an Asia reluctant to repeat the consequences of the 1997 crisis, but they nevertheless bring into relief the prospect of consolidating further notions of Asian regionalisation in the face of external threats and challenges: 'From the Asian point of view there is a stronger recognition that regional initiatives can help maximise the benefits of globalisation while minimising the disruptive effects of global financial markets' (*Financial Times* 13/14 January 2001). Several European representatives have joined these calls, as can be seen from the joint French and Japanese proposal in Frankfurt in early 2001 to promote an intermediate currency band arrangement, based on basket of currencies including the euro, the US dollar and the yen (*Financial Times* 15 January 2001). The aftermath of the crisis has also precipitated calls for Asian countries to avoid becoming marginalised in the process of globalisation, and in February 2001 delegates from 25 Asian countries endorsed a declaration in Boao, China, establishing the Boao Forum for Asia – a regional version of the World Economic Forum held annually in Switzerland. This non-governmental, non-profit forum is designed to increase cooperation among Asian countries and to discuss important issues linked to regional economic development. In the opening speech, Chinese President Jiang Zemin stated: 'We Asian countries, though with different national conditions, are faced with the common task of seizing the opportunity, standing up to the challenges and working for a steady economic and social development' (*Associated Free Press* 28 February 2001; *Financial Times* 28 February 2001).

The End of a Colonial Era?

Dent is optimistic that the growing recognition of 'Asia' signals the end to the colonial legacy and the start of an interdependent relationship (1999a, p. 36). However, increased attention by the Europeans to the links between human rights, democracy, the reduction of excessive military expenditure, good governance and economic aid and investment have made this transition a difficult one (Dios et al. 1996, p. 6), since in this way, too, it is against a Western scale that Asia continues to be judged. The shadow of the colonial past continues to inform European perspectives on Asia, and in so doing collectivises a set of disparate experiences, in a number of ways. First, the legacy of Western superiority was challenged but not eradicated by Japanese successes in the region. The exchanges that take place in the ASEM negotiations demonstrate a continued urge for the Europeans to force upon Asia market opening measures and human rights requirements, which are couched in a rhetoric of Asia's need to improve its own record. Asian resistance to this kind of treatment, echoed most clearly in Mahathir's exhortations for Asia to say 'No' to the West, seem to bear out this defensive role for Asia in the face of European superiority, or at least towards European superciliousness. Second, anti-colonial movements and struggles for independence shaped both the nature of intra-regional relations as well as the collective recognition of an external threat. Bandung in 1955 demonstrated the need for small states to work together, while the establishment of ASEAN in 1967 illustrated the need to deal with regional problems within the region. This view has taken on a salient resonance since 1997, when a collective response failed to materialise. Third, the colonial period created a framework for underestimating the region. For these reasons, the 'modern history of East Asia has taken the West by surprise', since it continues to be underestimated by Western powers (Godement 1997, p. 274). Only now has the possibility of the EU as an anti-model started to take shape, yet it still wears the rhetoric of defensive posturing. From the European point of view, cultural arrogance led to the belief that Asian's own financial 'crony capitalism' could not happen in Europe. Finally, the colonial period set up a menu of 'universal' rights and values, which the Asian community has been fending off ever since. Mahathir accuses Europeans of arrogance (cited in Godement 1997, p. 280), but even China has engaged in the terms of the human rights debate, if only to present a non-conformist view. The agenda is set by the EU, because the Europeans behave as though their agendas are universal. What is important to understand, then, is not that a specific level of Asian integration had been achieved by a given date, but that it is being informed and influenced by interaction with a much more significant other that retains discursive authority within the region-to-region conversation. 'Asia' also became a unit in this crisis by becoming 'a proxy for debates between the IMF and World Bank factions' (Godement 1999, p. 2).

One of the impacts of this growing sense that an Asian region can be approached – in both practical and cognitive ways – is that major actors may potentially be excluded. Most salient in this regard is Taiwan. For the Europeans, Taiwan offers an important market, not least for weapons and military equipment, as illustrated by the sale of Dutch submarines and French fighter aircraft in the 1980s and 1990s. A rapid growth in Taiwanese exports to the EU since the 1980s has led to a trade surplus in Taiwan's favour and a number of trade disputes. Although relations between the EU and Taiwan have in some ways echoed those of Europe with South Korea, the unique political status of Taiwan means that negotiations have often been left to individual EU member states (Bridges 1999b, pp. 59 and 63). The consolidation of an 'Asian ASEM' community has the potential to marginalise this island state further. There are, then, both practical and cognitive consequences for the ways in which European views of Asia have coalesced around the Asian Ten of ASEM. Implications for this perception will be examined in the concluding section. First, it is important to examine how Asia perceives the more 'advanced' region of Europe.

IMAGINING REGIONS – ASIA ESPIES EUROPE

Issues of practice and perception also inform Asian views of Europe. Asian interest in Europe, with the exception of Japan, only really began in the 1980s, and was intensified by the EC's preparations for the single European market and the 1992 programme: 'The Asians – led by Japan – suspected that the single market project was at least partly aimed at them, because they were formidably competitive in those products, such as cars and electronics, which the European governments were most likely to protect' (Bridges 1999b, p. 126). As a result of the growing perception of the erection of a 'fortress Europe', Japan and South Korea especially worried about the future of their automobile exports. Asian investment in Europe has always been rather difficult, mainly due to the competitive limitations of Asian firms, their preference for other locations, regulations and language barriers in Europe, the costs of investment and home country policies. What is more, many businesses within East Asia are suspicious of the EU's development of trade and competition policy, trade-related investment measures, and environmental and labour clauses, since they tend to redound to the advantage of Europe and to the detriment of Asia (Dent 1999b, pp. 387–8). While there are available incentives for foreign investors to enter the EU, restrictions on certain sectors such as telecommunications, as well as general local content requirements and access to R&D and visas, make investment there difficult. For this reason, and despite the regional core networks established by firms such as Toyota within Europe, FDI from developing Asia between 1990 and 1993 accounted for only one per cent of inward FDI into the EU. The fragmented and differentiated nature of the European market also makes it less attractive than the US, while the fact that the policy framework in Europe is often set nationally makes it hard for outsiders to decipher. Furthermore, the nature of the EU makes it so that certain issues have to be dealt with bilaterally, such as the double taxation treaties and investment treaties.

During the 1990s several states, such as Singapore and Thailand, came to pay greater interest in Europe, seeing, in particular, investment in Central and Eastern Europe as a way of overcoming levels of current and projected protectionism. The geographical proximity of these potential host countries to the EU market, their preferential arrangements and imminent entry into the Union gave them prized regional access and made them lucrative targets for investment. Moreover, while local demand continued to increase, labour and raw material costs made it cost effective to locate production plants there. At the same time as offering potential opportunities for Asian investment, however, many countries of Central and Eastern Europe are near rivals to Asians, in terms of what they produce, for example chemical and low-technology manufactures. There is concern within Asia, therefore, that European economic attention will continue to be directed at this region, to East Asia's detriment (Dent 1999b, p. 385). More significantly, ASEAN continues to be more concerned about, and interested in, the future of APEC than that of the EU, since its economic interests are tied more closely to this forum. In addition, APEC is premised upon a form of 'open regionalism' which is amenable to Asian (and especially ASEAN's) way of doing business, in contrast to what are often perceived as incompatible rigid rule-based negotiations by the EU.

That is not to say that individual firms from within Asia have not engaged successfully in Europe. Best known are Japanese and South Korean investment strategies in the region. In particular, the location of Japanese production plants in the UK (especially in the automobile industry) since the 1980s meant that by 1995 the UK held two-fifths of all Japanese FDI stock. Thai, Singaporean and Taiwanese investment has also concentrated on the UK. Most Japanese FDI in the EU is trade-related (commerce) and finance. European leaders increasingly tour a range of countries in Asia to solicit investment: during one trip to Asia in 1993 Chancellor Kohl signed US$4 billion in contracts; and in 1996 Belgian Prime Minister Jean-Luc Dehaene likened ASEM 1 to a trade fair, because of the number of contracts being signed at the time. British Prime Minister John Major used ASEM 1 to garner a contract for Davy International Ltd to construct a brand new steelworks near Bangkok, while Chancellor Kohl helped Siemens conclude a deal for the construction of a natural gas electricity centre, a Spanish–South Korea deal over a Daewoo washing machine factory was achieved and the French and British lobbied Thailand for a deal to supply the rolling stock for the Bangkok metro (*Le Soir* 4 March 1996). On the whole, however, in the mid-1990s the EU attracted only one-tenth of Asian FDI.

The role of the euro is also important for influencing these mutual investment trends, for a number of reasons. For Asian partners, an accessible, stable euro offers a reliable alternative to the role of the dollar in the region. Its importance can be gauged from the vocal discussions between Japanese firms and the UK government regarding the UK's current non-participation in the euro-zone. Japan has most of its investments in the UK and in January 1997 Toyota chairman Okuda Hiroshi observed that UK prospects for greater Japanese investment could be endangered by not joining the euro. Since then, a number of similar calls have been made. When British Prime Minister Tony Blair met his Japanese counterpart Yoshiro Mori on his way to the G8 meeting in Okinawa in July 2000, he assured Japan of the UK's commitment to the euro. In July 2000 Sir Stephen Gomersall, UK Ambassador to Japan, allegedly leaked a memo saying that Japanese investment could be threatened if the UK weakened its commitment to the euro. Nissan's European president, Carlos Ghosn repeatedly warned that sterling's strength and future currency uncertainties might force Nissan to move production of its Micra replacement, scheduled for 2003, to the continent (*Financial Times* 1 August 2000; *Financial Times* 11 June 2001). Nevertheless, Nissan eventually agreed to produce its next Micra model in the UK rather than in France, in response to a £40 million injection from the British government, which was approved by the European Commission. At the very least, then, the issue of the euro can be used by Asian firms in their dealings with European firms and governments, and as a spur to greater Asian cooperation, as noted above. Japanese Vice-Minister of Finance, Haruhiko Kuroda, said that the euro is undervalued against the yen and the dollar, and similar remarks have issued from others. In March 2000 the French finance ministry asked Japan to intervene in currency markets, whereafter the Bank of Japan (BoJ) bought dollars in Tokyo markets and euro in European markets, on the orders of the Japanese Ministry of Finance (*Financial Times* 23 March 2000).

The fabric and rules of the EU make it easy to represent itself as a collective unit, especially in the economic dimension. The very fact that these varied relations have become subsumed within the overarching EU process, particularly from the view of outsiders, further reinforces the EU's international identity on the global stage, a process which is bolstered by the need to compete in region-to-region and globalising environments. These integrating mechanisms of the EU have acted as an important incentive for the development of collective Asian responses to mutual concerns over Europe. In this way, changing European structural conditions have highlighted the growing global impact of the EU and increased Asian attention towards this now eponymous EU region. The following section examines some of the major implications of this growing region-to-region perception and set of contacts.

ASEM AS FUNCTION AND IMAGINING

Beginning in the 1970s as a various assortment of ad hoc bilateral engagements and agreements, relations between Asia and Europe from the late 1980s and especially into the 1990s started to function on dual levels of bilateral and region-to-region interaction. The quasi-inter-regionalism of the EU–ASEAN dialogue, premised clearly as it was upon a donor-recipient hierarchy, set many of the parameters later to be adopted within the ASEM framework. At the same time, the longevity and range of experiences within the EU-Japan dialogue provided for the Europeans a list of stock answers to proliferating Asian questions, as the remaining geese joined Japan's formation. The 1990s brought with them a plethora of new institutional arrangements that came more and more to regard an inter-regional or pan-regional (as in APEC) level of activity as the norm in the face of rapidly changing global trends. Since that time, a region-to-region approach has become dominant in a range of sectors, particularly in the economic field. The nature and structure of such inter-regional explorations, however, have been dependent to a large extent on the functions and perceptions of any one given set of inter-regional exchanges; thus, in the case of Asia–Europe relations, it has clearly been difficult to negate the colonial underpinnings of much of the post-war period, and to act in the face of a still powerful US orientation. Nevertheless, the EU–Asia relationship does differ from, for example, EU–ASEAN, EU–Lomé, EU–MERCOSUR, or intra-APEC relations, by setting side-by-side in an explicit and codified way, two 'regions' of 'equal' stature. Whether the practice or perception of relations lives up to this definition is a different question. Notwithstanding constant tensions, however, it remains the case that in 1996 two-way trade between East Asia and the EU was greater than that between the EU and the US. ASEM built on this growth to create a set of channels to deal with specific issues of interest and concern involving Asia and Europe in particular. In turn, these proliferating inter-regional channels created and sustained the perception that inter-regionalism was real and that, by extension, both Asia and Europe were coherent regions in that process. Because of this level of perception alongside functional aspects of Asia–Europe relations, it is important to go beyond comparativist studies, since perceptions only obtain through their mutual exchanges and subsequently feed back to inform ideas of each other and self as economic regional entities. Not only have 'Asians' and 'Europeans', through their processes of interaction, come to demarcate new lines of 'Asian' versus 'European' ways of doing business, they have also collectively recognised the need to garner leverage in the face of perceived 'others', whether they be globalisation or the US. This section addresses both the functional and perceptual outcomes of the ASEM economic process to date.

ASEM provides an important exchange of capital, resources, R&D, ideas and personnel in the field of trade and investment, and has provided the channels through which representatives of each region have confirmed a need to develop priorities under the principles of commitment to market economy and reform, government–business sector dialogue, liberalisation and transparency, compliance with international rules, including those of the WTO, and the recognition of economic diversity. Asia and Europe may deal with problems specific to their own economies and find areas of compromise on issues such as investment and labour. On such issues, moreover, the inter-regional forum offers an opportunity to air intra-regional differences of approach and opinion. For the Europeans, moreover, it offers a forum in which to voice blanket concerns over investment promotion and opportunities without singling out particular target countries and without having to undertake the same kinds of negotiations repeatedly. For example, the EU has consistently pushed ASEAN to conform to uniform IPR and quality standards and attempted to deal with the region in order to gain national concessions. In return, European representatives have come explicitly to acknowledge ASEAN as a 'viable and cohesive grouping', thereby lending continued international credibility to an association that has been searching for a raison d'être in recent years (www.europa.eu.int).

For the smaller economies of each region, and of Asia in particular, ASEM offers a voice with which to lobby the Europeans and ensure that their interests are not neglected in the face of attractive big economies. In addition

to addressing specific bilateral (Asia–Europe and country-specific) issues and
creating ad hoc and permanent mechanisms by which to deal with them,
ASEM also provides the opportunity for participants to garner 'minilateral'
support prior to multilateral meetings. For example, economic ministers from
ASEM discussed in their first meetings how to solidify mutual support prior
to the WTO ministerial meeting in December 1996. The WTO also carries a
heavy agenda, so that the inter-regional forum can be more focused on key
issues of mutual concern. The *Financial Times* proposed that ASEM should
agree targets (as APEC has) for free trade, in accordance with the WTO,
suggesting that region- and issue-specific fora (for example on investment)
offer a less unwieldy form of dealing with these subjects (3 March 1996). The
different levels of economic development within and between the two regions
make agreement difficult to achieve, but minilateral encounters prepare each
side for the multilateral wrangling to follow. The Meeting also provides an
important setting for the exchange of technological know-how and
innovations, and sets up the framework for an ASEM 'technomart' (Jung and
Lehmann 1997, p. 57). During the financial crisis, ASEM was used as a
channel to discuss the problems of Asia, how Europe could assist, and to
pledge (through the World Bank) a large contribution through its own Trust
Fund. In addition, the novel structure and recent timing of ASEM, as shown
at ASEM 3 most clearly, offers both regions the chance to deal with a new
economic agenda, which includes environmental concerns, global warming,
the protection of water resources, deforestation and desertification,
biodiversity and the marine environment, the spread of drugs trafficking,
nuclear energy concerns, economic migration and issues of oil security. Most
of these issues have a trans-continental impact and affect economic relations
between Asia and Europe (see also Chapter 4). Dominance of European
agendas also mean that close linkages are have now been established within
ASEM between economic exchange and issues such as good governance and
human rights.

The WTO also forms the background against which ASEM derived, and it
is within its boundaries that the inter-regional relationship functions. The
Chair's statement at ASEM 1 underlined that ASEM must be WTO-
consistent, and much of the discussion at ASEM 1 was geared towards the
completion of the first WTO Ministerial Conference in Singapore December
1996. Other areas covered by ASEM clearly overlap with WTO agendas,
such as science and technology cross-flows, agriculture, information and
communication technology, energy and transport, human resources
development, education, management training, poverty alleviation, the role of
women, the public health sector, global efforts to combat AIDS and the
promotion of AIDS prevention. ASEM in this way offers a minilateral forum
to develop 'embryonic WTO accords' (Dent 1999b, p. 389). In this way,

regional agreements can serve to codify rules or practices and 'constrain national discretionary power' (Woolcock 1996, p. 125). While it provides many of the agendas for Asia–Europe exchanges, however, it also acts as a target against which Asia and Europe collectively form a 'site of resistance'. As Dent notes for the case of the EU, ASEM's strategic value 'in geoeconomic terms should not be understated, given its [the EU's] potential for marginalization in the 'Pacific Century' (1999a, p. 245). At the same time, however, while 'the structure and politics of global trade governance plays an important part in conditioning the EU–Asia Pacific relationship ... its impact is not always clear-cut' (Smith, M. 1998, p. 309). It is in the face of such uncertainty that the bonds between Europe and Asia come to be strengthened. So great is the need for such mutual strength, in fact, that the Vision Group (of 'wise men', set up to advise the whole ASEM process) proposed free trade in goods and services by 2025 for ASEM member states through progressive stages. In the face of these external challenges, ASEM 3 made globalisation a key theme in its closed session on economic and financial issues, and an annual ASEM Roundtable on Globalization from 2001 was proposed. ASEM does offer a means of state coordination in an internationally active economic environment, and the very mechanisms of that interaction may also be important in determining the types and modes of cooperation (and conflict) that dominate Asia–Europe affairs. It was created in the context of a growing role for GATT/WTO fora and, especially, in an era of proliferating 'regional' fora, such as the EU, European Free Trade Area (EFTA), Latin American Free Trade Area (LAFTA), ASEAN and NAFTA, and in an era in which the state is no longer recognised as the 'sole provider', but has become 'facilitator and regulator' (World Bank 1997, p. 1). Thus, globalism, sectoralism and regionalism could all fit into contemporary international relations alongside one another (Aggarwal 2000, p. 187).

One key factor in ASEM's global environment is the role of the United States. The US provides both an important marker for Asia–Europe relations, and a target for joint cooperation. On the one hand, the US is represented as the apex of the perceived geo-economic triangle underpinning global relations today. In this way, it offers the measure against which relations between Asia and Europe must be assessed. On the other, the US also functions as a mutual threat to Asia–Europe interests, by dominating world markets with its currency, playing key roles in international financial institutions and shaping a particular (and often sanction-led) mode of negotiation. ASEM, then, retains, if its representatives choose to transcend trilateral limitations, the latent potential to create an alternative mutual discourse to counter that threat, through 'open continentalism' (Fukasaku 1995), in contrast to APEC's system of 'open regionalism'. In some ways this process has already begun, as the EU, unlike the US, has prepared to carve out a long-term dialogue with Asia in a non-confrontational form (Ferguson 1996, p. 16). In these small ways, Dent's observation may be rather precipitous, but indicates future trends: 'What has become clear is that East Asia's developing economies are moving beyond a dependency on the USA and Japan, thus helping create a more independent momentum for the region' (1999a, p. 18). In fact, inter-regionalism is beginning to develop a level of accommodation with US internationalism: the EU and Asia both have a vested interest in ensuring that the US does not turn away from their respective regions, but at the same time need to plan for a more diversified future. Although McGrew observes that increased economic activity of the US in the Asia Pacific 'erodes the boundary between the foreign and the domestic' (McGrew 1998, p. 165), there is simultaneously a movement within East and Southeast Asia – 'Asian ASEM' – to carve out the region's own destiny. While CAEC (unofficial 'track two' process of ASEM) may be rather too hasty to dismiss US and APEC influences, a supplemental channel of inter-regionalism is nevertheless becoming increasingly important (CAEC 1997, p. 15).

CONCLUSION: REGIONAL VOICES?

ASEM not only consolidates Asian and European interests in a loosely institutionalised way, it also provides a rationale and target for intra-regional consolidation. In Asia this is most obviously the case, where ASEM provides its Asian participants with an opportunity to project a regional voice for the purpose of inter-regional interaction, rather than in order to take a regional lead per se. This is especially important for the ASEAN countries, in the face of growing Japan-China economic competition. In Europe, too, however, it is interesting to note how the inter-disciplinary nature of three-pillared ASEM spans the range of competencies of the EU – from European Commission-based economic interaction to Council of Ministers' inter-governmental political interests – to help shape and reshape the nature of the political and to confuse further the boundaries of economic relations.

In addition to enhancing intra-regional interests, ASEM should not be seen to be eroding bilateral concerns. As shown throughout this chapter, a number of bilateral initiatives have developed in response to, and on the periphery of, inter-regionalism. Once again, this subject tends to be located in the realm of those scholars and practitioners who posit regionalisation and globalisation as zero-sum encounters. On the contrary, ASEM's mixed and varied agenda is amenable to a range of flexible approaches; thus it serves to legitimise the centrality of the role of ASEAN, to act as a spur to national deregulation activities and to bring into the regional and global folds a growing Chinese economy. At the same time, however, ASEM's boundaries are sufficiently clear to exclude a number of economies, with the effect that they do not benefit from its particular and growing sets of initiatives. The danger for them is that as ASEM becomes better established it could become a favoured target of investment promotion and developing trade ties, to the detriment of former and alternative beneficiaries. A focus on the Asian Ten could have implications for the relations of Asian ASEM and Europe with South Asia for example. It is no coincidence that India and Pakistan, among over twenty other countries, have applied for membership.

In addition to its practical value, ASEM also facilitates a growing cohesion among Asian members, although the form which that cohesion will take remains unclear. Some observers maintain that an Asian future is more likely to be an APEC-based one, rather than an EAEC one, feeling that it is more 'natural' a grouping than the uniquely East Asian one (*Far Eastern Economic Review* 27 January 2000). However, within ASEM the perennial 'Asian values' debate can be heard more and more strongly, especially in the wake of an economic crisis that almost split the region. In spite of separate paths towards recovery, the voices for collective economic management have grown in salience. Asian values also continue to be used by individual Asian leaders to justify their non-agreement to the forms of Western economic models with which they disagree or which are politically too difficult to impose. Japan has utilised this Asian values debate well, by demonstrating active interest in proposals such as the Economic Ministers' Meeting and appearing to take a back seat, while simultaneously playing a quiet role as regional leader. This issue will continue to be integral to economic discussions for the foreseeable future, and will be taken up in Chapter 4.

Godement sagely remarks upon the power of practice and perception in influencing Asia's relations vis-à-vis Europe: 'The dialogue between East and West, and the models each holds up in the mirror for the other, or believes it sees in that mirror, will continue for a long time, regardless of the more mundane economic reordering brought about by the Crash' (1999, p. 115). ASEM locates each set of economic structures firmly face to face with one another, thereby reifying their respective forms (Western capitalism, Asian 'crony capitalism', and so on) and setting them on course for mutual and self reflection. In one concrete example, the introduction of the euro has not only prompted further calls within Asia for the creation of a regional currency there, but has also been advanced as a model within Asia, in order that the region might secure an identity for itself in the face of US dollar dominance: 'Europe's example of closer economic integration has planted the seed in many Asian minds that their region too must forge closer ties and co-ordinate exchange rate regimes' (*Financial Times* 16 January 2001). Similarly the 2000 Treaty of Nice pledged further moves towards closer economic integration for member states, in view of EU enlargement. This view is more instructive than regarding the EU system merely as a model for Asian development. Indeed, there have been very few suggestions that any Asian currency alignment should follow strictly in the euro's wake. Rather, Europe's regional activities as a clearly determined region prompt Asian representatives to respond with a collective *regional* voice, suggesting that eliciting a response is more important than the nature of that response. As Japanese Finance Minister Kiichi Miyazawa noted in early 2001, 'talks with Europe are helping us build up our own Asian identity' (*Financial Times* 16 January 2001).

If the EU may be regarded as a 'significant other' for Asia (see Chapter 1), APEC is often viewed as an alter-ego for ASEM. Aggarwal's approach is misleading when he compares the two regions, to conclude that APEC has not led to a strengthening of ASEM, because the latter in its un-institutionalised state offers no forum for APEC-scale liberalisation (Aggarwal 2000, p. 191). Rather, despite appropriating a number of APEC initiatives within its own structure (such as the Non-Binding Investment Principles, increased cooperation in customs, simplified travel for business people and increased business dialogue), ASEM does not replicate APEC, because it retains a novel region-to-region format. Moreover, and following the discrediting of APEC's role during the financial crisis and greater Asian regionalisation (Higgott 1998b), the path between APEC and ASEM is becoming increasingly grassed over. Godement, perhaps mistakenly, asserts that ASEM is 'largely a tribute to APEC's effectiveness' (Godement 2000, p. 120). Instead, there is increasing recourse to a need for Asian participants within ASEM to carve out their own approach to international affairs, by having to behave as a region.

ASEM is more than a practical mechanism for engagement; it also functions at a cognitive level to provide a regime for creating consensual knowledge, while also developing the nature of the knowledge makers and knowledge receivers. This growing mutual discourse builds upon triangular interpretations of contemporary international economic structures. As Aggarwal notes, the principles and norms which underpin various international arrangements can not only give overarching purpose to the encounter, but may also underpin fora for the exercise of indirect control (2000, pp. 174–5). This can be seen in the role of Japan and the European Commission to date within ASEM. While Aggarwal is able to observe that meta-regimes can only derive through consensual knowledge in different issue areas (2000, p. 175), such regimes also require a locatable discursive framework to create the possibility of that consensual knowledge. For this reason, it is inevitable that the vocabulary of ASEM will draw from pre-existing international organisations and model 'regions'. In the case of economic relations between Asia and Europe, this framework to date has relied heavily upon the terms utilised within fora such as the WTO, APEC and the perceived triadisation of the global economy.

The role of regional development within an inter-regional context is important, for the very nature of the framework sets one region *qua* region against a like body within this 'vital level of analysis' (Cammack and Richards 1999, p. 683). This inter-regional identity is further enforced by embedding social practices mythologised from history as the bedrock of contemporary identity. Between 1990 and 1994, global exports by the ten Asian members of ASEM increased by 11.6 per cent, and the global dimension of their trade is becoming increasingly significant. At the same time, the EU's own international position continues to grow dominant, despite the lacklustre (or rather, over-estimated) performance of the euro to date. The growing dialogue of the EU with Asia now gives them jointly a new language of discussion and, as a consequence, a more coherent identity for Asia within that context. As the global environment continues to press them to resolve joint action problems in a more imaginative way, the growing importance of inter-regional economic engagement will become clearer. Indeed, globalisation can be seen to create new challenges requiring state, regional and even inter-regional responses. In addition, ASEM's tri-pillared structure enables different issues to be discussed across a range of perspectives, thereby integrating the political aspects of economic affairs. It is to the political dimension that Chapter 4 now turns.

4. Political Dialogue

Any notion of a 'political' dialogue among the countries of Asia and Europe during the cold war was subsumed by the constraints of American and Soviet concerns. For this reason, as shown in Chapter 3, only a variety of bilateral economic relationships could be sustained between the two continents. Events of the 1970s, such as disagreements with the superpowers over the Vietnam war, the oil crises and later the Soviet invasion of Afghanistan, did create a sense that Europeans should be kept engaged in Asia, in order to moderate inter US–USSR excesses, but no concerted effort was made to attract European interests to the continent as a whole. From a European perspective, the diverse issues and problems of Asia led member states of the EC to focus on specific post-colonial relations and upon growing common concerns over the penetration of European markets by Japanese and later Southeast Asian imports. From a broadly Asian point of view, the insubordinate role of Europe to the American superpower combined with stagnation in the EC process at the end of the 1970s to create little interest in this distant continent. Only with the 'relaunch' of the European project in the mid-1980s, and particularly the *1992* project of a Single European Market (SEM) would 'Europe' as a whole become interesting. This chapter examines how discussions over a range of issues under the heading of 'political dialogue' reflect and respond to changing notions of 'Asia' and 'Europe' as political partners in the ASEM process. It goes on to analyse the security dialogue within this pillar of ASEM, and to assess formulations of exclusion and inclusion which accompany this process. The final section re-assesses how the growing framework of inter-regionalism informs understandings of political actors in contemporary world affairs.

POLITICAL DIALOGUE AND ASEM

ASEM has woven into its fabric a suitably polysemic definition of the term 'political dialogue'. When it comes to defining the nature of that dialogue, however, the picture become much fuzzier. One fundamental difficulty is that ASEM is underpinned by an informal structure and therefore relies rather heavily on goodwill. As part of the ASEM process, political dialogue is dealt with at the level of the two-yearly summits and Foreign Ministers' Meetings, as well as meetings of senior officials (SOM) who prepare for them. For example, the first SOM meeting in Dublin in December 1996 discussed the future of ASEM, while the first Foreign Ministers' Meeting talked about political and security issues. By the time of the Berlin meeting of foreign ministers in March 1999, questions of arms control, disarmament and the Nuclear Non-Proliferation Treaty (NPT) were also under discussion. Summits are also supported by a coordinators' meeting (involving two representatives from Asia and two from Europe). As with the economic domain, a number of institutional arrangements were established to set up long-term strategies for political dialogue, and include the Asia–Europe Cooperation Framework (AECF) mentioned in ASEM 1 Chairman's statement, and initiated to stimulate long-term cooperation in political, economic, social and other areas. Those involving non-government organisations and movements, such as the environment, will be dealt with in Chapter 5. The subjects of political dialogue within ASEM are varied. At the first summit meeting, for example, issues on the discussion table included a nuclear weapons-free Southeast Asia and the proposed reform of the UN, which were prepared at a preliminary meeting in New York in June 1996 between the Troika (Spain, Italy and Ireland) and Singapore/Japan coordinators. Inter-regional support was garnered when British Prime Minister John Major won strong support from Thailand for his proposals to streamline the UN (*The Independent* 2 March 1996). Other, more complex matters, such as the question of Kashmir and an emphasis on nuclear non-proliferation, were trickier to deal with. Conducted, according to the Chair of ASEM 1, 'on the basis of mutual respect, equality, promotion of fundamental rights and, in accordance with the rules of international law and obligations, non-intervention, whether direct or indirect, in each other's internal affairs', its ambitious aim is to formulate a 'Common Vision for Asia and Europe' (Chairs' Statements at ASEM 1 and 2). Mutual vision suffers from short-sightedness, since representatives of this sphere of ASEM have failed so far to articulate a common set of goals for political engagement. At the same time, however, the broad remit of this element of dialogue does provide a forum for wide-ranging discussions on a number of issues, including contemporary debates over the nature of security. On the whole, ASEM 1 was represented as a 'feel-good summit', demonstrating the goodwill of its participants but bringing to fruition few concrete initiatives. While ASEM 2 was dominated by economic and political fallout of the Asian financial crisis, dialogue over political issues covered discussions concerning the Korean peninsula, Bosnia, Kosovo, Cambodia and UN reform. ASEM 3 focused around the newly raised question of North-South Korea rapprochement, since the summit in October 2000 followed the June 2000 historic summit between South Korean President Kim Dae-Jung and his North Korean counterpart, Kim Jong-Il, which reignited hopes at reconciliation mooted between Kim Il Sung (Kim Jong-Il's father) and Kim Young Sam of South Korea during the early 1990s. Shortly before the inter-regional summit, Kim Dae Jung had also received the Nobel Prize for Peace. As a result, ASEM 3 was able to produce a separate statement on the developments on the Korean peninsula, known as the Seoul Declaration for Peace on the Korean Peninsula, and which was adopted without discussion (*Financial Times* 21/22 October 2000). At ASEM 3, the French president, in his capacity as representative of the Council Presidency, outlined the goal of setting the 'broad direction' for ASEM, prior to the fourth summit in Copenhagen in 2002. Some countries, especially in Asia, hope to play down any political edge to the political dialogue. The Korean organisers of ASEM 3, for example, were very keen, as their Thai predecessors had been, to remove any controversial political items. At ASEM 3 it was noted that future meetings should focus on specific issues, not areas already covered by common ground, but China expressed concern at the prospect of opening the floodgates to discussions of issues such as human rights. EU participants, for their part, were divided over the issue of the recognition of North Korea, and some national leaders took their own (non-EU) line. British Prime Minister Tony Blair decided en route to Seoul unilaterally to re-establish diplomatic ties with Pyongyang, and used this initiative to justify a trip for which he apparently had little enthusiasm and which was seen to have no other domestic or foreign policy value. Given the different political agendas brought to the ASEM table, the Chair's Statement in Seoul was characteristically vague:

> Leaders reaffirmed their commitment to pursuing a secure international environment for all countries and to intensifying cooperation between Asia and Europe with a view to contributing towards international peace, stability and prosperity, and respect for international law. From this standpoint, they engaged in detailed discussions on regional and international issues of common interest. (Seoul 2000)

As with economic relations, political commitments within ASEM are underpinned by a range of international agreements, which include the United Nations Charter, the Universal Declaration on Human Rights, the 1986 Declaration on the Right to Development, the 1992 Rio Declaration on Environment and Development, the 1993 Declaration of Vienna and Programme of Action of the World Conference on Human Rights, the 1994 Cairo Programme of Action of the International Conference on Population and Development, the 1995 Copenhagen Declaration on Social Development and Programme of Action and the 1995 Beijing Declaration and Platform of Action for the fourth World Conference on Women. It is from this broad pool of activities that the agenda for ASEM is established. This broad dialogue provides an opportunity to discuss, or at least to present, a range of subjects from nuclear non-proliferation, the reform of the United Nations and environmental protection to child welfare, alongside economic standardisation and cultural exchanges. In so doing, it also offers the opportunity, as the title of a Singaporean TV documentary in January 2000 suggested, of 'Building Bridges' between Europe and Asia. One example involves the Child Welfare Initiative Resource Centre promoted by the Philippines and the UK and established at the University of Glasgow, Scotland following proposals made at ASEM 2. The centre facilitates access to legal documents relating to criminal justice and child protection, as well as providing contacts in each country for police, prosecution services, the health service and social welfare service, and offering advice on mutual legal assistance (including extradition) and issues relating to customs and immigration (http://eurochild.gla.ac.uk).

Overseeing the ASEM process has been the Vision Group, set up by Korea and resembling the Eminent Persons' Group within APEC, but with a broader remit. It was launched at the Dublin SOM in December 1996, produced an initial text in March 1997 and redistributed the revised version of *For a Better Tomorrow* in July 1997, to be finalised by September that year. According to the Vision Group, obstacles to greater cooperation include debates over human rights and questions about the nature of open markets. The group proposed 'open solutions', by reinforcing notably the role of the multilateral trading system, while improving infrastructure and increasing the role of NGOs and education in order to redress social imbalances. The group's report was rather hurried and ironically somewhat lacking in vision, since ministers were keen to have the report before them and subsequently picked out from the menu of its recommendations the parts they liked. Unfortunately, it still went nowhere towards answering the question of 'What is ASEM for?'. In its 1997 working document, the European Commission suggested that 'ASEM's key comparative advantage would lie in its ability to stimulate and facilitate work in bilateral and multilateral fora, to promote dialogue and understanding in areas where views with Asia might differ, and to foresee more active cooperation in areas where a commonality of views can be identified' (reported in European Parliament 1999). In the European Commission's 'Perspectives and Priorities for ASEM' document, which was drawn up to clarify the nature and function of each of the three pillars of ASEM activity, specific concerns in the political field were noted to be a need for enhanced exchanges of views on regional and global security issues, more educational exchanges and the possible enlargement of ASEM

(European Commission 2000). All of these attempts at designing the framework of a political dialogue usher from a growing recognition that Asia and Europe have grown in their respective political statures.

Three summit meetings later, mutual perceptions of the regions involved have been consolidated. The prominence of the EU within Europe has been reinforced by the fact that most of 'peripheral' Europe has also applied to join the Union. Such external perceptions of the EU's role persist in spite of the difficulties of achieving a 'European' position at the discussion table (Camroux and Lechervy 1996, p. 446; Patten 1998, p. 108), and among Asian participants the idea that 'Europe' is synonymous with the EU has become widespread. These developments have impacted upon a number of areas of Asia–Europe concerns. First, and perhaps contrary to expectations, this group-to-group mechanism has served to enhance and develop bilateral interests between European and Asian partners. For example, by the late 1990s France and Japan had developed a 'diplomatic, commercial and cultural love affair', as the best efforts of French Prime Minister Lionel Jospin and well-known Japanophile President Jacques Chirac took roadshow after roadshow to woo Japan away from its preferential relations with the UK (*Financial Times* 16 December 1999). What is more, President Chirac used an Asian trip prior to ASEM 1 in order to repair some of the damage caused by the 1995–6 French nuclear tests in the Pacific, which had resulted in a Japanese boycott of many French goods, and he declared that 'Asia is the new frontier of the foreign policy of France' (*Thailand Times* 26 February 1996). For its part, China has benefited from the ASEM to develop its own relations with the EU. The first EU–China Summit was held in London in 1998 and led to the proposal on 'Building a Comprehensive Partnership with China' in June 1998. A high-level EU delegation to China in October and November 1998 that included European Commission President Jacques Santer with Commissioner Sir Leon Brittan and Commissioner Yves Thibault de Silguy further demonstrated that the ASEM structure is important in European attempts to make China more multilaterally oriented. In this way, the political dialogue of ASEM is important for bringing into greater relief existing national and bilateral interests and concerns. The second role of ASEM in the political sphere is that it provides a potential balance to the global and regional position of the US over particular sets of issues and interests. This is not, however, to suggest that an Asia–Europe alliance is set to replace respective relations with the US; rather, that on an issue-led basis, Asian and European representatives may increasingly come to support one another in the face of mutual threats and challenges. In this context, for the French, unsurprisingly, 'Le partneriat avec l'Extrême Orient est vital' (*Le Monde* 4 March 1996). However, while 'Europe–Asia relations are now entwined with primary relationships with the USA and Russia' (Ferguson

1996, p. 3), it is not yet clear to Asian and European practitioners how this relationship might be strengthened. Third, the partnership between Asia and Europe also serves as a 'minilateral' mechanism for coordinating responses and positions prior to participation in larger fora. In this way, ASEM offers an additional forum to address post-cold war power structures, 'not simply in terms of the shifting balance between the EU and the Asia Pacific countries, which has been fundamental to the evolution of the EU's new strategy and to the approach taken by ASEAN members and others, but also in terms of the channels through which bargaining takes place and leverage can be exerted' (Smith, H. 1998, p. 312). A brief overview of the topics covered at Seoul in 2000 demonstrates the potential for this aspect of inter-regionalism, since ASEM replicates many of the political items for discussion already found in institutions such as the ARF, the ASEAN PMC, the G7 and the UN. The types of issue encountered to date have included: the question of East Timor and the role of UNTAET; the need to implement fully UNSC Resolution 1244 regarding Kosovo; UN reform; arms control; the review of the NPT; promoting the completion of signatures to the Comprehensive Test Ban Treaty (CTBT); calls for an immediate start to negotiations on the Fissile Material Cut-Off Treaty in the Conference on Disarmament; and measures to increase the Biological and Toxin Weapons Convention. Fourth, closer recognition of Asia and Europe as partners within a dialogue has engendered a number of debates about whether or not ASEM should be formally institutionalised. Despite the Chair's statement at ASEM 2 that 'as an informal process, ASEM need not be institutionalised', by its very existence ASEM in some ways already institutionalises a set of recognisable patterns of interaction. Debates over this issue have at times bordered on both the farcical and fantastical, as though the presence of an ASEM secretariat would lead to the diminution of state power in both regions. Those in favour of creating more formal structures note that while each leader might bring a list of aspirations to the summits, nothing is controlled or discussed in detail. Attempts have also been made to develop 'informal meetings' between national representatives, but attendance at the pilot effort was poor and heads of mission were sent in place of representatives from capitals. The idea of a secretariat of various types has been proposed on numerous occasions, including by the Vision Group. So far such moves have been resisted, leaving the European Commission as the most institutionalised collective voice within ASEM, and therefore attempts to 'avoid spontaneous and inappropriate proposals made by officials during ASEM meetings' have so far been unsuccessful (European Parliament 1998). At the same time, however, the continual interaction between representatives of Asia and Europe serves to provide an umbrella framework under which to locate the multi-level meetings of various economic, cultural and political committees that now occur in the periods between ASEM summits. For this reason, Dent is mistaken merely to refer to the 'underdeveloped socialization of a Eurasian dialogue' with such a definitive flourish (1999b, p. 380). The effects of the inclusion/exclusion nexus are in many ways far more important than debates about levels of institutional structures, and will be examined below. Before that, the following section looks at how Asia and Europe have come to regard one another within the structures of this political dialogue.

EUROPE CONFRONTS A GROWING 'ASIA'

Discerning 'Asia' as a political entity is not as easy as recounting its collective economic achievements. Nevertheless, European practitioners are able, here too, to draw upon a history of bilateral and region-to-region dialogues, which have cemented various understandings of 'Asia' among European interlocutors. At the core of these dialogues is the EU–ASEAN relationship that was formalised in 1978. This arrangement, which issued from a range of economic and security concerns, set a novel precedent for inter-regional engagement, by initiating a formal and regular ministerial channel of dialogue (Yamakage 1980). Since the ending of the Vietnamese occupation of Cambodia and the removal of explicitly cold war determinants in East Asia, however, leaders of ASEAN have been searching for a new role for the regional grouping, and initiatives such as the ARF of 1993 and ASEM focus on larger units of participation while retaining (nominally at least) the ASEAN group at their core. At ASEAN's Singapore summit in 1992, it was agreed, inter alia, that in addition to the Framework Agreement on Enhancing ASEAN Economic Cooperation, there was a need for greater cooperation between ASEAN and third countries (McMahon 1998, p. 237). In these and later endeavours there slowly emerged a grouping of the 'Asian Ten' member states, which included the first seven member states of ASEAN alongside Japan, China and South Korea: it was this formation of 'Asia' which would participate as the 'Asian ASEM'. In addition, a formal ASEAN+3 mechanism began on the periphery of the ASEAN leaders' meeting in Manila in November 1999. Although McMahon's assertion that ASEAN has become an 'economic and political force to be reckoned with' may be over emphasising the regional impact of the Association (1998, p. 238), documents relating to ASEM are swift to repeat the mantra that ASEAN remains the cornerstone of European relations with Asia and is the putative driving force within Asia for the ASEM process. At the Asia level, an East Asia Vision Group was proposed by Korean President Kim Dae Jung at an ASEAN meeting with its partners in December 1998 in Hanoi, to find a vision for the region in the wake of the financial crisis and to expand political and social cooperation.

While ASEAN may remain notionally at the core of many of these initiatives, as the 'Asian Ten' or 'Asian ASEM' the region brings with it greater political strength vis-à-vis Europe than ASEAN could conjure alone. This larger collective of 'Asia' both responds to (see below), and is utilised by, EU member state representatives in their dealings with the region. While many of the loose and informal mechanisms of ASEM, such as its policy of non-interference, draw upon ASEAN experiences, the sub-region's categorisation within a broader regional unit may also have a diluting effect. Indeed, this dilution of interests has been encouraged by Europeans and Asians alike, as a means of subsuming the contentious issue of Burma within a broader setting. Positions over Burma have been viewed in two ways. The first view acknowledges the intra-regional role of ASEAN as an agent in promoting stability: 'By accepting Myanmar as a member despite Western opposition, ASEAN in effect accepted the responsibility of trying to bring about political change in that country' (Zakaria 1999, p. 772). In addition, even with the onset of the ASEM process, the EU–ASEAN framework was strengthened from 1995 by the addition of regular SOMs, a channel of communication simultaneously utilised within ASEM. The second view asserts that ASEM provides a target for collective identification on the part of ASEAN, whose member states may coalesce in the face of collective Western criticisms (as in the case of the financial crisis, see Chapter 3), or may subsume difficult external problems (such as modalities for dealing with Myanmar) within the larger forum (Forster 1999, p. 752). Alongside their region-to-region encounters with ASEAN, EU officials have built their relations with Asia through a broadening economic and political dialogue with Japan since the early 1980s (Gilson 2000). The templates of both types of dialogue have been replicated in recent years within ASEM, EU–South Korea and EU–China encounters.

In the 1980s it became clear to Europeans, especially those inhabiting the European Commission and the Council of Ministers, that benefits could accrue from dealing with East Asia as a group. From an economic vantage point, the growing regional success of Asia beyond Japan signalled the fact that a rising Asian voice had to be taken seriously. Political issues took much longer to become embedded into inter-regional dialogue, but by the mid-1990s, and following the 1994 paper on 'Toward a New Asia Strategy for Asia' (European Commission 1994), at some level an Asian unit was beginning to be recognised. The strategy was endorsed by the European Council in Essen in 1994 and was to form the basis of European approaches to the ASEM proposal (Dent 1999b, p. 394). The rather promissory statement of intent set down in the paper identified EU relations with the Asian region as representing a 'partnership of equals', although it was designed primarily as a way of managing EU economic relations with East Asia and Southeast

Asia within a broad format facilitating the discussion of non-economic issues (Dent 1997/8). For some observers, it offered still another means by which the EU could 'attempt to enforce its economic and political presence in Asia' (see Palmujoki 1997, p. 274). It also linked the Asian strategy to the Common Foreign and Security Policy (CFSP) of the Union, partly in response to the expectation that the political weight of Asia as a grouping was likely to increase (Palmujoki 1997, p. 274). The overall strategy of the EU towards Asia was cast in general aspirations: to promote in Asia global issues such as sustainable development, the protection of the environment, the development of the information society, forest preservation, and research on AIDS; and develop cooperation towards global economic stability, China's full participation in the WTO and open and equitable competition. These are, in short, many of the same issues that were raised at the ASEM forum itself (Europe Documents, 1954/1955, 12 October 1995). In addition, the formal association of requirements for good and green governance with the EU's trade agreements since the 1990s means that economic issues can rarely be contained within a clearly defined economics-only sphere, and incrementally political and economic overlap had already begun to occur. The strategy itself, which divided 'Asia' into East Asia, South-East Asia and South Asia was to form the basis of the development within the EU of the notion of an 'Asian ASEM' (McMahon 1998, p. 233). Although subsequent EU documents related to Asia in still confused and all-encompassing terms (such as the 1995 brochure on *The European Union and Asia*, which made reference to 26 countries from Afghanistan to Japan), the late 1990s did witness a growing trend towards identifying this Asian ten when making reference to 'Asia'. In September 2001 the 1994 strategy paper was updated, with the clear goal of establishing a range of 'partnerships' with the different economies and governments of Asia, in order to strengthen the 'EU's political and economic presence across the region' of 'Asia', and to raise 'this to a level commensurate with the growing global weight of an enlarged EU' (COM (2001) 469 final). Among its priorities, the paper pinpoints the need to enhance European engagement in Asia, especially in the pursuit of 'peace and security', and to spread 'democracy, good governance and the rule of law'. Many of these activities, it acknowledges, will be addressed within wider regional, inter-regional and global fora.

On the level of EU policy making, the inter-governmental General Affairs Council (namely the 15 foreign ministers) oversees ASEM affairs, while Common Positions towards Asia (within the structure of the CFSP) continue to relate only to specific areas of shared concern, including to date Burma and East Timor, and an agreement over the role of EURATOM in the Korean Peninsula Energy Development Organisation (KEDO) process (see below) (Asia Strategy Project 1999, p. 166). In spite of a growing sense of Asia as a unit, then, reinforced especially in European documents of convenience, and despite calls for Europeans to 'drop the Marco Polo mentality' (*Financial Times* 7 January 1998), approaches to Asia as a whole have been at best patchy. In other words, an APEC-style mode of negotiation prevails, which prevents the development of a fully articulated inter-regional political dialogue. As a result, many of the subjects involved in formulating EU 'foreign policy' have been thrust into the ASEM ring without necessarily the agreement of the Asian contingent: 'It is impossible to avoid the linkages between material economic welfare, assumptions about the role of government and the cultural factors, such as those attaching to human rights and the role of the individual, which are central to the study not only of the Asia–Pacific itself, but also of the EU as another very different form of regionalism' (Smith, H. 1998, p. 307). The best known and most contentious of these is the human rights issue (see below), but other subjects such as the question of enlargement, non-interference and security are also dominated by intra-European debates.

ASIA WATCHES EUROPE

From an Asian perspective the integration processes within the EU have produced a European entity now able to voice collective opinions on a whole range of subjects. Prior to the ASEM meeting, the EU per se had been involved in a number of specific Asian issues, which ranged from aid to China, Mongolia and Cambodia, to humanitarian aid to North Korea. Within the ASEM framework, moreover, the European Commission is represented independently in the person of its president, who participates alongside national leaders. There are moves under way for the High Representative for the Common Foreign and Security Policy, a post currently held by Javier Solana (also head of the Western European Union, WEU) to join the ASEM process, thereby bringing greater EU weight to bear on its political international position. The growing role of the EU now means that the Union is most often represented by the Presidency and the European Commission, and the whole mechanism of the Troika has more or less become redundant in relations with Asia (CAEC 1997, p. 27). However, since many (trade) matters have already been given over to EU competence, in order to discuss the political implications of economic issues the EU per se cannot be excluded. The solution for this strange state of affairs was to make ASEM an informal gathering, while the problem of the Troika was resolved in 1999, by bringing together the Presidency, the High Representative of the CFSP, the Secretariat General of the Council of Ministers and the European Commission Vice President (responsible to himself, the Commission College and the European Parliament), with the possible addition of the incoming Council. In this way, the foreign ministerial representative of the Presidency could become the 'natural' spokesperson with the Secretary General of the Council representing the Council and with the role of assisting the Presidency. Thus, economic issues would be directed via the European Commission and overall EU policy and political issues would be channelled through the (inter-governmental) Presidency. Whatever the intricacies of the EU, this would all ensure greater continuity of some form of European voice.

This international exposure of a political EU continues to deepen external perceptions that the EU retains a political voice to match its economic competencies. National governments still determine the foreign policy agenda and remain influenced by the US, but there is concurrently a growing number of issues upon which the EU member states have come to agree. By the time of the first ASEM, moreover, 'Europe' had been prominent in the international media since the fall of the Berlin Wall in 1989 and the success of the Maastricht Treaty of 1992 which outlined the arrival of the single currency. In addition, years of incremental achievements for the EC/EU, especially through the Commission and its delegations in non-EU member states, had given the EU a de facto international political as well as economic role that Asia could not ignore. By the second ASEM summit, the launch of the euro had reinforced this growing image abroad of the EU as a coherent and powerful international actor. For many Asian participants, the continuing threat/benefits of a 'fortress Europe' were a significant factor in promoting increased links with Europe. Asian representatives have viewed ASEM as a means collectively to lobby the EU for the advancement of national strategies and initiatives. For example, while Malaysia was initially reluctant to respond to the proposal for ASEM, a cost-benefit consideration soon led its government to use ASEM to promote Asia–Europe rail links, a project which would subsume the existing ASEAN one of Thailand, Singapore and Malaysia and that would provide financing for Malaysia to upgrade its national railway system. For similar strategic reasons, Kuala Lumpur agreed to house the Europe–Asia University and at ASEM 2 Prime Minister Mahathir announced that Malaysia would host the Asia–Europe Centre for research activities. Similarly, leaders of the Philippines, 'faced with the task of recasting its foreign policy' since the end of its special relations with the US (Dios et al. 1996, p. 2), have come to make a number of presidential visits to Europe since the mid-1990s in the hope that the EU would apply its new strategy to improve relations with Manila.

Some observers claimed that Europeans saw at ASEM 1 the 'Asian mentality of flexibility, informal, non-institutional and consensus-seeking' (Tanaka 1999, p. 41). Indeed, the need to act collectively vis-à-vis this growing European entity has, particularly within the confines of the ASEM context, served to consolidate an 'Asian' voice over several issues. As mentioned above, leaders of ASEAN had already recognised the necessity of joining a larger Asian collective in order to gain leverage in the face of globalising challenges. What is more, while internal stability remains a goal of ASEAN, as demonstrated by its significant enlargement to include Brunei (1984), Cambodia (1999), Vietnam (1995) and Laos and Myanmar (1997), 'it now has to be attained in a manner that rides more on the vigor and self-confidence of open societies than on the claustrophobia of national security-obsessed states' (*Asiaweek* 14 April 2000). The coming to terms with intra-regional concerns among the ASEAN member states has been accompanied by growing external pressures on the region to respond collectively to new international issues, most notably in the wake of the start of the financial crisis of 1997. On the one hand, the crisis elicited international criticism that 'Asian' modes of behaviour – encapsulated in the term 'crony capitalism' – were based on an absence of democratic rights and the rule of law (*Far Eastern Economic Review* 27 January 2000). On the other, a collective response to such criticisms encouraged a greater intra-regional need for cooperation and prompted the view by the time of the Manila meeting of ASEAN in November 1999, that in fact the region was going through a 'revival in self-confidence' (*Financial Times* 29 November 1999). For a country such as Japan, participating as part of a wider regional bloc gives it the ability to shape regional concerns without itself taking a contentious leading role. As part of this strategy it has announced a 'Commitment to Peace in Asia' alongside specific projects (like the 'Frontier Spirit for Manufacturing' and the 'Frontier Spirit for Building Information and Developing Information Technologies') to develop technology in the region (Bowles 1997). When Japanese Prime Minister Obuchi attended the ASEAN+3 (Japan, China and South Korea) Summit Meeting held in Manila at the end of November 1999, he announced what came to be known as the 'Obuchi plan', a programme to enhance human resource development with Southeast Asia. At the following Japan-ASEAN Summit Meeting, Obuchi announced that Japan would actively extend assistance to develop a cooperative entity through which ASEAN could promote internal cooperation such as in the ASEAN Free Trade Area (AFTA) and contribute to the peace and prosperity of Asia. In particular, Japan announced cooperation to narrow economic disparities in the ASEAN region, centered on assistance to newly acceding ASEAN countries. Japan has also presented itself as the 'voice of Asia' more generally, and ASEM in many ways has furthered its intra-regional interests (Gilson 1999). Foreign Minister Yohei Kono in January 2000 stated that Japan sought 'to play more of a leadership role in Asia, and, through collaboration with Europe, to help keep the US responsive to international issues' (*Financial Times* 14 January 2000). More importantly,

Japan not only sees itself as the voice of Asia within the ASEM process (Bridges 1999b, p. 151), but also receives more and more support from its Asian neighbours in so doing, such as garnering support for Eisake Sakakibara (former Japanese Vice-Minister of Finance) to become the Managing Director of the IMF (*Financial Times* 29 November 1999).

Indeed, the ASEM process has necessitated regular gatherings on the Asian side, such as the pre-ASEM Asian foreign ministers' meeting in Phuket in February 1996 which 'was also significant in fostering dialogue and cooperation within Asia' (MOFA 1998, p. 57), and the informal meeting of economic ministers in Chiang Rai in February 1996 to examine mutual concerns for economic improvement. The more radical statements of cooperative Asian intent include former Philippine President Estrada's proposal for an East Asian common currency, market and community, which was supported as a long-term objective by Singapore Foreign Minister Richard Hu (*Financial Times* 29 November 1999). Clearly, practical advantages to greater inter-regional cooperation include the sharing and development of technology (*Financial Times* 11 January 2001), but Singapore Minister for Communications and Information Technology Yeo Cheow Tong's insistence that it should be achieved by developing an Asian model for regional growth is commonplace in Asian statements to Europe. Interestingly, this growing Asian coordination has led to a multiplicity of references to 'Asian values' and an 'Asian way' of conducting affairs, in relation to what is regarded as a European 'other'. Voices like those of Malaysia's Mahathir and Singapore's Goh Chok Tong have warned repeatedly against Western ideas of democracy and governance being forced on to Asia, and Mahathir's EAEC is indeed the constituency of the Asian side within ASEM.[1] While the concrete representation of a coherent set of 'Asian values' is impossible to uncover (Pape 1997, p. 1), recourse to an Asian values debate does offer a politically loaded means of facing the growing region-to-region requirements of modern interaction. The effects of the ASEM process upon the intra-regional cohesion of the Asian representatives have yet to be tested fully. However, it is clear that ASEM is shaping for them a channel of dialogue previously unavailable to the Asian Ten.

SECURITY QUESTIONS

Asia–Europe relations tend to be characterised by a lack of security dialogue at the inter-regional level, although collective security fora involve a number of member states, and include the Five Power Defence Arrangement (involving Australia, New Zealand, Malaysia and Singapore and Great Britain) as well as bilateral agreements, such as the security treaty between the UK and Brunei. In the post-cold war era, a 'definitional sleight of hand' has come to shroud notions of security (Thakur 1995, pp. 33 and 35): not only does the term relate to a host of 'new' issues, but the security alliances formed today (such as the ARF) are not locked into cold war rhetoric or dependent uniquely upon military capabilities. Former European Commission President Jacques Santer emphasised the problem of these 'new security issues' as a key to security dialogue (1998, p. 13). A lengthy discussion of the ways in which the idea of security might be (re)interpreted in a post-cold war era is not the aim of this section. We start, rather, from the premise that the notion of security is now as much about 'conditions of existence' as survival (Buzan 1991, p. 432), and, to that end, Buzan et al.'s five factors are indicative of what such a concept might contain; namely, military, political (organisational stability, systems of government, and so on), economic, societal (language, culture and so on) and environmental security (1990).

The Chair's statement at ASEM 3 outlined, under 'Fostering Political Dialogue', how ASEM would address specific issues of security concern, from Bosnia to Korea, rather than develop a broad security dialogue mechanism of its own. Even these subjects were deferred to mutual information exchange and to the auspices of organisations such as the UNSC, the NPT Review Conference and the CTBT where appropriate, rather than proposing initiatives for Asia and Europe to adopt on their own. The declared particular issues of interest were very wide-ranging:

> Leaders expressed their commitment to addressing global issues of common concern such as managing migratory flows in a globalized world and transnational crime, including money laundering; smuggling and exploitation of migrants and trafficking in persons, in particular of women and children for the purpose of sexual exploitation; international terrorism and piracy; racism and xenophobia; the fight against illegal drugs; the welfare of women and children; community health care improvement; the fight against HIV/AIDS, infectious and parasitic diseases; as well as food security and supply. (Chair's Statement, ASEM 3)

This lengthy wish-list reflects different member state interests and also demonstrates how ASEM is attempting to accommodate a non-traditional security role. At the same time, however, there is a growing feeling that Asia and Europe must reflect seriously upon the waning military interest of the US administration in each region, while intra-European inadequacies evident during the Kosovo crisis and Asian confusion over East Timor, as well as joint concern over Russian intervention in Chechnya have all signalled that the time may be right for greater inter-regional cooperation on the military periphery. Developments within each region further support this contention.

On the one hand, the EU is pressing ahead with a debate over proposals to add a defence arm and a corps of up to 60 000 personnel for peace-keeping operations, while the status of EU–NATO links continues to be renegotiated (*Financial Times* 13/14 January 2001). This proposal has been stimulated by a recognition in Europe of a need for the EU to play an increased role in the post-settlement issues of Kosovo and to deploy a rapid reaction facility (*Financial Times* 31 May and 4 July 2000). The WEU pledged in the Petersberg Declaration of June 1992 to deploy WEU military units on peace-keeping operations (PKO), dispatched naval forces to the Adriatic in July 1992 and later established a single command with NATO in June 1993 (Dobson 1999, p. 157). At the European Council meeting in Cologne in 1999, the EU decided to develop its own capacity for action in military crisis management, and to underscore the so-called Petersberg tasks, by focusing on humanitarian and rescue operations, as well as peace-making. The inter-governmental nature of this agreement means that although the EU is the largest contributor to the regular and peace-keeping budgets of the UN, it in fact supplies no EU contribution per se, thus illustrating the fragmented nature of the EU as an international interlocutor. Within Europe itself, the deepening of the CFSP process and the rejuvenation of the WEU have enabled the EU to play a greater role in a range of regional institutions. All institutions designed to run the military capability will be in the Council, with little European Commission involvement. The European Council in Helsinki set the goal for military capabilities to be achieved by 2003, and the proposed European Security and Defence Policy (ESDP) will take the EU into a new realm. For an EU trying to broaden its international profile in the light of the deepening and widening of its integration process, extending the remit of the CFSP procedure has become important, and one way of doing this has been to develop its relations in regional fora dealing in 'soft' power issues. On the other hand, there is no regional security forum in Northeast Asia. Thus, for now, no security cooperation, but only security dialogue, is possible, and ASEM can only contribute to that dialogue. Discussions over security within Asia have concentrated since 1994 upon the role of the ARF, whose foundations have also provided the framework for security discussions within ASEM. The ARF emerged in the 1990s from the development of a 'cooperative security' mechanism for multilateralism in the Asia Pacific, which was to be premised upon inclusivity and equality (Acharya 1999a, p. 87). Now composed of nearly 20 members, including the countries of ASEAN, its work has also been complemented by a mechanism of communication with Dialogue Partners including the United States, the EU, Japan, Russia and others. In the mid-1990s the key for the ARF remained transparency in information over arms transfers, acquisitions and production, as well as military deployments and exercises and defence doctrines (Simon

1995, p. 19), and it also moved towards working with UN PKO activities, and providing training, seminars, places, financial assistance, and cooperation, as well as dialogue and information technology (IT) for peace-keeping (Dobson 1999, p. 163). The ARF now brings together defence as well as foreign policy spokespeople (Cheeseman 1999, p. 334), and its multidimensionality has also ensured Chinese support. It is important to remember that in setting up the ARF, a number of calls were made for it to be modelled on the structures of the Conference on Security Cooperation in Europe (CSCE), which later became the Organisation for Security and Cooperation in Europe (OSCE). While this path of development was rejected at the time, in practice the ARF has become more like the OSCE than any other European institution including NATO, the EU or the Concert of Europe. The financial crisis was also instrumental in moving the ARF to supplement traditional issues (such as nuclear weapons and regional security in Korea) with new ones of a non-military nature in 1998. At the same time, however, complaints within the ARF in July 2000 by China and Russia over US proposals for a missile defence system, and regional discontent over the NATO bombing of Kosovo and the attack on China's embassy in Belgrade in 1999 illustrate that such 'traditional' concerns remain important (*Financial Times* 28 July 2000). At the same time, ASEM member states are aware of the need to keep US involvement within their respective regions. Equally, the need to avoid destabilising the power vacuum during a period of transition means that it is still important to retain a US presence. In adopting many of the tenets already found in the ARF, ASEM may be hamstrung by the same failing: 'the fledgling ARF has yet to demonstrate that its consensus-oriented approach to security cooperation will be sufficient to defuse the many potential territorial conflicts among East Asian states' (Ravenhill 1998, p. 267).

Within the ASEM context, there have been proposals for Asia to adopt a number of European models, most notably that of the CSCE/OSCE, and ASEM has contributed to the debate surrounding the idea that an OSCE-type security arrangement could be transferred to Asia. In existence in its present form since 1994, the OSCE is a regional arrangement of the UN under Chapter VIII of the Charter, and is a pan-European security organisation, whose 55 participating states cover a geographical span from Vancouver to Vladivostok. It is renowned for its comprehensive and cooperative format, and for addressing a wide range of security-related issues including arms control, preventive diplomacy, confidence- and security-building measures, human rights, election monitoring and economic and environmental security (Flynn and Farrell 1999, pp. 506–7; Dobson 1999, p. 157). It works closely with other international and regional organisations and maintains close links with numerous NGOs. There has been considerable support, notably from the Vision Group, for Asia to benefit from European experiences of establishing confidence-building measures (CBMs), preventive diplomacy and conflict resolution (Verdi 1999, p. 13).[2] What is more, Japan and Korea have been in the OSCE meetings since 1996 as 'Partners for Cooperation', so there is already an awareness in Asia of what it actually does. Japan, like many of its neighbours, does not want to be isolated in the face of NATO expansion and closer EU–Russian relations. The potential benefit of the OSCE model is its flexibility, broad membership and cooperative approach. However, both the US and China have reservations about the idea of an OSCE for Asia: the US fears it would undermine bilateralism and China is worried that it would become an anti-Chinese camp (Acharya 1999a, p. 96). While being regarded in many ways as a model, there is also the view that Europeans could also act as a 'moderator' for intra-Asian conflicts (CAEC 1997). In some ways, the financial and political strength of the European defence mechanism can serve both to support and act as a potential model for Asian defence integration. However, not only does Asia tend to be driven by bilateralism in matters of security, and demonstrate the dominant influence of the few (Harris 2000, p. 502), there would also be suspicion that Europeans would behave with the hubris recently shown by Australia (see below). In addition to the prospective European model, there are also tangible issues for Asians to confront, including the need to ensure that Europeans keep open sea lines in Asia. In these and other growing ways, some observers note that the EU has and can become a 'new' element in Northeast Asian security (Verdi 1999, p. 19) and can offer new forms of security dialogue (Harris 2000, p. 505), since its current relations with Asia were formed in a post-cold war milieu (Simon 1995, p. 17). In this context, the promotion of 'soft', or 'human' security, previously linked with particular speeches by statesmen such as Obuchi, has become more widespread on an inter-regional scale (Cheeseman 1999, p. 336). The need to deal collectively with the complex and trans-regional responses to the terrorist attack on New York on 11 September 2001 also offers new opportunities for Asia and Europe.

Problem Areas

In security dialogue, then, ASEM is able to combine both specific and general agendas within which to confront the distribution of power and to address distorted mutual perceptions. A number of issues have been discussed within ASEM, and include the subjects of environmental protection, East Timor, KEDO and Kosovo.

One increasingly recognised area of security involves the environment, which has become a three-pillared issue in the ASEM context (European Commission 1997a). First, there is an attempt to increase and improve environmental management capabilities in Asia, to ensure the sustainable use of resources and a more sustainable pattern of wealth creation. Second, there is a growing emphasis on market-based approaches to environmental protection, with a particular need to address questions relating to pollution reduction and prevention and the protection of natural resources. Third, the establishment of environmental research and development (R&D) networks involving Asian and European representatives is being called for, in order to strengthen environmental awareness and training. These three areas are underpinned by a commitment to international standards and in particular the Kyoto Protocol, which facilitate the ongoing discussion of environmental concerns among developing and developed countries. The most tangible expression of their joint interest to date is the Asia–Europe Environment and Technology Centre (AEETC) that was opened in Thailand in April 1999, and which is funded principally by the EU. Its creation followed in the wake of the ASEM 1 Statement, which outlined environmental issues as one of the six key areas of Asia–Europe dialogue, and of a 1997 European Commission paper on 'Europe–Asia Cooperation Strategy in the Field of Environment' identifying four criteria for environmental cooperation; namely, mutual interest, complementarity, synergy with international donors and lenders and sustainability. Based on an existing research centre at Pathum Thani, the remit of the AEETC is to examine and assess the impact of a number of specific issues, such as megacities and biodiversity, to raise public awareness in environmental concerns, to enhance trade flows in environmental services and technologies, to promote the exchange of scientific and technological expertise and to increase understanding of tropical environmental and ecological systems. In addressing these and other subjects, the AEETC monitors situations, defines problem issues and pursues their resolution in a multilateral context. In the context of increased Asia–Europe cooperation over environmental issues, the EU Presidency in early 2001 expressed its determination to stand firm in the face of US refusal to implement the Kyoto Protocol: 'We hope that [the] United States will participate in the Kyoto process. We are however prepared to find a solution also without [the] US' (eu2001.se/eu2001/news, 13 March 2001). One report maintains that ASEM can play the role of creating 'possibilities of pressing demands for sustainable development' (Asia Strategy Project 1999, p. 248). In these ways, the structure of ASEM provides greater international leverage with which to address these newly salient issues.

In the case of environmental issues, there has been a trend towards utilising European skills in Asia, in areas such as water and waste management, technology, policy analysis, technical engineering, environmental consulting, management services and the application of IT. In addition, the EU's Communication on Trade and Environment (COM(96)54 final, 28 February 1996) emphasised the role of environmental protection as part of its drive towards resource efficiency, competitiveness and employment. In an instructive mood, the European Commission has proposed to work on the three areas of increasing Asia's environmental management capacity (including the need for clear rules, assistance in creating institutional frameworks, the encouragement of a broad dialogue and bringing in NGOs), facilitating market-based approaches to environmental protection (promoting environmental products, identifying key polluters, advising and sending missions) and promoting the development of an R&D network (through cooperation and institutions). As with the case of trade and human rights, it is the European side which is setting much of the agenda in this field. Clearly, there is also a markedly economic rationale behind European interests in Asian environmental issues, since OECD estimates suggest that Asia's share of the global environment market is likely to rise from four per cent in 1992 to 14 per cent in 2010, reflecting an estimated annual growth rate of 12 per cent (cited in European Commission 1997b). As a result, connections between trade and environmental issues are becoming ever more tightly drawn and an Environmental Impact Assessment is written into trade projects, with indicators being developed to monitor cooperative procedures.

Asian participants in this field thereby become driven by regulations requiring new equipment and the need for exporting firms to adhere to external standards, and by global pressures for eco-efficiency. While they may not subscribe fully to the complete raft of requirements, there is nevertheless a concern within many parts of Asia with the need to counter the serious environmental problems caused by rapid economic development. From polluted rivers in China, Japan and South Korea, to oil spills and depleted natural resources, 'the question of how the concept of "sustainable development" is interpreted and implemented is one that is crucial to the long-term stability of the region' (Schreurs 1998, p. 88). In addition, a number of trans-national problems have been worsened by the fact that inter-state cooperation is not always possible among countries with different levels of pollution control, standards, environment agencies and NGO activity (Schreurs 1998, p. 90). In addressing these dilemmas, European cooperation can assist in two ways: by providing practical assistance in the form of trained engineers able to set up and maintain equipment; and by offering a forum in which the nature of the subjects under discussion and the different types of pressure to conform will be altered. The net effect is to bring together a disparate range of environmental policies and interests in a body better able to address communal problems, and further to develop within Asia certain 'norms of multilateral citizenship' (Higgott 1998a, p. 337). Moreover, the European side comes well versed in the international regulations of bodies such as the OECD, so that a different set of expectations also enters the negotiations. Finally, environmental concerns in many ways remain a 'safe' subject on the ASEM agenda, because they are popular with domestic and international audiences and embrace a whole spectrum of different topics. As domestic networks attain regional and even inter-regional recognition, however, their bargaining power in the face of national governments, as well as in international fora such as the UN, is likely to be strengthened, with the net effect that 'regional issues' may find their way to domestic and international environmental agendas (Schreurs 1998, p. 98).

Other issues relate to specific geographical episodes, and include the problem of East Timor. After Portugal changed its colonial policy and following Indonesia's decision to annex East Timor during the 1970s, fighting continued between pro-independence and pro-integration groups in East Timor. In response to a new proposal by the Government of Indonesia in January 1999, however, agreements were reached in May among Indonesia, Portugal and the United Nations for the East Timorese people to vote in a direct ballot in August on the acceptance of an autonomy proposal. The United Nations Mission in East Timor (UNAMET) was established to implement the direct ballot, which was conducted on 30 August 1999 in generally peaceful circumstances, and it was announced on 4 September that close to 80 per cent of the East Timorese favoured separation and independence from Indonesia. Just after the announcement, however, violence by groups dissatisfied with the result intensified, and the security situation in East Timor deteriorated severely. Measures taken by the Government of Indonesia did not prove effective enough, and Indonesia finally announced that it would accept international peace-keeping forces into East Timor. A multinational force authorised by UN Security Council Resolution 1264 was then deployed to East Timor to restore order on the ground. In response to the demonstration of the East Timorese will for independence in the direct ballot, the United Nations Transitional Administration in East Timor (UNTAET), a body responsible for the administration in East Timor until its independence, was established by UN Security Council Resolution 1272 in October. Even before 1999 demonstrations had also begun to occur elsewhere, and in 2001 protests continue in other states such as Aceh, Kalimantan and the Moluccan Islands. It became clear in East Timor that the problems of reconciliation, economic development and the safe return of displaced persons could not be dealt with by Asian nations alone, and the EU issued a number of resolutions and decisions on the whole problem of governance in Indonesia. For example, prior to the 1999 elections, the Council extended electoral assistance in the form of financing and personnel and sent a number of high-level envoys to the country. The Presidency and Parliament have made a number of resolutions, dealing with issues from the general political and economic situation in Indonesia, to specific concerns relating to East Timor. The latter include a series of condemnations of the killing of unarmed civilians in Liquiça and Dili in early April 1999 and calls for the immediate release of political dissidents (see Bull EU 4–1999, pp. 62–3). One of the earliest EU initiatives regarding East Timor was its first Common Position (CP) on East Timor, released on 25 June 1996, with the aim, inter alia, of stressing the EU's support for peace talks under UN auspices and commitments undertaken in the UN Commission on Human Rights, and pledging to allocate resources to strengthen respect for human rights and improve the situation of the Timorese people. While the CP disappointed some activists by not committing the EU to curtail arms sales to Indonesia, the EU began consulting European NGOs with experience in East Timor and drafting proposals for an assistance package. Problematically, however, in January 1997 Indonesian Foreign Minister Ali Alatas stated at the World Economic Forum that no aid to East Timor would be accepted unless it was channelled through Indonesian agencies. Without Indonesian consent no EU assistance could be delivered, but any assistance channelled through Indonesian agencies would be incompatible with the EU's non-recognition of Indonesia's claim to sovereignty over the territory. Many NGOs, along with the EP and some member states, opposed the Indonesian demand.[3] Human rights groups were also critical that the EU was unable to obtain an EU Council declaration applauding the award of the Nobel Peace Prize to Monsignor Belo and Mr Ramos Horta. In the event, domestic moves towards free elections prompted the EU to adopt a more generous position towards Jakarta and to issue a Common Position on the support for popular consultation of the East Timorese. In issuing this position, the Presidency emphasised the 'need for a visible EU presence during the consultation process' (Bull EU 7/8–1999, p. 87). As a result, a European Observation Mission and European Election Observation Unit were formed (Bull EU 6–1999, pp. 18 and 90). The violence that escalated in the wake of the elections, however, precipitated European condemnation of the pro-Indonesia militias, calls for the return of refugees and demands for an International Commission of Inquiry to be set up. From September 1999, the EU also imposed a four-month embargo on the supply of arms, lest they be used for terrorist or repressive purposes (Bull EU 9–1999, p. 85). At the same time, EU representatives pursued the development of closer relations with Indonesia, in the belief that a 'dialogue would also help to anchor human rights, the rule of law and national reconciliation' (Bull EU 1/2–2000, p. 113). A Commission communication to that effect was presented at the end of 2000 (COM (2000) 50). This issue demonstrated not only a European interest in Asian affairs, but also the importance of determining an EU position, setting human rights as a 'cornerstone of EU foreign policy' and recognising the central role to be played by ASEAN member states (Bull EU 3–2001, p. 25). The Presidency even reported that ASEAN contributions to the establishment of the international force sent to East Timor 'clearly shows their interest in the maintenance of peace and security in the region' (Bull EU 9–1999, p. 70). By 2000, this issue had also come to be an important component of ASEM discussions (Bull EU 6–2000, p. 116).

Another area of limited Asia–Europe cooperation has been within KEDO. Established as a result of the October 1994 Geneva agreement between the US, South Korea and Japan, KEDO also garnered financial support from a number of other states and on 30 July 1997 the EU signed an agreement to provide contributions over five years of ECU15 million annually to the organisation. The thawing of relations between the two Koreas and the potential for the reunification of the peninsula have important security implications for the region and beyond. While Kim Dae Jung's 'sunshine policy' towards the North serves to lessen some of the intra-Korean tensions, nuclear testing and the missile programmes in the North, linked to the lack of transparency and available information about North Korea, mean that it remains a difficult country with which to negotiate. The historic inter-Korean summit of 2000 went some way to allaying fears, although the intentions of the North Koreans beyond this move remain unclear. In addition, a range of other forms of security issues, such as the need for financial aid, possible implications for migration and so on, must be borne by other nations. The foreign ministry in Seoul is keen for Northeast Asian dialogue to match that of ASEAN, but there is as yet no consensus and there remains the need to talk to Pyongyang.

A conflict on the European continent has also attracted attention within ASEM; namely the Kosovo crisis, which in February 1998 escalated into fighting between Kosovo Albanians and the authorities of the Federal Republic of Yugoslavia (FRY). Although a cease-fire was achieved in part, fighting was rekindled at the end of 1998. In February 1999, a Contact Group – comprising the US, the UK, Germany, France, Italy and Russia – submitted a peace proposal and urged the two parties to the conflict to accept it, bringing them together for negotiations in Rambouillet and Paris. At the negotiations, although the Kosovo Albanians signed the proposed peace agreement, the Yugoslav authorities refused outright to do the same. The fighting in Kosovo intensified under these circumstances, and with the Yugoslav military and police forces bringing in reinforcements, it became evident that a further increase in refugees and internally displaced persons would occur. In response to the situation, NATO launched air strikes against the FRY, which only ended on 20 June 1999, following the acceptance by FRY President Slobodan Milosevic of a peace proposal and the UN Security Council Resolution 1244 and NATO announcement of a halt to its air strikes. Over 800 000 refugees were displaced to the neighbouring countries of the

Federal Republic of Macedonia and the Republic of Albania as a result of the conflict. Asian responses to the bombing were largely negative, although Japan, given its close ties to the US gave the rather unsurprising response that it understood that the NATO air strikes were an unavoidable step taken in order to prevent the humanitarian tragedy of further increases in victims. The Kosovo Force (KFOR) was created to conduct peace-keeping operations in Kosovo, and the United Nations Interim Administration Mission in Kosovo (UNMIK) was set up to deal with civil administration. Concern among Asian states following the ending of the bombing translated into a number of concrete gestures of solidarity, including a Malaysian contribution of troops, and Japanese finances: 'While some Japanese wondered why Tokyo should respond with economic assistance to distant Eastern Europe, official circles answered that Japan is not only an Asian country. As a member of the West it must strive to cooperate in defense of common values. The widened Japanese role in East-West relations indicates a new sense of Japan's international responsibilities' (Rozman 1992, p. 319). In contrast, China provided assistance to Yugoslavia, as humanitarian assistance, and Beijing-Belgrade ties grew closer after the NATO bombing of the Chinese embassy, when three people were killed (*Financial Times* 10 December 1999 and 13 June 2000). This demonstrated a level of Asian disunity, but also the difficulty of achieving Asia–Europe agreement. This crisis was especially important for opening discussion about the nature and limits of 'humanitarian intervention' and non-interference. When Li Peng visited Yugoslavia in June 2000 he attacked NATO, saying that one political bloc could not impose its values on the rest of the world (*Financial Times* 13 June 2000). The Chinese government expressed fears that such disrespect for the non-interference in domestic affairs could be all too easily transferred by the West to the Asian continent. He said: 'This constitutes a violation of the purposes of the UN Charter and the universally recognised norms governing international relations, and poses a serious threat to stability in Europe and peace in the world' (*Financial Times* 13 June 2000). When the Chinese embassy in Belgrade was bombed by NATO planes, the Japanese government, too, was quick to reassure its Asian neighbour of its solidarity in the face of Western hostilities.

These issues share a number of characteristics. First, they demonstrate how Europeans and Asians have already begun to engage in one another's areas of tension, and in particular have demonstrated a willingness to play a role in conflict prevention and resolution, and peace-keeping and building projects. This emphasis locates the purpose of developing closer ties between Europe and Asia within the post-cold war need to address new situations (such as the widespread problems associated with international drugs trafficking) within localised spheres. Second, they demonstrate how ASEM's comprehensive structure enables the discussion of alternative forms of security, from a range of political, economic and military perspectives. Third, they illustrate how the bilateral structure of ASEM tends to polarise interpretations and responses to different events. In particular, the question of non-interference, seen most potently in the cases of East Timor and Kosovo, has, on the one hand, led Asian leaders to express collectively their fears regarding potential Western interference in their own affairs. The Chinese saw a dangerous precedent in the NATO decision to circumvent the UN and bomb Kosovo, fearing that a future Taiwan incident may elicit a similar response (*Far Eastern Economic Review* 8 April 1999). In this way, European actions draw collective Asian responses and non-interference becomes a prized Asian norm. On the other hand, in the wake of the financial crisis and the intra-regional disarray it demonstrated, as well as Asian participation in the East Timor crisis, cracks have appeared within Asia's commitment to non-interference and a number of prevailing norms have come to be challenged. ASEM offers a fruitful forum for the renegotiation of these norms and has already begun to show its utility, in facilitating discussions over the ways in which intra-regional border disputes and issues might be addressed. For example, Thai concern with its Burmese border, and the trafficking of drugs and people which continues there, led the Thai foreign minister to suggest that Thailand would be willing to reconsider the now outdated norm of non-interference for certain issues. Clearly, in the case just cited, ASEAN's policy of non-interference hampers initiatives which include the training of the Thai Karen community to wage a war on drugs by the British SAS corps, and attempts to dissuade China from continuing to protect the United Wa State Army which controls the regional production of heroin and metamphetamines (*Far Eastern Economic Review* 1 June 2000; see also Dupont 1999, p. 434). These issues illustrate how security concerns form part of ASEM's multilayered inter-regionalism, by involving a range of different actors and non-conventional initiatives and concerns (Pelkmans and Shinkai 1997, p. 82; see Okfen 1999, p. 78). Particularly important in this context is the emphasis on CBMs and the transferability of a European model for implementing them to an Asian collective. To date, concrete proposals for ASEM-specific activities have been limited to ideas for peace and cooperation institutes to be set up and the need to improve mutual understanding between the two regions (*Bangkok Post* 13 November 1997). This, in turn, has implications for how each region substantiates its own security position in a world of increasing and diverse security challenges.

Asians and Europeans share a mutual concern over the changing role of the US. For the Europeans, a rejection of observer status to APEC left them with a weak position in Asia compared to that of the US. Within Asia, particularly, the past few years have witnessed a greater questioning of the role of the US. Japan has paid almost all the costs of maintaining US troops on its soil since 1995, and Korea has contributed 35 per cent of US costs on its own peninsula (Simon 1995, p. 13). What is more, former US President Bill Clinton utilised the role of the military as leverage for his market-opening measures throughout the Asia Pacific. In other words, protection has been offered in exchange for enhanced trade. During the period of the Clinton administration, regionalism came to be seen as another strand of exerting US structural power, and Washington ensured its continued status as the 'linchpin of the Asia–Pacific security structure' (Mak 1998, p. 101). The US continues to act as '*status quo* power' in the region, by keeping intra-regional animosities down, and maintaining stability in the Taiwan Straits and Korea, particularly through the presence of the Seventh Fleet in Southeast Asia and the Security Treaty with Japan (Mak 1998, pp. 101–2). For these reasons, both sides share an interest in keeping the US predictable and stable in the region (Shin and Segal 1997). The US is not only a dominant military presence in the region but is also the largest arms supplier to the Asia Pacific, providing important weapons and weapon technology (McGrew 1998, p. 161), and thereby ensuring a continued regional role. Small inroads have been made jointly by Europe and Asia to balance this role, but they tend to depend upon the level of coherence of the EU's approach to Asia, rather than any proposals issuing from the Asian side. Thus, ASEM 3 and its Korean peninsula agenda 'boosted the European Union's goal of playing a more assertive foreign policy role in east Asia to balance US influence in the region' (*Financial Times* 23 October 2000). Moreover, as is the case with Japan–EU relations, this novel form of interaction within ASEM may serve to strengthen their hand in their relations with the US (Drifte 1998b, p. 11), particularly over the kinds of particularistic issues outlined above. In ideational terms, of course, it is in the context of their respective relations with the US that Asia and Europe jointly form ASEM, one of whose remits was to 'strengthen the weak side of the triangle' (Bridges 1999b). Once again, this places Asian regionalism on a par – at least a theoretical one – with the US and EU.

AN EXCLUSIVE DOMAIN?: THE CASE OF AUSTRALIA

ASEM is by all official accounts an 'open and evolutionary' forum (European Commission 1997a, p. 7), and yet to date the question of enlargement has repeatedly been addressed only to be dismissed from official agendas. This section will not examine the position of the more than twenty prospective applicants (which include India, Pakistan and Russia), but rather seeks to examine how the inter-regional structure of the process is utilised as a political tool for particular sets of interests. In this respect, the position of Australia (which along with New Zealand, India and Pakistan is at the top of the prospective candidates' table) offers an interesting case study in the role of identity and exclusion within the ASEM process.

Arrangements for membership to the ASEM forum have been discussed and refined, so that the current system requires the application of the so-called 'double key mechanism', whereby a country must be proposed by two countries and agreed upon independently by the Asian and European sides before being agreed upon by heads of state. The Asia–Europe Cooperation Framework (AECF) sets down this mechanism in writing and further reinforces the region-to-region foundation of the whole ASEM process. This mechanism is designed so that automatic membership is not extended to new member states of ASEAN or the EU, and was initiated in particular due to European concerns over Myanmar. However, European Commission assertions that the Union must 'remain at the core of the ASEM process' (European Commission 1997a, p. 8) implies a European desire to ensure that the integrity of the EU itself is not undermined by an inability fully to participate as a unit in this process, thereby demonstrating the utility of the meeting for further reinforcing the idea that Europe is, indeed, one entity. Several participants have also raised the possibility of inserting a clause to state that only Asian and European countries should be allowed to join, but this proposal raises the question of what 'Asia' and 'Europe' comprise. Australia applied to join ASEM even prior to the first summit. As a member state of APEC, ARF partner, Commonwealth member and with important links to Asia through, for example, the security treaty between Australia and Indonesia, it was in a prime position to join. Specific problems dog several applicant member states. But while India and Pakistan are hampered by their non-ratification of the NPT and continued fighting over Kashmir, Australia for its part is stymied by a range of issues of its own and others' making. While its admittance, along with that of New Zealand, India, Pakistan and Myanmar was close to becoming accepted at the December 1997 East Asian leaders' meeting in Kuala Lumpur, continuing European opposition to the entry of Myanmar prevented the accession of Canberra, too.

The question of inclusion and exclusion illustrates more than simply a widening versus deepening dichotomy within the whole process. From an Australian perspective, participation in the ASEM offers a means of bridging the gap in approaches to Asia that was opened by differences in the Keating and Howard administrations. While the former prime minister pursued an 'Asia First' policy, his successor has insisted on the need to work with, but not as part of, Asia (McDougall 1998, p. 109). Indeed, in no small part to distance his administration from that of Keating's, Howard insisted that Australia's 'frantic' period of obsession with Asia was over, and that 'The most important long-term consequence for Australia is the growth of a new sense of East Asian regionalism – which does not include Australia, Canada or the US' and the revival of the idea that Australia is a Western enclave (*The Australian* 6 March 2000).

In the context of ASEM, Australia would benefit from being able to exchange views about the CFSP and the new initiative on European defence, and to develop with ties with the EU. In recent years, while negotiations with Europe have remained mired in tensions over Europe's Common Agricultural Policy (CAP), Australia has focused on Asian interests. For example, in 1987 an Australian Defence White Paper declared Southeast Asia and the South-West Pacific as areas 'of primary strategic interest' (cited in Baker 1998, p. 201), and Canberra even proposed a Conference on Security and Cooperation in Asia, along the lines of the CSCE in Europe. However, not only was this proposal rejected by the US (which did not wish to see a diminution of its own power in the region), but ASEAN member states were also hostile towards it since it came with certain institutional and regulatory prerequisites. Nevertheless, in 1989, Australia promoted APEC in order to avoid trade blocs and exclusion and reduce tensions with East Asia and the US (Ravenhill 1996, p. 181). The context of Australia's attempted engagement within ASEM, then, is the story of a middle power: 'those small and medium-sized states which perceive a strong correlation between their national well-being and the maintenance of regional (or global) order, and which also have the capacity and the commitment to pursue a measure of defence policy independence and foreign policy influence' (Baker 1998, p. 190). ASEM offers a forum in which to locate and resolve its regional and global challenges. From ASEM participation, Australia could gain 'significant integration with the Asian region as a basis for future participation in discussions which have relevance for the region's economic and political relationships', at the same time as strengthening ASEM as a 'launching pad for greater European trade and investment in Asia' (Australian Parliament 1997, p. 27). Ironically, however, the primary motive for applying to join ASEM was to allay Australian fears of being excluded from a future East Asian bloc at a time when Australia was 'increasingly concerned about losing its regional relevance and its economic and military edge' (Baker 1998, p. 199; Wesley 1997, p. 524), but, in the event, Canberra's application was rejected for the very reason that it did not, indeed, fit either bloc of the forum. Like its Turkish counterpart in Europe, perhaps, Australia thereby obtains only 'second-tier status' and is excluded ostensibly in terms of cultural (rather than geographical or economic) criteria (Wesley 1997, p. 525).[4] However, when its membership was initially proposed, it was clearly judged to belong to the Asian side. This was a misjudgement, for it does not fit so easily into either category. In other words, the narrative of Australian participation does not fit the inter-regional model, leaving its policy making orientation somewhere between the US-dominant, state-based forum of APEC and the culturally determinate, anti-Western Asian club of the EAEC. Of course, prior to ASEM this situation had already arisen and Australia had attempted on numerous occasions to express its Asian linkages, through, for example, proposals for Closer Economic Relations (CER) with New Zealand and AFTA, as well as the 1995 proposal for the East Asian Hemisphere (Wesley 1997, pp. 530–52). But the advent of ASEM brought additional pressures for government and business representatives painfully aware that the Meeting offers an important trade-enhancement facility and that if 'an East Asian bloc develops as a node of both the APEC and ASEM processes, the current dominant definitions of the East Asian region emphasizing solidarity against Western states would leave Australia on the outer'. One of the misreadings made by the Australians, however, was to believe that East Asians had in fact 'acquiesced to the "Asia Pacific" definition of the region' (Wesley 1997, pp. 530–33). In order to redress this, too, increased contacts by Australian government officials and business representatives form part of Canberra's ongoing attempt to develop 'cultural convergence' with its neighbours (Wesley 1997, p. 539). In many ways, this locates much of Australia's position close to that of Japan's: in but not of the region.

The biggest problem, however, issued from resistance to Australia's entry by Malaysian Prime Minister Mahathir. In practice, so long as Mahathir is around, Australia and New Zealand will not be able to join ASEM. The most recent clashes began in December 1993 when then Prime Minister Paul Keating used the term 'recalcitrant' to describe his Malaysian counterpart, an adjective which was subsequently translated to mean 'ignorant' or 'ill-educated'. At the Brunei meeting of ASEAN in August 1995 the message was given that Australia would attend ASEM 2 (*Thailand Times* 27 February 1996), but in December 1995 Mahathir said that regional membership of ASEM was only to be for countries which are 'Asian of culture' (Wesley 1997, p. 540). What is more, Mahathir was also keen to use the forum of ASEM to reassert the de facto existence within that process of his EAEC (the 'Asian Ten'): Australia's presence would have destroyed that image. In spite of a relatively cordial visit by Mahathir to meet Howard in Australia in 1996, the Malaysian prime minister was soon back in Kuala Lumpur complaining about Australian racism and actively lobbied in December 1996 against Australian entry to ASEM. Shortly before and immediately after Alexander Downer became foreign minister in the new Howard administration in 1996, he stated that he wanted Australia to join ASEM, and considered Malaysia's rebuff as Malaysian punishment for the 1993 incident (*The Australian* 7 March 2000; *Thailand Times* 28 February 1996). In February 1997, Howard overlooked Malaysia during a tour of Asia, and made a point of criticising

Mahathir over his treatment of Ibrahim Anwar during the APEC meeting in Kuala Lumpur in November 1998 (*The Australian* 7 March 2000).

In September 1999 Mahathir opposed Australian leadership of an East Timor peace force. Nevertheless, Australia led the International Force in East Timor, a move approved by the UN at the request of the Indonesian Government (which nevertheless, was suspicious of Australian motives for its involvement, *International Herald Tribune* 23 January 1999). When Australia led an armed task force to restore peace there with 4500 of its own troops, Howard's triumphalism got the better of him (*The Australian* 5 March 2000; *International Herald Tribune* 20 September 1999), not unlike his 'strong man of Asia' speech in the wake of the Asian financial crisis, and in the eyes of external observers 'confirmed an impression that the government is more comfortable with American and European partners than with Asian ones' (*Far Eastern Economic Review* 8 June 2000). Once again, during the crisis in East Timor Prime Minister Howard's unfortunate reference to Australia as the regional deputy sheriff (to the US) was not well received in Jakarta or Kuala Lumpur, leading the Indonesian Government to wonder at the 'aggressiveness with which it [Australia] has assumed the leadership role in the peace-enforcement operations' and to cancel the Australia–Indonesia security pact (Zakaria 1999, p. 778), and prompting Mahathir to call Australia a 'regional bully' (*Financial Times* 18 May 2000) and to express the view that Australia was no longer welcome in Asia (*Far Eastern Economic Review* 8 June 2000). Even the Singaporeans, long-time supporters of Australia in the region, were aghast at the Australian blunder. The so-called 'Howard Doctrine' and the rift with Indonesia were the key reasons why Australia was not invited to join the ASEAN+3 process (*The Australian* 7 March 2000). Australia's actions have pushed Mahathir to find accommodation with Indonesia, and its US$1 billion contribution to the IMF bailout fund for Thailand has secured good relations there. Meanwhile, the Japanese government is baffled by greater Australia moves towards Europe and the US and away from Asia. China, on the other hand, prefers Australia's quieter approach to Asia and sees Australia potentially as an East–West bridge (*The Australian* 9 March 2000). The fiasco in East Timor led to domestic articles examining how 'Australia's relations with Asia are drifting' (*The Weekend Australian* 11–12 March 2000). These added to previous unfortunate episodes, such as Howard's 1988 tirade on the need to curb Asian immigration (continued with current anti-immigration trends), and strengthened the feeling within Asia that the 'Howard doctrine' was an attempt to impose Western values on the region (*The Australian* 3 March 2000).

At the same time, Australia has been making inroads into improving relations with the EU, and signed the EU–Australia Joint Declaration in June

1997, which emphasised 'shared commitments to the respect and promotion of human rights, fundamental freedoms, democracy and the rule of law which underpin our internal and international policies'. Similarly, a European Parliament delegation saw Australia as a bridge between East and West (Australian Parliament 1997, p. 15). This was a change from a position taken in 1993 when, asked to participate in peace-keeping operations in Bosnia, Australia declined, saying that Europeans should deal with European problems (McDougall 1998, p. 112). Historical roots and the English language mean that Australian relations with the EU tend to be informed by the Euro-sceptical British press and continue to be overshadowed by perennial problems related to agricultural subsidies. Now accepted as an insurmountable issue, however, CAP problems have been supplemented by the discussion of issues such as the new proposals for a common European defence mechanism and work on issues such as humanitarian intervention, crisis management capacities and financing, and the role of EURATOM, which all offer potential models for Australia's engagement in its own region. Developments since the Maastricht Treaty have also given Australia a more coherent EU to deal with. One of the results of the ending of the cold war and the imminent accession to the EU of a number of the states of former Central and Eastern Europe, however, has been the redeployment of EU personnel from Australasia to the European continent, suggesting a down-grading of Australian relevance to the EU and further reinforcing a need for Australia to keep European interests in the region alive. All of these questions are somewhat redundant for now, and can only be revisited if and when the current ASEM member states reopen the membership question. Australia's identity within the region is buffetted by the question of membership within ASEM, since this process represents an explicitly region-to-region format. Continuing Australian schizophrenia over this subject can be seen in Canberra's response to European insistence on including in the joint agreement (as with all others, since a Council decision of 1991) a human rights clause. This clause, which applies to all EU relations with third countries, including the member states of ASEM, provoked a dispute over Canberra's treatment of Aborigines and human rights' issues relating to it. In many ways, the tone adopted by Australian representatives in response to the clause, suggested that as an (advanced) member of the West (and, implicitly, not of Asia) Australia should not be exposed to such scrutiny. The framework of inter-regionalism makes it difficult to resolve this issue, since the cultural and political are employed alongside the geographical to form a boundary of exclusion emphasising clearly differences between 'them' and 'us'.

CONCLUSION: IMPLICATIONS FOR INTER-REGIONALISM

This chapter has demonstrated how the inter-regional structure of ASEM builds upon, and further reinforces, mutual representations of region within a broadening agenda for 'political dialogue'. On the one hand, this pillar of ASEM ensures that a range of non-trade discussions can be sustained, on the other, it reifies notions of self and other, by positing a European-led agenda alongside disparate Asian characterisations of the political. In the first place, then, the three-pillar structure of ASEM enables participants to talk about a number of non-trade subjects and to engage in a larger stock-taking exercise of what might be achieved collectively. From an EU standpoint, the inclusion of political dialogue alongside the economic pillar facilitates discussion of those facets of social and governmental responsibility now deemed within Europe to be inextricably linked to trade affairs. These include issues relating to environmental protection, the sales of military equipment and related materials, and questions of good governance, democracy and human rights. While critics continue to claim that the weaknesses of the EU prevent it from playing a major political role above that of 'modérateur sur divers thèmes qui intéressent la sécurité régionale' (*Le Monde* 4 March 1996), efforts within the political realm have been made to offset Asian criticisms levelled at the EU in the wake of its inadequate response to the Asian financial crisis. For the Asian contingent, the pillar of political dialogue has proved more problematic to date, since issues of democratic accountability have frequently elicited joint recourse to the distinctiveness of 'Asian values', which goes as far as locating a form of 'Oriental wisdom' alongside 'official decisions and procedures' of the West (Watanabe 1993, p. 53). For its part, the Asian side has benefited from encouraging its European partners to forge a political dialogue with Asia that does not include the US, with the result that, for example, novel forms of security cooperation have been proposed. In reality, the track record of this rather neglected area of relations is unimpressive, and to date the leaders of ASEM have been averse to using this pillar for more than benign purposes. As the *Financial Times* wryly observed: 'Government leaders do not need to travel half way round the world to organise exchanges between students' (*Financial Times* 3 March 1996). In fact, the loosely organised structure of political dialogue and the necessity of functioning as regional units at present means that only apparent consensus can be achieved (*Le Figaro* 2 March 1996). For this reason, too, American observers of the Asia–Europe process have tended to view the enterprise with disinterest (Bobrow 1999). Nevertheless, the fact that the US indeed remains present as a Banquo-like figure does provide stimulus for the Europeans and Asians to cooperate in response to its actions, particularly in order to persuade Washington to remain engaged politically and in security terms in both (but especially the Asian) regions (Gilson 2001). For Asian nations (especially Japan) which rely upon cooperation with the US, the positive encouragement by Washington for the creation of further regional cooperation has been an important factor in pushing the nations of ASEM together. What is more, reactions against the so-called Washington consensus in the wake of the financial crisis have stimulated (still to be embraced) opportunities for Europe to carve a novel niche in its relations with Asia.

Secondly, the inter-regional structure of the ASEM process is now firmly embedded in the rhetoric and documents which surround it. Thus, 'ASEM is a bilateral relationship between Europeans on the one hand and Asians on the other' (CAEC 1997, p. 4). In this way, the meeting departs from other regional models such as APEC and the ARF, in that it explicitly recognises two sides engaging in region-to-region dialogue. The application of regional understandings also locates a coherent 'Asia', side by side with an institutionally recognisable 'Europe' of the EU, an application which has implications for both 'sides'. In this way, questions pertaining to the Balkans and Korea share air time at summit meetings and are open to collective ideas for resolution. In practice, however, the less than enthusiastic attendance of the European representatives at the summits and the European tendency to put forward their own models (OSCE, EURATOM, EU and so on) and agendas gives little opportunity for tangible cooperation in these fields. What is more, the European representatives rarely stray too far from their commitment to pursue their own commercial interests in Asia, while their Asian counterparts, too, focus predominantly upon their own regional dilemmas of adhering to global trade negotiations and encouraging inward investment. These tensions are further exacerbated by the loose and non-binding nature of the ASEM framework (Smith, H. 1998, p. 307). The putative equality of the relationship within ASEM, therefore, is undermined by the requirements of regional advancement within a changing global environment.

Despite these inherent tensions, the inter-regional structure of political dialogue is important for offering lessons in 'bloc-think', with the result that questions of regional identification play an implicit role within this pillar (*The Economist* 2 March 1996). In practical terms, the collective approach to this meeting derived on the European side from the need to find a voice in the already overcrowded region of Asia (particularly the Asia Pacific); while for Asia it had become clear that ASEAN alone could not provide sufficient leverage on the global stage to represent the interests of the region. In order to play this regional role, Asian participants are required to formulate a collective response prior to the inter-regional encounters, and thereby establish some kind of 'soft institutionalism' (Soesastro and Nuttall 1997, p. 84). Within the EU, the post-Maastricht merger of two (political and economic) groups for Asia within the Council and the rare use of the Troika system for ASEM activities mean that the region-to-region structure promotes greater internal cohesion here too (Soesastro and Nuttall 1997, p. 83). The consolidation of regional positions within ASEM extends increasingly to collaboration between the two regions in the face of external structures, so that a 'minilateral' role for ASEM is also visible. In the economic pillar, the first ASEM summit was used to seek a joint approach to the forthcoming WTO ministerial meeting; in the political field, too, ASEM offers a framework for other activities, such as within the UN or with regard to Korea (Smith, H. 1998, p. 304). In ideational terms, the process also introduces an important development, as its very mechanisms require each region to 'prepare separately in advance to engage in shared activities', thereby reinforcing 'the regional identity of each partner, which in turn helps create the realisation of shared interests – the "ASEMness" of the process' (CAEC 1997, p. 5). However, ASEM's inter-regional structure has the effect of perpetuating the discursive dominance of a Western-led agenda, and reinforcing the inequality evident in the economic pillar, and within other inter-regional frameworks maintained by the Europeans (such as EU–Lomé, EU–ACP or EU–MERCOSUR agreements). What is more, the Asia–Europe parallel tends to encourage contrasts of (caricatured) 'Asian' versus 'European' styles of decision making (Segal 1997a, p. 126), and the dominant discourse of European notions of 'region' in this regard leads to conclusions regarding Asian inadequacies in the face of a superior Western model. As a result, the apparent failures of ASEM, such as its loose and non-binding nature and the sidelining of human rights issues, come to be associated with a need to propitiate 'Asian-style' negotiations (Bridges 1999b, p. 184). The increasing application of an 'Asia versus Europe' discourse further embeds these notions and removes any need to problematise the very natures of the regions in question. Rather, this formulation leaves many observers with the idea that Asia indeed has the 'mirror' of Europe through which to view its potential self (Camroux and Lechervy 1996, p. 450). This process of interaction simultaneously informs Asian participants of the presence of a coherent regional body within Europe.

Maull asserts that 'ASEM in practice should be seen as twenty-six actors (including the EU), rather than two effective teams' (Maull et al. 1998, p. xiv). At the level of both practical and ideational effectiveness, though, the evidence presented here suggests that, in fact, ASEM should be seen additionally as a nascent inter-regional dialogue and as a supplement to a range of existing 'collective Imaginaries', which transcend traditional ideas of inter-state activity (Jameson and Masao 1998, p. xii). Without acknowledging this dimension we cannot appreciate the dynamic nature or the potential future for ASEM. Moreover, in the context of new ways of thinking in this globalising age (see Booth and Smith 1995; Gill and Mittelman 1997), inter-regionalism may offer an alternative route for responding to the exigencies of an increasingly complex international political economy, and ASEM may even operate as an inter-regional integrating mechanism to this end. In this regard, inter-regionalism remains an untested dimension, but continues as an experiment in a novel form of cooperation. Part of this experiment also involves a move away from state-level actors and towards the influence upon them of civil society linkages that transcend continental divides. It is to this element which the next chapter now turns.

Notes

1. Indeed, Mahathir observed that Japanese financial woes were due to its being too westernised. 'Even Japanese youths want to be blondes, work less and play more' (cited in the *Financial Times* 19 January 2001).
2. Ultimately, the draft of the Vision Group's proposal dropped 'security' from paragraphs 4 and 8 (p. 111).
3. See www.tni.org/asia/wath/asem33.htm.
4. Interestingly, the Turkish prime minister solicited Mahathir's support for ASEM membership! (Wesley 1997, p. 544).

5. On the Margins of Summitry

> Our understanding of the presence of diversity tends to be somewhat undermined by constant bombardment with oversimple generalizations about "Western civilization", "Asian values", "African cultures" and so on. Many of these readings of history and civilization are not only intellectually shallow, they add to the divisiveness of the world in which we live. (Amartya Sen, *Development as Freedom*, 1999)

The Chair's statement at ASEM 3 records the rationale for the third pillar of 'Promoting Cooperation in Other Areas, including Social and Cultural Issues':

> Leaders underscored the importance of enhancing mutual understanding between the two regions through closer people-to-people exchanges of various kinds in the social and cultural areas. Leaders also recognized the vivid and diverse cultures of Asia and Europe as a source of vitality to enliven the mutual cooperation between the two regions and noted that ASEM is an excellent vehicle to achieve this end. (Seoul 2000)

This pillar becomes the repository for issues of indeterminate status and includes subjects from science and technology (which, in fact, span all three pillars), to human resource development, education, environmental protection and cultural exchanges. As such, it is often regarded as the light refreshment of the ASEM process: after all, student-to-student exchanges are easier to organise than inter-state trading agreements or political dialogue. ASEM speech writers make frequent reference to promoting the involvement of 'civil society' as an integral part of developing overall relations between Asia and Europe. Indeed, when the British government hosted ASEM 2, a glossy brochure accompanying the event placed the role of civil society at the top of its list of ASEM priorities. The civil society role envisioned by the hosts of the formal structure, however, tends to focus on a benign face of cultural activities, as a means of introducing each region to one another's artistic, literary and societal heritage, and supporting the status quo of the government-led agenda. For this reason, non-governmental groups (especially non-governmental organisations, NGOs) tend to be excluded from formal ASEM discussions, since state leaders are unwilling to tackle the sometimes contentious agendas raised by them. At the heart of ASEM's cultural programme is the Singapore-based Asia–Europe Foundation (ASEF), which was inaugurated in February 1997 in response to a decision made at ASEM 1, and whose remit is to promote inter-regional cultural exchange. While it is the clearest expression of how civil society may be understood in the formal context of ASEM relations, in fact it forms part of a more complex mosaic of non-governmental interests which lie within and on the edges of the ASEM process.

This chapter examines several key components of the third pillar, and assesses the value of the inter-regional engagement for incorporating civil society representatives. First, it examines the differing notions of what civil society may indeed mean in the context of Asia–Europe relations. Second, it analyses the role of the People's Forum which has formed itself in response to the ASEM summit, and in particular considers the constituency and goals of this mechanism and how it compares to other, increasingly vociferous, civil society movements activated in response to international meetings. The final part of the chapter assesses the impact of inter-regionalism on the civil society component of Asia–Europe relations.

DEFINING CIVIL SOCIETY ON THE MARGINS OF ASEM

Given the range and complexity of the involvement of non-state actors in the ASEM process, it is not straightforward to determine how 'civil society' should be understood in this arena. A conventional (Western) definition of civil society delineates institutions and groupings that reside outside government, but which may include business, NGOs, other social groups and for-profit organisations. The ASEM process reflects a mixture of these actors, some of whom are closely associated with formal proceedings (such as business interests and ASEF), and others who remain outside official channels. To understand this juxtaposition of different societal interest groups, it is necessary to go beyond Hall's notion of civil society as the 'self-organization of strong and autonomous groups that balance the state' (1995, p. 15) or Ferdinand's 'collectivity of inter-dependent and inter-influential organisations not part of or controlled by the state' (1999, p. 4), to acknowledge not only that at the inter-regional level there is more than the state to be challenged, but that there may also arise alliances among these different levels. As a result, it is instructive to reject the concept that the 'other' for non-governmental actors represents simply the state. In fact, collective attention may be drawn towards (or, indeed, against) local, sub-national, national, sub-regional, regional, inter-regional or global 'others', thereby transcending the 'politics of identity and difference' (Gill 2000, p. 138).

The nature of interaction at the non-governmental level suggests that overlapping and multiple interest groups, or different nodes of engagement, coalesce at given moments to present a web of interlaced demands in the face of a common set of causes. For this reason, the concept of the non-ephemeral pursuit of the common good (www.tni.or/asia/watch/asem23.htm) must be set aside, to be replaced by a nuanced understanding of non-state actors gathering simultaneously for long-term or transitory purposes, as isolated moments of collective resistance by disparate groups (Gill 2000, p. 138). Some of these groups may be granted controlled inclusion (Richards 2000, p. 9) in the formal political arena where 'political players struggle, debate, negotiate and decide on policy issues and, in doing so, are bound by given rules' (Arts 1998, p. 55); others are left to function on the periphery, but are constrained by the same rules in challenging the political norms within them. It is at this level, within the context of Asia–Europe relations at least, that different groupings of non-governmental actors diverge, leaving a number of non-governmental groupings to militate on the margins of official structures.

DEFINING INTERESTS

Social groups in their many guises (NGOs, 'global social movements', interest groups and the like) are difficult to define, since they vary, for example, according to types of organisation, membership, duration, budget, staff, geographical locus, ideology and political conditions (O'Brien et al. 2000, p. 3). NGOs are easier to pinpoint, since they retain a fixed and visible identity, which may be supported by significant finances (for example the World Wildlife Fund), media attention (Greenpeace), great communications, or scientific and specialist knowledge. The term 'social movement', which encapsulates 'groups of people with a common interest who band together to pursue a far-reaching transformation of society offers a further means of understanding groups that function beyond state parameters (O'Brien et al. 2000, p. 12). The functions of these groups may also vary, although they tend to provide civic education and may serve either to legitimate or delegitimate the multilateral meetings whose periphery they inhabit. More importantly, they may act as points of reference around which forms of 'social learning' develop (Princen and Finger 1994, p. 18 footnote 46). Participation in parallel conferences activated on the edge of formal summitry not only brings together interest groups in a communal voice of opposition, but also renders visible previously unheard of movements. While they may not form part of the formal negotiating process, interest groups and NGOs may influence conferences (as they did at the United Nations Conference on Environment and Development, UNCED) by lobbying governments collectively, and by placing representatives on national delegations (Finger 1994a, pp. 207–8). In turn, the official stratum may recognise the role of the interest groups as part of its own remit and thereby enhance further the global voice of non-state actors, forcing them, in turn, to organise themselves through a coherent strategy in response to this official level recognition. One word of caution is worth sounding: namely, that the influence of interest groups should be neither overestimated nor romanticised (Scholte 2000, p. 116). Hence, while parallel conferences may be important, they may in fact serve as no more than 'jamborees' and 'theatrical exercises', where they 'influence delegates only indirectly through the media and through demonstrating their ability to mobilize a large constituency' (Lindborg, cited in Princen and Finger 1994, p. 18 footnote 46).

The social dimension of ASEM does not fit neatly into these existing analyses, and may more adequately be posited as a coalition of interest groups, which brings together a range of locally active advocacy and lobbying bodies, to create mutual leverage and international awareness in the face of a common threat or challenge. This formulation raises two key questions: namely, what is the nature of the interest coalition?; and how, in an inter-regional structure, does it function in relation to the state? In responding to the first question, the coalition may arise from a medley of concerns and will therefore lack formal and cohesive roots, while deriving its membership quite simply from those who happen to be present at the outset: 'In negotiations that have few precedents, little predetermined structure, an ill-defined agenda, and fuzzy outcome expectations, simply sitting at the table confers influence' (Princen 1994, p. 37). As a result, it may function in one of two ways: as a body containing multiple nodes of interest, which may be salient at different times according to the nature of the particular issues under discussion (O'Brien et al. 2000, p. 15); or as a 'swarm' of 'amorphous groups' that collectively attack a given target, such as environmental degradation or 'globalisation' (Pieterse 1997, p. 82). According to the RAND study that formulated this concept, a swarm has no 'central leadership or command structure; it is multi-headed, impossible to decapitate. And it can sting a victim to death' (*The Economist* 1999). The force produced by this agglomeration of multi-level interest groups subsequently creates 'civil energy' within specific loci or fields of activity (Schmit 1996, p. 178). These socially derived groupings often issue directly from moments of perceived crisis, such as environmental dangers or human rights abuses, and from the recognition that citizens alone cannot combat a given problem. Actors within this non-governmental field may build coalitions, in order to create bargaining capabilities with respect to the state, and set long-term goals for fundamental change, ideals which are usually beyond the reach or concern of fixed-term governments (Princen and Finger 1994, p. 11). Solingen's work on coalition analysis provides a useful tool for understanding how such groups originate against the background of domestic institutions and function across state and society. By extending the analysis, it is also possible to determine how these groups operate at the trans-national level, where they encounter institutions that negotiate forms of international activity (1998, p. 9). If his location of actors in *for* or *against* coalitions, however, is rather too neat in suggesting a uniformity of opinion and purpose, it is instructive to supplement coalition analysis with the concept of band-wagoning, whereby groups climb on or alight, according to whether or not their own local needs are being served at a given moment.

The second important question raised by the unique nature of this interest coalition pertains to the nature of the state, against which 'civil society' by definition is situated. On this point, O'Brien et al.'s work provides a starting-point, by identifying a lack of cohesion within global social movements as a major difference between them and their domestic counterparts (2000, p. 13). For this reason, it is useful to conceptualise global social movements as umbrella coalitions that pool issue-specific expertise and fill a niche of activity, 'by building expertise in areas diplomats tend to ignore and by revealing information economic interests tend to withhold' (Princen 1994, p. 41). In relation to the states that constitute the inter-regional agenda monitored by these groups, there are two factors worth considering in an inter-regional context. First, while they are often seen to play an oppositional role towards the government, interest coalitions (or the groups that constitute them) may be funded in part or whole by those same state bodies, in order to create the legal, financial and political organisational structures that give them recognition and legitimacy (Smillie 1999, p. 11). So, while interest coalitions create networks of dependencies among themselves, they may also incorporate links with government in the process (Princen 1994, p. 33). As Pieterse observes: 'Civil society empowerment comes to a point where either it pursues the path of local autonomy, a path of de facto state substitution, or it accepts being a player in a pluralistic field, side by side with state and market forces' (1997, p. 83). However, in obtaining tacit or concrete support from the state or states they purport to oppose, interest coalitions face a paradox; for, while they may 'provide a counterforce to short-term decision making, to the grow-at-any-price imperative, and to the tendency to find ever more creative means of externalizing costs, they must be able to counter the obvious strengths of governmental and corporate actors without becoming such actors' (Princen and Finger 1994, p. 11). By becoming integrated – if only loosely – into state structures that are often premised upon notions of an ideal of political pluralism, the 'success' of a civil society movement may result in its absorption into the political processes it professes to monitor or oppose. This form of co-option by the state has not only become acceptable, but has also led to the institutionalisation of a set of rules of 'fair play' – which determine the parameters of 'good governance' – for actors who have been playing different games (Miller and Meier 1998, p. 53). The second factor regarding the interface between interest coalition and state pertains to the nature of inter-regionalism itself. As has been noted throughout this book, inter-regionalism increasingly has to be conceptualised as a separate level of interaction, with the result that it may indeed be the *region* rather than the state that is in question. On the one hand, this factor tends to reify regional behaviour (with regard to globalisation or human rights, for instance); on the other, it requires the functioning of intra-regional groups to respond – if only for logistical purposes – to the demands of an inter-regional framework. It will become clear below that these factors often confuse debate at the level of civil society engagement within ASEM. What results is that, just as interest coalitions may be swarm-like, the targets against which they articulate their concerns may also lack central authority (Arts 1998, p. 21). Pieterse rightly observes in this context 'a political gap from the local to the global which is only partially being filled by the stretch from local networks to planetary social movements, international NGOs or global civil society. This is not merely an institutional hiatus but as much a programmatic hiatus and a hiatus of political imagination' (1997, pp. 86–7).

The cumulative effects of the actions of social movements can only be measured on a case-by-case basis, but it is clear – simply from looking at policy pronouncements by heads of state – that their role in general has gained media attention and a level of international credibility. Increasingly, they are seen to offer a 'different form of politics', by bringing on to agendas different terms of priority for a range of issues (Princen and Finger 1994, p. 12), and adding 'legitimacy, transparency, and transnationalism', since they are freed from the yoke of national boundaries, which governments, by their very definition cannot be (Princen 1994, p. 34). O'Brien et al. go as far as to discern a transformation at the global level where formal institutions encounter global social movements (GSMs) to produce 'complex multilateralism' (2000, p. 3). The 'peculiar contribution' of these groups affects not just structures of power and institutions, but may indeed have a transformative effect on processes themselves (Princen and Finger 1994, p. 1).

More and more frequently, the diverse sets of actors behaving as part of NGOs or interest coalitions draw upon a lengthening historical narrative that joins them in common cause against the forces of a vaguely defined notion of globalisation. Thus, they are linked in an instrumental way in their collective engagement through, inter alia: the International Tropical Timber Organization (ITTO) and 1987 Montreal Protocol on Substances that Deplete the Ozone Layer; protests in late 1999 in Seattle against the WTO; demonstrations against the WTO Ministerial conference in Lac Leman in 1999; anti-debt action outside the G7 in Birmingham in 1998; resistance to the 2000 (and 2001) Davos meetings of the World Economic Forum (WEF); and anti-capitalist demonstrations outside the EU meeting in Göteberg in June 2001 and the G8 in Genoa in July of that year. The ephemeral nature of their disparate actions is thereby substantiated within an ongoing *process* of non-state activism. In this way, too, each can lay claim to form part of a force for resistance against the threats posed by globalisation and free trade regimes (Pieterse 1997, p. 82). The growing global dimension of this force of resistance draws domestic groups into a new realm of activity and casts them as part of a quasi-institutionalised 'global NGO community' (Princen and Finger 1994, p. 18 footnote 46), or even as a nascent 'super NGO' (Smillie 1999, p. 17), in which they all come to be connected, as a collective voice articulating the 'basis for an alternative world order' (Cox, cited in Devetak and Higgott 1999, p. 492). Impressively, some observers note their potential to become the 'principal actors in the reconstruction of political authority at the global level' (Devetak and Higgott 1999, p. 492). This phenomenon corresponds, according to Finger, to a post-modern condition, which sees the rise of these new forms of actor 'within the context of eroding traditional politics and the corresponding fragmentation and erosion of the project of modernity' (1994b, p. 61). What is novel, is the way in which locally derived and issue-specific NGOs join the ranks of non-governmental activity previously reserved for *international* NGOs, with the net result that interest coalitions come to represent significantly more than a mere aggregation of the oppressed from national contexts (Finger 1994b, p. 59). The growing role of these voices enables them not only to influence, but also to create anew, the structures in which they locate themselves.

CIVIL SOCIETY AND ASEM

The idea of civil society within ASEM may appear to be no more than a chimera. Not only do inter- and intra-cultural differences impede the development of a coherent social voice to monitor and challenge official pronouncements by ASEM's leaders, but the difficulties inherent in running parallel conferences within an inter-regional framework also militate against the organic development of an ASEM interest group stratum. There are, nevertheless, two types of civil society within the ASEM framework: an official and an unofficial one. ASEM planners have crafted an intentionally vague definition of 'civil society', enabling them to reflect the interests of the people of Asia and Europe, while simultaneously ensuring that many of the groups which represent grassroot issues continue to be excluded from the formal process.

The official story of non-governmental cooperation between Asia and Europe draws on a history of inter-cultural interaction between Asia and Europe, which began in its present region-to-region form in the late 1970s when the EC and ASEAN agreed in their 1980 cooperation agreement to undertake together a range of activities. These actions, such as the provision of student scholarships and the promotion of cultural heritage, were reaffirmed at their Karlsruhe meeting in September 1994 and now also form part of the cultural events pursued under the ASEM framework. In addition, business interests and European parliamentarians can be included in this broad understanding of civil society within ASEM. For their part, business communities are not part of the government structures of ASEM, but their representation and feedback are, nevertheless, integrated into the formal structures of ASEM. A range of channels, such as the Asia–Europe Business Forum and initiatives designed to assist small and medium-sized enterprises (SMEs, see Chapter 3), ensure that business interests are integral to the goals of the ASEM leaders, while fora such as the regular Evian Group meetings lobby ASEM leaders, in an attempt to prevent trade policy from being treated simply as a 'technical' matter that is too complicated to garner public understanding and support. On the one hand, business interests utilise the structures of ASEM to put forward their concerns over government decisions. On the other, they place themselves clearly in opposition to other areas of the non-governmental stratum, and argue that, for example, the Battle for Seattle was 'led by people who had been left in the dark while globalization continued' (Evian Group 2000, pp. 5–6). Members of the European Parliament (MEPs) play a somewhat different role, and initially did not request participation in ASEM, but monitored European Commission and Council preparations for the summit. The Parliament (EP) has been associated with the formal process, through the Asia–Europe Young Parliamentarians' Forum and EP reports on ASEM activities resulting from scrutiny by EP Committees on Foreign Affairs, Security and Defence Policy and on External Economic Relations. As the ASEM process has taken root, the EP has called more and more often for parliamentarians to be fully included in the ASEM framework. In April 1996, for example, delegates of the European Parliament–ASEAN Inter-Parliamentary Organisation (AIPO) proposed inviting a few parliamentarians from Japan, China and South Korea to join them, in order to ensure that parliamentary scrutiny of ASEM could be made possible. In March 1998, the EP passed a resolution to establish an Asia–Europe Parliamentary Partnership, which would, nevertheless, have no direct input into the senior discussions of ASEM. To this end, the eve of the third summit witnessed the first steps towards the establishment of an Asia–Europe inter-parliamentary dialogue. In October 2000 in Seoul, members of an ad hoc inter-parliamentary group called for the creation of an official Asia–Europe Parliamentary (ASEP) dialogue within the ASEM process by ASEM 4 in 2002, and insisted that all matters relating to ASEM be reported to respective national parliaments, as well as to the EP, in order to provide 'a critical role in contributing to a more democratic, participatory and cooperative ASEM process' (Statement of Inter-Parliamentary Dialogue 2000; Bull-EU 1/2–2000, p. 7). The trend has been for the EP to make formal statements and resolutions about specific issues, and to encourage fora like ASEM to include them in their remit. Specific concerns include calls for the drafts of TFAP and IPAP (see Chapter 3) to integrate requirements for democracy, fundamental rights, the environment and the fight against poverty into their principles and objectives. Although many of the EP's discussions related to ASEM have focused on the need to ensure fundamental workers' rights and to raise human rights on the formal agenda, it continues to support the IPAP and TFAP (see Chapter 3) without advocating the insertion of accountability clauses, and tends on the whole towards a reactive rather than innovative position when faced with this novel inter-regional arrangement. Rather than challenging prevailing concepts of the status quo, therefore, the EP plays a role in promoting non-governmental liaisons and has paid particular attention to imbuing a social dimension into pre-existing trade-related activities. Hence, for example, it supports governmental initiatives for a new WTO trade round, but advocates the inclusion of discussions on subjects such as sustainable development and the protection of the environment, as well as employment, child labour and social security (European Parliament 2000). It has made 'causes célèbres' and issued resolutions with regard to particular issues such as human rights' abuses in Burma (for instance, 22 October 1996, 16 September 1999, 18 May 2000, 7 September 2000), and has urged the European Commission and CFSP High Representative to make a determined effort to visit Mrs Aung San Suu Kyi and for the EU and its member states to implement economic sanctions against Burma. At the same time, consultations continued among the various parliamentary delegations, towards the preparation of ASEP. On the whole, the reports produced by them have supported ASEM initiatives, welcoming in particular the multi-sectoral cooperation of ASEM and noting that the 'step by step institutionalisation of the relationship between the EU and the ASEM partners would pave the way for the achievement of more concrete results' (European Parliament 1999). The Parliament's relations with NGOs is somewhat ambiguous. While it has expressed strong support for the work of the People's Forum and has supported the Forum's inclusion in the official

ASEM process, it also makes frequent recourse to debates played out elsewhere. For example, by claiming that 'the European institutional model is a framework that can be exported, as already shown by the creation of MERCOSUR and the Latin-American Parliament' it rests upon state-led agendas, while simply noting that it encourages the development of an 'organisation capable of acting collectively' for civil society interests (European Parliament 1999). In other words, the EP works within both formal and informal agendas, with the result that it articulates the interests of officialdom and potentially sanitises other civil society concerns. Its members have expressed the need to include the discussion of human rights within ASEM, while at the same time supporting trade projects such as the TFAP without insisting on accountability clauses that would ensure the protection of such rights. In fact, in its repeated references to the need to involve civil society within ASEM, it, too, rests on a vague notion of what civil society is and what it can and should achieve.

As noted above, ASEM's cultural remit is most closely associated with the work of ASEF. This Foundation, which comprises a director alongside a number of staff and advisors, reports to ASEM leaders through the SOM (see asef.org.sg). It receives contributions from ASEM states (initial funding was set at a voluntary US$5 million per year for the first five years after which time its costs would be mandated, excluding the accommodation costs borne by Singapore) and its remit is to promote exchanges between think-tanks, peoples and cultural groups of the two regions, in order to enhance mutual understanding. Concretely, it focuses on the five key sections of intellectual exchange, people-to-people exchange, cultural exchange, public affairs and the role of the Executive Office, and to date has organised a host of conferences, seminars, a summer school and the Asia–Europe Young Parliamentarians Meeting (AEYLS), held for the first time in March 1997. At that first meeting, junior scholars and practitioners participated in workshops on issues as varied as international co-existence, security cooperation, inter-regional cooperation, the WTO, economic development and the role of the private sector, welfare and multimedia. These and other such ASEF flagship events are paralleled by numerous activities aimed at promoting educational exchange, including the sponsorship of events such as the November 1999 conference at INSEAD, Fontainebleau, which brought together representatives of about 60 universities, and where it was agreed to create a Europe–Asia Education and Research Network (EARN). These educational pursuits through ASEF are complemented by state-sponsored proposals such as Austria's idea for a 'Uninet' university network, and Singapore's proposal for ASEM Education Hubs (AEH) and an Asia–Europe University. In addition, ASEF promotes and plays a part in other fora, such as the Asia–

Europe Cultural Forum in Paris in February 1998 and the Europe–Asia Civil Society Summit held in Lisbon in June 2000.

As the very establishment of ASEF testifies, even this area of activity is not without complications. For, while Singaporean law permitted ASEF to be established either as a private foundation or as an international organisation, since the latter was susceptible to international agreement it was decided to create a foundation, with the legal capacity of a body corporate working on a non-for-profit basis. The very decision to locate ASEF in Singapore also demonstrates a political motivation by the Singaporean Government to be at the centre of this new project, while debate over whether or not to make a permanent secretariat for ASEM also focuses upon the existing and potential role of Singapore as a regional hub. ASEF is important, not only for providing the focus of a range of activities, but, like ASEM itself, for creating a discursive framework as to what is – and, by extension, what is not – an 'ASEF' project. Funding is therefore directed towards activities seen to promote the ASEM 'corporate image'. For these reasons, the ongoing debate over whether or not to create an ASEM secretariat, and whether or not to create it within ASEF, brings with it a range of issues which transcend simply identifying levels of competence, but which also raise questions about inclusion and exclusion within ASEM, as examined below.

A further group that maintains close association with the ASEM process is the so-called 'track two' process, of the kind already embedded within APEC (through channels such as the Pacific Economic Cooperation Council (PECC) and the Pacific Basin Economic Council (PBEC)) and the ARF (through the Council for Security Cooperation in the Asia Pacific (CSCAP)). This level of activity provides a 'soft' channel of power, through which expertise is exchanged, ideas are tried out, information is gathered and the political climate is judged. In the case of ASEM, the track two forum is the Council for Asia–Europe Cooperation (CAEC), which brings together a number of academics and advisors from different institutions within Asia and Europe. Its plenary sessions, which began in June 1996, have brought together over 50 representatives to discuss themes such as 'Bringing Two Major World Actors Closer Together', and 'Europe–Asia: Strengthening the Informal Dialogue'. This channel of dialogue is not able to represent track two of ASEM officially, since it includes among its number a representative from Australia. For this reason, and in spite of considerable lobbying by the Japanese, its role as the official track two channel was vetoed by Malaysia. CAEC is an information gathering and idea-generating forum, whose key remit to date has been to formulate a 'rationale' for the ASEM process. ASEM was, after all, established as a novel inter-regional gathering with no formal history prior to becoming a summit (unlike, for instance, APEC). An early CAEC Task Force Report, entitled *The Rationale and Common Agenda for Asia–Europe Cooperation*, outlines the five elements of what it regards as the 'logical structure' for ASEM activities: namely, the geopolitical, political and economic security, economic and business, institutional and societal dimensions (CAEC 1997, p.vii). In their contribution to the same volume, Maull and Tanaka offer a number of functions for ASEM including: advocacy (as a forum for lobbying); the role of 'regional integrator' (requiring intra-regional coordination); a means of separating foreign policy from the constraints of domestic demand; and a potential mechanism for creating leverage to engage the regional great powers of Japan and Germany (1997, pp. 34–6). Similarly, ASEM is seen to serve functions in the economic realm, by supporting the WTO agenda and creating opportunities to redress inter-regional imbalances in economic performance (Jung and Lehmann 1997, pp. 56–8), and acting as a means of 'understanding the interface between culture, history, and society' in the societal sphere (Hernandez 1997, p. 92). Discussion of these functions is supplemented by calls for the ASEM agenda to include security issues in their broadest sense, an area of concern which is now coming to be introduced at the official level, too, particularly in the light of the apparent North-South Korean rapprochement in 2000. This group also contributes to a dialogue regarding the nature of inter-regionalism per se, although it tends to remain focused on its role as an intermediary framework 'between pure bilateralism and multilateralism', rather than delineating what that level might actually contain (CAEC 1997). The CAEC, nevertheless, offers a further forum for a discussion of the potential value-added contribution of ASEM.

The somewhat airy notion of civil society embedded within the official process reproduces two trends. On the one hand, it enhances the apparent 'multidimensionality' of ASEM (European Commission 2000). On the other, the very vagueness of its definition creates for those excluded actors a new space in which to articulate novel interests (Carver 1999). Both trends bear out Gill's notion that there exists a 'new set of democratic identities that are global, but based on diversity and rooted in local conditions, problems and opportunities' (2000, p. 140). For these reasons, the civil society movements on the periphery of ASEM should be regarded not simply as a pressure group for short-term political gain or change, but may also be associated with long-term social and cultural change, whose advocates may eventually obtain a longer lasting source of power (Arts 1998, pp. 51 and 58). At the centre of these movements is the People's Forum, which was established directly in response to the ASEM process.

The People's Process

The so-called 'people's process' lies beyond, but mirrors, the formal structures of ASEM. The existence of this group of actors, most frequently defined through the 'People's Forum', highlights two important issues: how international summitry is being utilised by local interest groups; and the role played by the inter-regional structure of ASEM in affecting civil society actions. This section outlines what the People's Forum is and what it does, before going on to consider these two questions. The ASEM People's Forum (AEPF) brings together a host of disparate, (often) locally active movements under one umbrella interest coalition, and bears the support of other groups, such as the EP which regards the Forum as a legitimate means for integrating issues of trade unions, women, migrant workers, young people and the environment into official ASEM concerns. The first Forum took place on 27–29 February 1996 in Bangkok, in parallel with ASEM 1, and brought together over 350 participants representing 100 people's organisations and NGOs to address the theme of 'Beyond the Geopolitics and Geo-economics: Towards a New Relationship between Asia and Europe'. It addressed the social impact of economic decisions, and also turned its attention to political agendas, including the endorsement of France's withdrawal from French Polynesia and New Caledonia and that of Indonesia from East Timor. Other issues dealt with in 1996 included Northern Ireland, former Yugoslavia, East Timor and Burma, with particular attention to the need to look at transnational migration, especially human rights' violations against women migrant workers, and trafficking. This first meeting was a direct response to the new ASEM framework, and it was decided that a follow-up task force should be constituted to formulate a mechanism for developing an ongoing movement. A number of groups, including Focus on the Global South (Thailand), the Transnational Institute (TNI) (Netherlands), One World Action (Britain) and the Asia Foundation (Germany) were subsequently instrumental in forming the AEPF in 1997, as a loose network of Asian and European organisations able to provide an umbrella structure for working on Asia–Europe concerns, and to relate to the ASEM process.

This group ran a number of conferences and workshops (such as the one on the Social and Political Dimensions of the Asian Economic Crisis at Chulalongkorn University in Bangkok in March 1998), in the run-up to the second AEPF in London from 31 March to 1 April 1998. On that occasion over 150 civil society groups gathered to discuss the theme of 'ASEM and Crisis: Peoples Realities and Peoples Responses'. They rallied for greater recognition of interest groups within the exclusive club of ASEM, as part of their 'People's Vision: Towards a More Just, Equal and Sustainable World'. Through its theme of 'Solidarity and Action Challenging Globalization', the

Forum also addressed the social impact of globalisation, focusing on issues related to environmentally, socially and economically sustainable patterns of development, and of greater economic and social equity and justice including equality between men and women. A key subject of the Forum was to address the social effects of the Asian financial crisis, thereby mirroring the principal theme of the official Meeting. The AEPF claimed that the World Bank's Asia Trust Fund was no more than a smokescreen designed to divert attention from the radical policy changes necessary to tackle the causes of Asia's financial crisis and the need for greater democracy and respect for human rights in Asian countries. It also criticised planned assessments of the effects of the crisis, noting that detailed information on the human impact of the crisis had already been collected by civil society groups and NGOs working in the region. In addition, the proposed fund was observed to represent a contradiction: on the one hand, the financial rescue packages of the IMF, endorsed by the EU, intensified the poverty caused by the crisis; on the other, the Fund would be set up to study that poverty. The Forum's spokesperson, Yi Daehoon Francis of the People's Solidarity for Participatory Democracy in South Korea, was critical: 'What NGOs in Asia really want from Tony Blair, and other heads of government, is for Europe to take the lead on fundamental reform of the IMF and other international financial institutions' (www.tni.org/asia/watch/asem32.htm). Concretely, the Forum called for EU governments to use their 29 per cent share of voting power within the IMF, and their influence on the IMF Executive Board, inter alia, to press for a review and restructuring of the IMF to make it more transparent, accountable and democratic, and to reverse contradictory stabilisation programmes being imposed by the IMF on East Asian economies. What is more, and as with IPAP and TFAP, the AEPF urged greater transparency and accountability with regard to the Trust Fund, while several workshops during the second Forum discussed how ASEM's economic interventions in the post-crisis development debate tended to be focused on engineering and legitimising neoliberal reforms. In particular, it targeted the IMF for dealing only with the structural and not the social problems caused by the crisis (Richards 2000, p. 8). The final statement of the 1998 Forum reiterated the need for social safety nets and for the respect of fundamental workers' rights, and insisted that migrant workers should not be used as scapegoats for economic problems. This contention formed part of the broader debate regarding the potential consequences of ASEM's goal towards the rapid liberalisation of trade and investment (Brennan 2000). In the final analysis, then, the AEPF pushed for the replacement of the World Bank, the IMF and the WTO, declaring them to be unacceptable and de-legitimised parts of the architecture of the global economy. Most interestingly, and in contrast to ASEM 1, there was a greater sense within official circles of the growing utility of this form of representation. For example, European Commission President Santer expressed his support for greater civil society participation, while the UK Minister for International Development, Clare Short, provided the keynote speech at the parallel conference.

Events accompanying ASEM 3 followed a similar pattern, and during the concluding months of 1999 and January 2000 over 130 Korean civil society movements and organisations developed the Korean organising committee for the ASEM 2000 People's Forum. Likewise, organisations involved in the ASEM process from Europe had been working together to formulate their own initiatives, and overall a number of thematic groups was established, including labour, agriculture, trade, poverty, development, culture, women, peace, security, human rights, environment, media, adolescence/youth, spirituality and globalisation. In addition, lobby tours of Europe and Asia were arranged for May 2000, to highlight the concerns of civil society with respect to ASEM, to stimulate public debate on ASEM in parliaments and the media and to profile the issues articulated within the 'People's Agenda'. The Forum took place on 18–21 October 2000, just prior to the leaders' summit, and once again key themes addressed included: economic, social, cultural, civil and political rights according to international human rights and humanitarian law; environmentally, socially, economically sustainable patterns of development; greater economic and social equity and justice including equality between men and women; and the active participation of civil society organisations at ASEM. In particular, Hilary Coulby of the Catholic Institute for International Relations, which participates in the Forum, cautioned against economic agreements being struck 'at the expense of the immediate and long-term welfare and rights of ordinary people' (www.tni.org/asia/watch/asem33.htm). While the Korean government provided over 40 per cent of the funding for the Forum (about US$150 000 in addition to other state contributions and funding from NGOs), state-level responses to the NGO gathering were ambivalent. Although AEPF organisers liaised with national embassy officials, Asian embassies (China in particular) seemed to prefer a 'wait and see' position, particularly watching official Korean behaviour. While openly supportive of the Forum, however, the Korean government did throw an untimely spanner in the works, by raising objections, only days prior to its commencement, to their planned venue in a Buddhist temple. Situated directly across the street from the venue of the official summit, the government claimed to be concerned about the security risks, but there were obvious reasons for keeping potential demonstrators as far away from the media glare as possible. The AEPF in Seoul in 2000 followed its now familiar pattern, adding particular emphasis to the need to increase educational exchanges between Asia and Europe, in order to give greater mobility to scholars and students and to develop further the mutual recognition of diplomas and credits. By the third summit, attitudes towards the links between unofficial and official exchanges had become rather confused. For, while the AEBF had initially been regarded as a useful model for civil society participation in the ASEM process, it had become clear that closer participation may, in fact lead to the co-option of NGOs into the official process. Nevertheless, at ASEM 3 an AEPF meeting with senior officials in Seoul resulted in a call for a Social Forum to be held, a request which will be followed up in Denmark in 2002.

The People's Forum, as indicated above, brings together a large number of disparate groups with a range of interests drawn from local, national and transnational concerns, and with a number of differing interpretations as to what an NGO actually *is* in each national context. In Northeast Asia, for example, the distinction between non-governmental and governmental organisations is difficult to make (Akaha 1998, p. 19), while in Japan NGOs are known as *koeki hojin* (public interest corporations) which may be subsidised by the government although they retain nominally independent status (Randel and German 1999a, p. 149). In Southeast Asia the situation is different, and it is still not unusual, in Indonesia for example, to find 'political opposition and the liberal-individualist notion of civil participation' to be incompatible with political culture (Schmit 1996, p. 178). As a result, European state leaders have tended to leave Indonesia alone and agencies are 'aware that making aid conditional on political changes modelled on European and American democratic traditions has not been effective' (Schmit 1996, p. 195). A number of social changes have resulted from the overthrow since the latter half of the 1980s of several authoritarian leaders and regimes (such as in the Philippines in 1986, South Korea in 1987 and Thailand in 1988), adding new socio-economic dimensions and opening spaces for civil society actors to play a more visible and often international role (Pei 1998, p. 67). Nevertheless, as contemporary Indonesia, China, Vietnam and Burma illustrate, there is no unified strategy in Asia towards these goals, and no regional authority to be lobbied in order to achieve them, which means that those NGOs with a voice have to militate principally on a national level. In contrast, NGOs working in Europe have invested heavily in EU-level advocacy, and the European Commission is the frequent target of attention (Randel and German 1999b, p. 263). This professional advocacy stratum has become necessary due to the complex distribution of labour within the EU (for example, while the Development Directorate-General deals with development cooperation, Asian, Latin American and Mediterranean countries come under the remit of the External Relations Directorate-General, and ECHO oversees EU humanitarian actions in non-member states). Having a channel such as the NGDO-EU Liaison Committee (CLONG) to represent

EU NGOs to the European Commission creates a region-wide target for NGOs, the like of which does not exist in Asia.

Many of the demands of the AEPF are similar to those made by other parallel conferences and international NGOs, whose agendas they often mirror. These range from criticising the lack of social concern in WTO proposals, to the need to protect natural resources and local interests; from the need to promote the social and political fabric for the sake of workers, democracy and development, to an insistence on incorporating international laws on core labour standards into trading arrangements. Similar to other international NGOs, the AEPF is also affected by the structure of the forum it shadows. For this reason, the parallel conference contains elements of the same regional stereotypes that are to be found at governmental levels, which can often lead to an implicit acceptance of ideas of Western versus Asian forms of capitalism, and of innate differences in approaches to human rights. On the one hand, participants can be saddled by this regional stereotyping, for practical as well as ideational reasons. In practical terms, while funding is available for Asian NGOs through European development funds, there is no such channel within Europe for the European NGOs themselves. On a perceptual level, this imbalance reinforces the notion of the developed versus under-developed civil grouping, thereby imbuing the (albeit sometimes poorer) European NGOs with greater discursive legitimacy. On the other, such stereotyping in fact also offers a useful tool for civil society movements to maximise the reach of their message. Thus, for example, in the wake of the financial crisis, as 'Asian values' came to be blamed for the crisis in the region (Acharya 1999c, p. 418), Asian NGOs in particular could gain credibility for their own attempts to push forward a project of democratisation: 'The current economic and political turmoil in Southeast Asia shows that the domestic forces that affect democratization often derive their strength from international ones, including the effects of globalization and the spread of democratic values' (Acharya 1999c, p. 419). In this way, the civil society grouping as a whole responded to the general 'democratic contagion' (Acharya 1999c, p. 419). While the 'retreat' of Asian practices of nepotism and business practices has still to be discerned (cf. Acharya 1999c, p. 422), greater public awareness and condemnation of such practices both builds upon and fuels activities at the inter-regional level.

Accompanying the role of inter-regional stereotyping is the question of the role of civil society towards the state, within the ASEM process. In the three conferences held so far, it is easy to discern a movement from neglect towards the 'controlled inclusion' of non-governmental actors (Richards 2000, p. 9). Even prior to the first meeting, civil society representatives (supported by European parliamentarians) were calling for involvement in the process. Participants in that official process have gradually come to recognise the utility of civil society for persuading suspicious and apathetic publics of governmental intentions. From recognition it is only a small step to full inclusion, which may in fact, be tantamount to co-option, as a result of which civil society groups have the choice either to become a legitimate and mainstream part of the process or to sever themselves from it altogether. Interest groups may come, in fact, to disseminate state interests (for example, by advocating 'Western' forms of human rights), and in this way any apolitical stance is usually compromised, since governments increasingly see interest group support as important for their own self-legitimation. Having begun their campaign with a demand to obtain the status enjoyed by the Asia–Europe Business Forum, several observers have recognised that such involvement would remove from non-governmental groups the legitimacy afforded by autonomy. The receipt at ASEM 3 of over 40 per cent of their funding from the Korean government demonstrates the potential difficulties of this trend within ASEM, as its civil society counterparts come to obtain limited access and the nature of their participation comes to be redefined. It is no coincidence that groups such as Amnesty International, while supportive of many of the AEPF initiatives, remain on the outskirts of the interest coalition, in order to retain their own independence of the process. Amnesty positions itself, rather, as a monitor and critic, calling on governments and civil organisations to link issues (such as human rights and trade) and to adhere to agreements already made. Part of the problem for AEPF participants is that they derive simultaneously from top-down and bottom-up origins. Hence, in challenging the tenets of ASEM, they begin from the inter-governmental agenda and either seek to improve conditions within the given remit or to develop their own epistemic communities to drive normative frameworks. At the same time their membership issues from local and scattered responses to particularistic issues, which may or may not become aggregated over time (Princen 1994, pp. 29 and 33). The following section examines more closely the principal benefits and disadvantages of parallel summitry.

Parallel Summitry

ASEM, like many of its inter-governmental predecessors, provides the space for a number of civil society interests to parallel the summit-level governmental format, and to address the same issues, as illustrated above. This type of summitry provides interest coalitions with a number of benefits. First, the spotlight afforded by the presence of government leaders addressing a range of economic, political and environmental concerns extends far enough to raise the profile of those associated with it, even if they reside on the periphery. In other words, the TV cameras were already in Seoul for the heads of state meeting, and so the People's Forum was able to gain some prominent media coverage. Prior to ASEM II, Amnesty International produced a document calling for the full ratification of the International Covenant on Civil and Political Rights, the International Covenant on Economic, Social and Cultural Rights, the Convention Against Torture and the UN Refugee Convention. In this way, Amnesty, too, uses the summit-level forum to promote its aims. Second, the nature of ASEM offers a useful framework against which to establish the constituency and interests of a disparate collection of civil society groups (cf. Rüland 1996, p. 75). In this way, not only does ASEM provide an agenda, it also creates a collective identity (the People's Forum) for a set of actors who would otherwise retain no cohesion. In other words, ASEM offers for them a clearly defined arena for debate and negotiation, which is itself 'bound by given rules' (Arts 1998, p. 55). ASEM is also useful in that its multi-headed structure facilitates the gathering of an incongruous group as part of the NGO forum. What is more, by raising the subject as part of a parallel conference, NGO bodies are able to present a common front in reaction to the Asian versus Western values debate which tends to prevail at the official level. Third, the presence of civil society on the edge of the ASEM process forms a mechanism for accountability of the inter-state process. In addition, the People's Forum brings issues such as human rights on to the shadow of official agendas, even if not on to the formal agendas themselves. Within the structure of summitry, the dialogue on human rights becomes subsumed within a broader political dialogue, so that links between (for example) business and human rights can be made more easily (see below). Fourth, the growing acceptance of a represented civil society coalition within ASEM may make the idea of civil participation more palatable to governments such as China's, while the participation of nine Chinese delegates to the AEPF conference in 2000 demonstrates growing representation for Chinese society within this forum. It also provides an agenda around which different conceptions of civil society and its political role may coalesce, so that, for example, China has become an important component of the human rights discussion, even while eschewing calls for its government to implement Western-style human rights' policies. While the Chinese continue to be sensitive to European attacks, and at an inter-parliamentary meeting of MEPs with its Chinese counterparts in October-November 2000 the EP was attacked for making 'irresponsible resolutions' (such as that on 20 January 2000 on human rights), practical endeavours (such as the EU–China Human Rights Small Projects Facility for small-scale human rights initiatives) provide a grassroots-level contribution. In this way, then, the parallel summit facilitates an Asian intra-regional debate about the possibility of NGO inclusion in official decisions. The NGO stratum of ASEM both represents and threatens the status quo: it represents it by talking on behalf of the local communities which governments pledge to protect; but threatens it by coming together as a force to challenge the very authority of those governments. Fifth, interest coalitions can be important to sustain dialogue in the face of official stand-offs, as occurred with the case of Burma and ASEM (see below).

There are also disadvantages for civil society groups in participating as part of ASEM. First, there are obvious problems with representing multiple interests and voices within one forum, however broad. This leaves local or national groups to campaign for specific issues in the context of changing national political environments. Second, parallel summitry requires a coherent response, but the very nature of the role of NGOs in each state, especially within Asia, makes for a rather incongruous grouping. Third, in terms of the issues covered, the need to compromise among a range of disparate interest groups means that calls for action can in fact become diluted. At ASEM 3, for example, over 100 Korean NGOs and a few other groups formulated a long wish-list of topics for discussion, but the lack of organisational structure made it impossible to pare these down to a manageable set of concerns. As a result, the 'Vision' offered to the leaders remained broad and aspirational. Fourth, the risk of co-option is great in a forum like ASEM, where the inclusion of NGO interests into the formal structures is not only practically possible (unlike, say for the IMF or World Bank), but also increasingly desired by the leaders who espy a possible function for NGOs with regard to their own goals. The contrast between 1996 and 1998 is interesting: at the first summit in Bangkok NGOs were 'asked to think twice' about having a meeting to coincide with ASEM 1 (*Bangkok Post* 28 February 1996; *Thailand Times* 27 February 1996); in 1998 the UK Secretary of State for International Development, Clare Short, attended as a speaker at the AEPF conference. This change in tendency was reflected in 2000, by the Korean government's willingness to provide considerable financial support to the People's Forum. NGO organisers also met with embassy officials from Denmark, Sweden, Italy, the EC Delegation, Germany, France and Portugal, as well as Indonesia, China, Thailand and Singapore. The potential result of such co-option is that pro-market policies can come to be passed off as pro-poor initiatives, when they may in fact be no more than an attempt to legitimise neoliberal reform (Richards 2000, p. 9). To this end, civil society interest groups may argue that a new form of thinking is required, but this is rendered difficult (if not impossible) by their inclusion in the existing modes of interaction. An inability to rethink the political gap between the local and the global returns us again and again to familiar strategies and structures (Pieterse 1997, p. 87).

HUMAN RIGHTS

To date, probably the most visible arena for civil society activity vis-à-vis ASEM has been the issue of human rights in its many guises. In particular, this issue illustrates well the ways in which paralleling summitry and acting within an inter-regional environment can affect the approach to particular issues and the kinds of actors who become involved. The general tone adopted by Asian governments within ASEM replicates a position that has been restated on a number of occasions; namely, that the issue of human rights has to take into account the specific historical and cultural background of each state (Tang 1995, p. 205). This contrasts with what is often presented as a legally based, universalising viewpoint expressed within Europe, and highlights a priori the inherent tensions underpinning any discussions. In Bangkok in 1996 the most visible human rights issue pertained to Indonesia's treatment of East Timor, particularly as it set Portuguese Prime Minister Antonio Guterres (who declared 'My voice will not be silent in defence of human rights', *Thailand Times* 28 February 1996) against Indonesian leader Suharto (who threatened to walk away from the talks if the issue was addressed). For his part, Thai Prime Minister and host Banharn Silpa-Archa responded to Belgian Prime Minister Jean-Luc Dehaene's request to address human rights, by saying they should be considered in informal talks but should not spoil the agenda (*Bangkok Post* 28 February 1996). In the end, a tête-à-tête was organised between Guterres and Suharto on 29 February 1996 on the periphery of ASEM 1. In other words, however, the formal structures of ASEM, due to their inter-regional nature, could only facilitate a number of 'pirouettes sémantiques' over this difficult issue (*La Libre Belgique* 4 March 1996). While the final declaration at ASEM 1 did not ignore human rights altogether, it rested on invoking the UN Charter and Universal Declaration on human rights (*Le Figaro* 4 March 1996). Although the *Thailand Times* observed in the EU a relatively 'go-easy approach on human rights with Asia' at the summit (28 February 1996), this issue has dogged parts of the inter-regional framework since that time. At ASEM 2 and 3, however, the question of human rights was only conspicuous by its absence, and although briefly mentioned at ASEM 2, it was left to the People's Forum to take it up fully. Issues related specifically to human rights have been addressed within ASEM, for example, at the first Foreign Ministers' Meeting in February 1997, when participants proposed a symposium on human rights and the rule of law. However, on the whole these efforts have tended to represent low-key and tentative approaches to this contentious subject. The principal problem is that, while all member states have been prepared to acknowledge the existence of shared universal values, views diverge as to the nature of democracy within which such values are located. As a result, the Chair's

Statement at ASEM 1 talked of 'fundamental rights' in the following way: 'the dialogue among the participating countries should be conducted on the basis of mutual respect, equality, promotion of fundamental rights and in accordance with the rule of international law and obligations, non-intervention, whether direct or indirect, in each other's internal affairs'. Leaving open to individual interpretation the exact nature of these 'fundamental rights', leaders at ASEM 1 were eager to remove from the discussion table any mention of 'human rights'.

During preparations for ASEM 1, civil society groups were quick to remind state leaders that they were all signatories to the 1992 Rio declaration, to the 1993 Vienna Declaration of the World Conference on Human Rights (underlining the fact that the 'promotion and protection of all human rights is a legitimate concern of the international community') and to agreements reached at Cairo (1994), Copenhagen and Beijing (1995). With specific reference to the European side, the Amsterdam Treaty of 1997 introduced a new chapter on fundamental rights and non-discrimination and on 10 December 1997, the 50th anniversary of the UN Declaration on Human Rights was used to recall the European Council's own Human Rights' Declaration of 1991. For their part, civil society groups have tended to focus on specific abuses of human rights in ASEM states, particularly Indonesia and Myanmar. In the case of Indonesia, persistent human rights violations were publicised by the 1996 Nobel Peace Prize, and its co-recipient, East Timorese resistance leader Jose Ramos Horta, has been a contributor to AEPF conferences. At the AEPF in 1998 he addressed more than 300 activists and accused leaders at the official two-day ASEM summit of ignoring the very root causes of the economic débâcle in Asia: 'If they want to avoid turmoil, if they want to avoid bloody confrontation in the streets, if they want to avoid violence, if they want to avoid revolution, then they must address the root causes of these problems – and that is the lack of freedom, of democracy, of rule of law'. His exhortations were accompanied by videotaped expressions of solidarity from fellow Nobel laureate Daw Aung San Suu Kyi of Myanmar: 'It is time everybody stopped trying to separate human rights from economics' (www.tni.org/asia/watch/asem33). In these ways, the AEPF has used the periphery of the summit to gain media attention and to raise the profile of debates over human rights, while Forum participants have also drawn on the work of other NGOs which have also participated in making particular demands to state leaders. Amnesty International has been especially useful, by acting as an institutional memory of past promises, so that, for example, at ASEM 1 it attacked European participants for acting in defiance of their own 1994 European Council paper, which stated that ASEM should contribute inter alia to the respect of human rights. Similarly, Amnesty reminds participants of their legal obligations and institutional pledges. Thus, in the case of the EU it draws attention to: the Maastricht Treaty's Article F2, observing the need to respect fundamental rights; Article J.1 (2), stating that one of the objectives of the Common Foreign and Security Policy (CFSP) is to consolidate the rule of law and respect for human rights and fundamental freedoms; Article 130u, noting that development cooperation shall contribute to the general objective of developing and consolidating, inter alia, the respect of human rights and fundamental freedoms; and the 1997 Amsterdam Treaty, which introduced a new chapter (Article F2) on fundamental rights and non-discrimination. The Council decision in 1995 to insert a human rights clause into all trade and cooperation agreements underpins this approach to external relations. This forms part of a carrot and stick approach, in that the new GSP scheme of 1998 offers development-oriented rewards and incentives to comply with international environmental and social standards (Amersfoort 1998, p. 139). Amnesty also gave a critical assessment of ASEM's contribution to the debate over human rights at ASEM 3: 'In the Bangkok statement ASEM governments repeated their commitment to international human rights treaties and declarations. Since then, some ASEM governments have openly challenged the universality and indivisibility of human rights, principles which are fundamental to the UDHR and the major human rights covenants. Others have distanced themselves from these attacks' (www.tni.org/asia/watch/asem26.htm). In addition, Amnesty's remit is to promote best practice among companies, so that business develops codes of conduct which include international human rights standards. Amnesty's Human Rights Principles for Companies (ACT 70/01/98) provides an introductory checklist and a basis for companies to develop their own codes of conduct. Unlike the AEPF, Amnesty organises itself on a global plain and utilises fora such as the People's Forum and ASEM itself as further channels for putting pressure on governments over their human rights abuses, and for proposing the adoption of existing models, such as the OSCE for Asia and Europe to 'develop their own regional security dialogue and mechanisms' (www.tni.org/asia/watch/ asem39).

In the brief history of ASEM, the case of Burma has exercised a number of anxieties with regard to human rights, and has become key to understanding how inter-group differences are played out at the inter-regional level. The situation in Burma was first raised in 1991 by the EU during a meeting with ASEAN in Luxembourg, and the EU banned SLORC officials from entering member states. When Burma joined ASEAN in July 1997, the EU refused to engage in EU–ASEAN meetings at ministerial level, and as a result of worsening relations, the EU imposed an embargo on the sale of arms to Burma, and in March 1997 forced a temporary withdrawal of tariff benefits under the GSP (Amersfoort 1998, p. 139). Not until November 1999 was the next official level meeting held in Bangkok, but further repressive actions by the Burmese government prompted the EU to impose further sanctions and to strengthen its Common Position on Burma in April 2000 (Reuters, Singapore, 23 January 1999). NGO positions on Burma, through Amnesty and the AEPF, have been accompanied by EP pronouncements. Resolutions on Burma (in particular those of 16 September 1999 and 18 May 2000) have strongly condemned the violation of the freedom of movement, expression and assembly of the Secretary General of the National League for Democracy, the intimidation against Daw Aung San Suu Kyi, her de facto house arrest since her return, and the fact that Western diplomats have not yet been allowed access to her. In a 1999 letter from the Burmese Foreign Minister Win Aung to Thailand's Foreign Minister Surin Pitsuwan, Burma signalled its readiness to discuss any issue Europe may want to raise in exchange for participation in an ASEAN–EU meeting in Berlin later that year (*Bangkok Post* 3 February 1999). There is, then, a growing recognition within Burma of the potential costs of non-compliance with human rights norms, and the need for countries like Burma to gain a positive spot in the international limelight, not least to enhance international understanding and encourage foreign investment which all but dried up during Asia's economic crisis.

The question of Burma is important for a number of reasons. First, it provides an issue that has been important for bringing together European and Asian NGOs in common cause. Somewhat ironically, the issue has polarised Asian versus Western viewpoints on a number of occasions. For example, in November 2000 the ten ASEAN leaders agreed on a policy to tell outside countries seeking meetings with the group to 'take all ten of us or none at all' (*The Nation* 25 November 2000). There was clear resentment at European high-handedness: 'Mahathir Mohamad's comment earlier this week that ASEAN might boycott the London meeting if Burmese officials are not given visas to attend the meeting was a reminder of the existing cleavage between the two groups' (*The Nation*, 4 September 1997). Intra-Asian responses to Western impositions have led to the statement that the basic key to human rights is economic development, which is fundamental to democracy (Mauzy 1997; Vatikiotis 1996, p. 96). Stalled negotiations over Burma also led to a call for the ASEM Asians to rally together against European injustices (Mauzy 1997). On such issues, there is clearly an NGO interest to ensure that they do not replicate the region-to-region structure of ASEM itself. By reinforcing the self/other dichotomy of inter-regional engagement, this issue forces the NGO stratum to rebut accusations of partisanship before taking practical steps towards the resolution of particular issues. As a result, while the AEPF has consistently pushed for the inclusion of discussions of human rights' abuses, and has at times shamed leaders into taking on board this sensitive subject, it has been forced – due to its own lack of organisation – to mirror in many ways the institutional and perceptual structures of ASEM and therefore to become embroiled in polarised debates. Second, while the question of Burma has become the central theme of EU–ASEAN concerns, within ASEM it may be subsumed as part of a broader dialogue, in terms of both membership and subject matter. For this reason, Mahathir could simultaneously threaten to boycott ASEM 2 for not admitting Burma and criticise Burma for not following certain international practices. NGOs may benefit from being able to address the broader picture, but this larger structure also makes it more difficult for them to pinpoint the target of their attacks. Third, the complex nature of this issue and the disparate actors involved in addressing it are conducive to the multilayered framework of ASEM, ensuring that there is a clear role for NGOs within this structure.

CIVIL SOCIETY AND INTER-REGIONALISM

While the ASEM summit provides a forum for non-governmental interests to gain international recognition, the inter-regional focus of this meeting both facilitates and constrains the way in which they put forward their arguments. For, even though the format of the AEPF itself is not premised upon the same east-west division as the formal summit, it is inevitably informed by those parameters on a number of levels. First, although Asian countries have the largest number of NGOs in the developing world, the experience of the non-governmental sector in Europe, in NGOs as well as the OSCE, has been held up as a potential model for enabling 'Asian' interests to cohere (Princen and Finger 1994, p. 2). The OSCE provides a model for monitoring elections, developing national electoral and human rights institutions, providing technical assistance to develop national legal institutions, promoting the development of NGOs and civil society and training human rights and election monitors and journalists. Indeed, the very foundations of the EC were based upon social concerns and equality in areas such as labour rights and health and safety, and have been pursued by actors such as the Council of Europe and the EP since the 1960s. What often occurs, however, is that the West is seen to be teaching Asia with regard to these issues, particularly by insisting that good governance projects are integral to a country's entry into the global market economy (Ferdinand 1999, p. 7). Second, while the ASEM process pays lip-service to the meeting of equals, the donor-recipient history of the two regions continues to pervade much of the economic and political discussion, and this is mirrored in the civil society process where a dialogue of the learned versus the learner still exists, which posits the experience of European NGOs and civil society traditions as a potential model for the Asian groups. As a result, moreover, a polarisation of Western (universalistic) versus Asian (particularistic) norms is created, which means that civil society groups are forced to address this label before undertaking any joint activities. On the one hand, the accepted Western position regards them as essential to good and fair government and social and economic development, wanting internationally recognised standards to be applied and conditionalities on trade or aid as pressure for compliance. This is a position, moreover, which is supported by a number of 'universal' texts, including the Universal Declaration of Human Rights (UDHR) of 1948, the ICCPR of 1976 and the ICESCR also of 1976, which have become part of what is 'legitimate internationally' (Vincent 1999, p. 132). The 'Asian' position, on the other hand, regards civil and political rights as retarding economic development, which needs a stable environment. In many ways, the Asian NGOs (many of which are, in any case, chapters of European organisations) adopt the 'Western' discourse to condemn the actions of their own governments, and in this way perpetuate the idea of the 'Western' versus 'Asian' views of human rights. As a result, debate at the level of civil society tends to be far more nuanced, due in part to the fact that many of the role models for NGO behaviour already come from the West and that chapters of international NGOs tend to have the fundamental human rights principles inscribed within them from the start. This trend has been strengthened by the effects of the Asian financial crisis, which witnessed the reconsideration of ASEAN's long-held policy of non-interference, thereby making the dichotomy between Western and eastern norms more difficult to sustain. Simply blaming Western human rights for societal ills is also no longer a sustainable argument (Chan 1998, p. 39). However, the 'Asian' NGO label continues to be dominated by issues of development and thereby leaves a less developed Asia to work alongside its advanced European partners. The division is made starker by the fact that in the EU organisations have developed to lobby the EU as a group through mechanisms such as CLONG, while half of ECHO's funding is distributed through NGOs (Randel and German 1999b, p. 267). CLONG even published the NGO Charter in 1997 to define the basic principles of non-governmental organisations. In Asia, there is no such cooperative framework and interpretations of what civil interest groups actually are continue to abound. Third, the NGO forum at ASEM 1 was noted for its contrast to the governmental positions adopted: 'Their stand was in sharp contrast to those of Asian governments, who have viewed attempts to link trade and investment with labor and safety standards a form of European protectionism' (*Thailand Times* 28 February 1996). Most of the NGOs also draw upon international texts in order to gain credibility and status for themselves, so that the tenets of the UN Charter, International Covenants on Civil and Political Rights and on Economic, Social and Cultural Rights are often written into their very definitions. By playing a part in that international framework, actors reflect the discourses set down by these texts. Fourth, as part of a broader historical movement, and in the wake of the conditions imposed by International Financial Institutions (IFIs) particularly since the late 1980s, civil society coalitions increasingly view their role as curbing further such impositions (Friedman 1994, p. 20). Within ASEM, and in response to this climate, the AEPF has developed inter-group facilitators to provide a counter attack against the region-to-region claims made at the official level. Fifth, if the polarisation at the summit level leads to an east-west dichotomy to which NGOs must pay attention, and posits an advanced Western model in the face of seemingly parochial or incoherent Asian groups, at the same time NGOs within ASEM draw on their international patrimony in the 'Battle for Seattle' tradition. This is in part due to the clear definition of ASEM motives within international parameters and the fact that it is based upon functioning within that international (be it the UN, International Labour Organisation (ILO) or WTO) environment. It is also due to calls from the NGO movements within ASEM to ally themselves for a greater voice with their international partners. By way of example, NGOs involved in child welfare within ASEM have called for links to be made with the August 1996 First World Congress against the Commercial Sexual Exploitation of Children, in Stockholm. If on the one hand, an east-west division fragments civil society movements into localised vested interests, on the other, the globalisation debate subsumes all constituents. They are simply working on precedents well established elsewhere and a growing international recognition of the valuable role civil society can and does play. However, by becoming part of a global agenda, they may lose their purpose in this more manageable region-to-region context, where their 'minilateral' collaboration could be formed to deal with the issues which then arise in the larger fora.

CONCLUSION: INTER-REGIONALISM AND CIVIL SOCIETY

This chapter has examined how the nature of the ASEM process – in both its inter-regional structure and three broad pillars – creates a number of different spaces for civil society actors to articulate their interests. While ASEF and business groups are built into the official structure, and the EP and CAEC are seen to inform the official process, however, the position to date of many civil society groups has been one of peripheral involvement with increasing negotiated access for their representatives. These complex narratives of civil society participation reflect and form part of the changing role of different kinds of interest groups in response to globalising trends. In this way, the internationally visible forum of ASEM offers yet another locus for the articulation of aggregated local dissatisfaction in the face of global change, as they 'erect barriers against inroads into local or national moral economies' (Pieterse 1997, p. 84). As a result, however, it becomes tempting to regard all collective regional action within this process (as with the official level itself) as a site of resistance against the evils of globalisation, and to allow 'globalisation' itself to provide the potential origins of a new inter-regional 'swarm' to develop: 'Tear gas, rubber bullets and police sweeps, the object of incessant media coverage, are the outward signs of impending change – that the guardians of the social order have grown afraid' (*International Herald Tribune* 13 January 1998). They are also influenced by, and in turn influence, the inter-regional structures of ASEM itself.

The civil society component of ASEM, then, is a hydra. Moreover, as the examples presented here illustrate, disparate groups of activists may forge temporary alliances to promote common interests and may identify themselves as belonging to a global movement, while simultaneously negotiating change and conditions for micro-interests. The emphasis and point of entry by each group, however, will define the terms of membership it adopts. Thus, the Seattle package comes replete with the need to protect fundamental human rights and environmental measures in the face of inexorable capitalist expansion, while groups borne of local needs may seek to minimise the costs of social change for economic expansion by functioning within extant parameters. ASEM accommodates these diverse positions, by gathering together sub-national, national, regional and global interest groups ostensibly under one rather uncomfortable umbrella within the AEPF. However, while it is therefore able to accommodate novel forms of civil society representation, its wide remit and the position taken by NGOs within ASEM to date tend to suggest that the interests of different groups may be at one and the same time fragmented and globalised. In many ways, the inter-regional level is the perfect foil for these competing levels of interest: it offers a manageable framework to represent disparate interests within two clear groupings which require intra-regional organisation, but which then may be collectively formulated to respond as a larger, more viable group at the international level. Practice to date has, unsurprisingly, proved to be more complicated.

Most importantly, civil society representation within ASEM turns on the issues of power and inclusion. With regard to power, the same concerns found at the official level prevail. First, Europeans command the dominant discourse and organisational clarity which the Asian contingent has been unable to match to date, so that even where Asian civil society groups are strong (as in the case of the Koreans at ASEM 3) there is no intra-Asian group formulation. Somewhat ironically, this apparent lack of organisation leads observers to conclude that an 'Asian' way of conducting affairs is being followed, thereby not only collectivising independent Asian pursuits, but also imbuing civil society participants with the notion that European values and practices are to be aspired to. Second, the power to determine the agenda of the AEPF enables civil society groups to include in their discussions issues that are taboo at the official level, most notably those pertaining to human rights. In their collective stance, moreover, the disparate groups are able to politicise agendas (such as the accountability of IPAP and TFAP) which otherwise may be passed without external scrutiny. As Pieterse rightly notes, however, the agenda becomes political when these groups converge, but when they are disaggregated the agenda is a social one and each group pursues its independent interests (1997, p. 83). The nature of the ASEM process makes this duality a likelihood. The third issue relating to power involves the role of the United States, which has not been covered in this chapter, but whose influence on NGO participation echoes that in the political sphere (see Chapter 4). For civil society groups, particularly those from Asia, both the source of the external threat (such as international capitalism and globalisation) as well as the models for how to address it (for example, Amnesty International and other groups which are active in the US) lie within the US. In this way, the NGO movements alongside ASEM are confined by the same trilateral parameters which determine the rules of the official game, and make it all the more difficult for civil society representatives to challenge those rules from an alternative platform (see Chapter 4).

The issue of inclusion is also key to understanding the role of civil society on the margins of ASEM. One of the principal effects of holding power within ASEM is to be able to determine rules of inclusion and exclusion, and in some ways the situation at present for civil society groups on the margins of ASEM parallels the debate over identity for Australia (see Chapter 4). Participants of the AEPF, supported by groups such as Amnesty but also the EP, have called continually for the NGO sector to be associated with the formal decision making structures of ASEM. Nevertheless, the 'negotiated access' they have come to obtain, the support for a greater voice and the funding for their events by the governments they claim to monitor, have led many in the movement to take stock and reconsider whether or not it is ideal to be on the inside of the process, in a way that the AEBF finds itself. On the one hand, the international spotlight cast by ASEM is an important platform to air civil society concerns, and the deepening links with the governments of Asia and Europe may be seen as part of state recognition of the role of civil society and of the reorganisation of 'state capacities on a different territorial scale to enhance their strategic capacities' (Richards 2000, p. 12). On the other, the association with partisan regional positions in a broad Asia-versus-Europe contest, and the concurrent dilution of regional interests within a global battle for Seattle and elsewhere, subsume differentiated civil society identities and goals within a greater collective with which they may not invariably be compatible. The 'Battle for Seattle' paradigm has intensified this tension, by portraying the role of civil society as simply the bottom-up rebellion against the top-down imposition of globalisation, with the result that NGOs become simultaneously vilified and romanticised (Scholte 2000, p. 116). It is undeniable that civil society movements at a range of international meetings have obtained important media attention: from Rio 1992, when NGOs roused enough public pressure to push through agreements on controlling greenhouse gases, to anti-Davos protests at the WEF in 2001. Their success, however, has engendered the aggregation of a range of concerns into what has come to be regarded as straightforward anti-capitalism, and has resolved simplistically the issue of what an 'NGO' is and what it stands for. For ASEM, too, the very globalisation of NGOs may highlight their presence but dilutes their (many and various) targets. In fact, as Seattle itself demonstrated, the lines of division between governments inside and social movements outside were not clearly marked, as US President Clinton's proposal to link environmental and labour standards to WTO trade sanctions was supported by Northern labour and environmental groups and opposed by similar groups in the South. Moreover, the organisers of anti-ASEM opposition groups have also used the Seattle–Davos continuum as a legitimation of their own struggle for 'critical engagement' against the global neoliberal agenda, but have relied upon the power of Seattle without articulating the shape and specific nature of their own form of engagement. In 1999 *The Economist* attributed the success of Seattle to the detailed organisation of the NGO movement there and the clear and specific goal of derailing the official talks. Participants of the ASEM NGOs have to date presented neither a coherent united front nor a coherent and targeted agenda: the swarm, rather than flying together, is scattered and directionless. Within ASEM, this fundamental tension between insider and outsider is being constantly (re)negotiated alongside a parallel issue, which brings notions of 'self' and 'other' into relief as 'Asia' meets its 'Europe' counterpart. The perceptual self/other dichotomy does not translate into intra-regional organisation among European and (especially) Asian civil society groups, thereby making it particularly difficult to sustain momentum among civil society agents in between the biennial conferences. It may be that their effects should be measured more effectively in terms of long-term social and cultural change, rather than as pressure groups for short-term politics (Arts 1998, p. 51), but current differences within the NGO community itself make it unlikely that civil society groups within ASEM and elsewhere will become a serious and sustainable form of 'discursive opposition' in the near future (Devetak and Higgott 1999, p. 493).

The inter-regional (Asia versus Europe) and the global (trilateral) discourses which surround ASEM also affect the civil society sector, and the closer their ties with the formal structures, the less likely will be their chances to challenge these discourses. Interestingly, the inter-regional nature of ASEM, being neither uniquely state-determined nor wholly buffetted by the winds of globalisation, is amenable to the accommodation of the local and global aims and objectives of ASEM-related NGOs. For, while globalisation is seen as a top-down phenomenon and civil society provides the bottom-up rebellion against it, ASEM is in fact a range of local groupings housed in an international forum. On a perceptual level, however, much work is still to be done. While some governments are becoming more amenable to the full association of civil society interests with ASEM, they are increasingly setting the terms of that inclusion in a way intended to co-opt those bodies as a means of disseminating their own political motives to people who are rarely able or inclined to listen to their governments. These issues hold a number of implications for the ways in which civil society groups might – by playing the region-to-region game – come to formulate novel responses to a new environment and thereby to question the very nature of the state-led agenda in an era of globalisation. This examination of the role of civil society movements within ASEM has attempted to draw attention to the difficulties of reconciling novel ways of thinking with the constraints of existing modes of acting. These tensions force NGOs to wrestle with the challenge of 'deciding how to fit into projects of collective and individual identity that presuppose inscription in a multiplicity of often incommensurable identity schemes' (Calhoun 1998, p. 12). In order to avoid being placed into this dichotomous format, civil society groups have begun to reject the explicit inter-regional perceptual mantle of ASEM, but to work in an organisational way so as to spar with the embedded discourse of its institutional structure. Already transcending national boundaries, without embracing the all-encompassing remit of the (anti-)globalisation debate, ASEM provides an institutional framework within which to rally regional concerns and to offer important international leverage for disparate local interests. In the case of Asia–Europe relations, the under-developed visions of alternatives from within their ranks, however, can only be remedied if the tensions between the institutional and perceptual parameters of their actions can be successfully and explicitly resolved. The key problem for civil society movements functioning on the margins of ASEM is that they comprise domestic civil society interest groups working to a global agenda, but within an inter-regional framework. In other words, unless and until the level of inter-regionalism is understood within its own parameters, the simplistic renderings of Asian versus European values will continue to prevent civil society coalitions from articulating an alternative form of behaviour from the official channels they confront. Only at that point can the anti-globalisation resistance of Seattle and Prague be seen not as a choice of resistance, but as part and parcel of the behaviour of social actors in their challenge to globalisation. Crucially, although the formation of ASEM was in many ways the outcome of a complex interplay of national, regional and international politico-economic developments of the early 1990s, civil society groups' responses to this body to date suggest that they have not decided what their actual role is, or to whom and what conditions they are responding. For some observers, the inclusion of a social dimension in ASEM is not an end in itself, but it provides a small terrain for challenging the bureaucratic niceties and undemocratic aspects of a neoliberal inter-regional regime. That terrain, however, remains contested by a range of disparate, disunited interests, and is not yet home to a solidarity of civil society feeling. Prior to that, an internal debate over the nature and validity of the universal versus the particular (or regional) will have to be resolved (see Somers 1994, p. 633), while interest coalitions themselves determine exactly who they are and what they are for.

6. Conclusion: Interpreting Inter-Regionalism

This book set out to provide an explanatory framework for understanding the economic, political and socio-cultural dimensions of contemporary Asia–Europe relations. It examined and illustrated how the three-pillared structure of the ASEM process is put into practice, by determining the lengthy foundations upon which they are based and demonstrating how the framework of inter-regionalism sets them into certain kinds of patterns of behaviour. Economic relations between Asia and Europe draw upon a history of disparate bilateral agreements issuing from the early postwar decades, and upon a growing recognition of the value of region-to-region engagement by the end of the 1970s. The 1990s added to these historical trends the ending of a cold war, European moves towards a single market and currency and the apparent rise and sudden fall of economic Asia. As a result, Asia and Europe find themselves in a spotlight under which common causes and interests unite them in the face of ever-intensifying trends towards globalisation. For these reasons, the economic pillar of the ASEM structure has become its most active area of cooperation, one which now brings EU and Asian representatives into frequent contact with each other at a number of high and lower levels of engagement. Political relations may not have quite the same pedigree, but nevertheless they have opened the way for the discussion of a whole range of contemporary issues related to 'soft' politics and security affairs. From child welfare and environmental degradation, to military cooperation and human rights' abuses, ASEM provides an umbrella framework for airing a spectrum of often contentious issues. In this pillar, too, and in spite of a lack of EU mechanisms to act on behalf of its member states in the (inter-governmental) field of foreign affairs, political dialogue has come to be institutionalised in regular meetings at a number of different levels. The third pillar of cultural and intellectual exchanges provides an opportunity to include people-to-people interests and grassroots involvement in ASEM affairs. To date, such events have been conducted in the main by organs such as ASEF, with frequent European Parliament and business input. All three pillars of activity continue to be informed by moribund colonial power structures, whose divisive legacies are often found to be embedded, not only within, but also on the margins of, this inter-regional setting. The Conclusion turns now to address two important questions to guide reflection on this subject:

1) What are the consequences of ASEM for Asia–Europe relations?

2) What does the experience of ASEM tell us about the role of inter-regionalism?

A FUTURE FOR ASIA AND EUROPE?

ASEM has only been around since 1996 and it is far too soon to make any final judgements on its relative success or failure. After all, were we to judge APEC by the same criteria, it would only just be approaching its second summit meeting after a number of years in the wilderness. For this reason, we should search instead to highlight the issues, problems and tensions visible to date, in order to discern any patterns of behaviour or modes of engagement which have cumulatively contributed to ASEM's brief history. Although ASEM has distributed a number of benefits and disadvantages among its members, this section focuses on six principal issues pertaining to the notion of the 'value-added' quality of its structures. In other words, what is important about ASEM per se that we cannot glean simply by looking at other forms of cooperation or conflict among representatives of Asia and Europe?

First, and at a most basic level, ASEM brings to many of its participants the glare of the international media that it is increasingly difficult to attain. While London (host of ASEM 2) may inhabit the world's televisions already, Bangkok (ASEM 1), Seoul (ASEM 3) and Copenhagen (ASEM 4) are less familiar to the global viewing audience. ASEM spotlights issues as well as places. But not only does it provide an additional forum to highlight now global issues such as the Kyoto Protocol or house arrest of Aung San Suu Kyi, it also facilitates the discussion of issues of concern among Asians and Europeans within their own backyards. From trade confrontation and cooperation, to intellectual exchange and possible peace-keeping reciprocity, a forum without the US and without an unwieldy number of members lays bare the terrain for greater mutual rewards. This lack of direct US participation – a focus only on one side of the triangle – also serves as an exercise in region-spotting. Hence, 'Asia' comes to be regarded among Europeans as the 'Asian Ten', while Europe and the EU are further entrenched as synonyms from an Asian point of view. On a positive note, this mutual recognition raises the profile of each region in a global context and serves to balance the interests of other major players, most obviously those of the US. Second, and on a less positive note, the idea that 'Asia' and 'Europe' meet within ASEM also raises questions of power and exclusion, despite the glowing rhetoric emphasising the equality of the relationship. Questions of power are subsumed within a range of dimensions: from the impact of disparate colonial legacies, to the potential for economic leverage (with, for example, the EU's Generalised System of Preferences and its human rights' clause); and from the (often European) loci of institutional modelling and agenda-setting, to the very idea that Asia and Europe are, in fact, comparable and identifiable regions. This is not to suggest that Asian participants have been sucked into a European-led Western neoliberal agenda which drags them into the muddy waters of globalisation against their collective will. Rather, it should evoke caution in naming regional representatives and identifying regional interests without taking into account the historical moment at which they originate and the issue-specific contexts for which such interests are pursued. Participants may also buy into this region-to-region framework for vested national or sub-regional motivations, since it empowers them to reject additional members whose interests they do not share. The case of Australia is instructive in this regard, since the clear economic advantages of admitting Canberra to the ASEM club were outweighed by political interests justified in cultural terms. Third, and linked to the previous section, such cultural terms further embed certain regional stereotypes issuing from colonial structures, adopted for pragmatic purposes and codified within the inter-regional structure that is ASEM. From an Asian perspective, this stereotyping has served as a protective screen in the face of European (read 'Western') intrusions, and as a justification for taking hasty cover in the undergrowth of lowest common denominators. Facing accusations of 'crony capitalism' during the Asian financial crisis, it became clear that the Asian values referent could as easily inculpate as exonerate Asian norms of behaviour. European participants, for their part, have utilised this inter-regional stereotyping further to advance justificatory schemas of developed versus underdeveloped lifestyles (from human rights to environmental concerns, to liberalisation and good governance). As a result, the 'ideal' models posited for Asian development usher from the histories of OSCE progress and European integration mechanisms. Like it or not, Asia has to accept or eschew the Single European Market as its own future, but in any case is forced to set its own future in terms of the European debate. The fourth important question for ASEM relates to its nature and to the role of informalism, which underpins its very raison d'être. In 2000, the European Commission outlined the key characteristics of ASEM as including its informality and multidimensionality (European Commission 2000, p. 15). This structure facilitates the three-pillared approach undertaken by Asia and Europe and allows for a wide-ranging discussion of inter-linked issues behind closed doors. At the same time, however, the list of interests of the 25 member states is so long that in many ways these discussions are destined to coat relations in no more than an aspirational gloss. The civil society activities accompanying ASEM are similarly prone to produce disorganised pleasantries. Linked to this point, the fifth issue to bear in mind relates to the costs of summitry and its trappings, and the question of who actually bears them. As the biennial summits compete to become bigger and better jamborees, the costs of hosting ASEM and of sending high-level delegations around the world for a friendly chat will not be tolerated for long if government leaders return with little or nothing to show for their efforts. In some ways ASEM was unfortunate to be launched with summit-level fanfare, leaving the cleaners at CAEC to coat the halls with a new sheen once leaders had departed. Opportunities have landed on each ASEM doorstep to date. In 1998 a financial crisis gave Europe and Asia the perfect chance to show that their mutual engagement was serious and strong. They did not take it. In 2000 the timely North-South Korean summit demonstrated that Europe can and should be involved in Asian security affairs, leaving further occasion for Asian participation on war-torn European territories. To date, only tentative and declaratory steps have been taken to exploit this potential.

Finally, ASEM is riddled with definitional deficiencies and dissonance, which pave the way for its members to open a fresh chapter in inter-regional relations, or to hide behind existing assumptions of what regional, and by extension inter-regional, behaviour is and should be. To date, square pegs have been stuffed unceremoniously into round holes, as vain attempts to measure Asia and Europe as comparable regions force developmental arguments to the fore and leave the Meeting hostage to the spectre of globalisation. From the Vision Group, to the CAEC, the European Parliament, NGOs, government agents and leaders and business communities, the purview of ASEM's planners remains patchy and stale. The principal reason for this, however, remains the fact that ASEM's novel structure is not embraced and the space it opens in contemporary action and decision-making is not explored. The final section examines how the very notion of inter-regionalism needs to be problematised and addressed within its own dimensions.

LESSONS IN AND FOR INTER-REGIONALISM

This book has insisted that inter-regionalism has to be taken on its own terms as a particular unit of enquiry, and has lamented the fact that studies to date have reduced its parameters to a supra-regional or sub-global phenomenon. Indeed, in a field of burgeoning literature about the role of regionalisation as a response to, or consequence of, globalising trends (Fawcett and Hurrell 1995; Hettne et al. 1999; Yeung et al. 1999), extant scholarship continues to locate globalisation at the apex of a hierarchy of interests which subsumes the region, the state level and substate actors at the lowest level (see Hirst and Thompson, 1996; Bhagwati, 1992), and which, as a consequence, neglects or casually dismisses inter-regionalism (cf. Hänggi 1998; Richards and Kirkpatrick, 1999). Such neglect continues even in the face of a growing number of inter-regional dialogues, from EU–ASEAN, EU–MERCOSUR, EU–Lomé to ASEM agreements. To date, these have been equated with, or compared to, pan-regional fora such as APEC, to the extent that some scholars consider that 'APEC was set up as the first recent important form of interregionalism' (Maull and Tanaka 1997, p. 32). This APEC trap condemns ASEM and other inter-regional arrangements to continued mis-categorisation.

While it is correct to pinpoint the relevance of ASEM as a lesson in the 'politics of identity' (Higgott 2000, p.15), it is also necessary to explore new ways of thinking about the nature and perception of new levels of interaction. In order to counter constant recourse to viewing ASEM as an 'outcome of (i) the dialectic of globalisation and regionalisation; (ii) the post Cold war search for a workable set of structures of global management; (iii) the new regional diplomacy being practised in East Asia' (Higgott 2000, p. 15), only a mezzanine level of thinking can identify the ways in which regions act towards other perceived regions, in an era when multiple identities inhabit contemporary agendas. To this end, there is a need for new themes and actions to examine in detail and to contrast the EU's numerous inter-regional engagements in a way that probes their substance, the mutual perceptions elicited by them, and the interests of the different actors involved in them. Is inter-regionalism designed to advance business and trade interests, to promote national economic or security agendas, or to garner leverage against the tide of globalisation? Ignoring inter-regionalism as a path of cooperation or conflict obfuscates the answers to such questions. Finally, to posit inter-regionalism against globalisation is to smooth the choppy seas of international relations and negate the potential for alliances or conflicts at the level of region-to-region engagement itself. Against this trend, inter-regionalism as outlined throughout this book provides the new promontory from which to witness a changing set of relations at the start of the twenty-first century.

Chronology

| | 20 | SOM (General Follow up), Dublin |

1997

January	16–18	Europe–Asia Forum on University Relations, Naples and Rome
	24	Coordinators' Meeting, Singapore
	30	1st ASEM EMM Coordinators' Preparatory Meeting, Makuhari
February	7–8	1st Enforcement Working Group of ASEM Customs' Meeting, Brussels
	11–12	SOM 2 (General Follow up), Singapore
	14–15	FMM, Singapore (after EU–ASEAN FMM, 13–14)
	15	FMM launch ASEF
	15	1st TFAP Shepherds' Meeting, Singapore
	17	Inauguration of ASEF, Singapore
	25	AEBF Steering Committee
March	10–14	1st Young Leaders' Symposium, Miyazaki and Tokyo
	21–2	1st Procedure Working Group of ASEM Customs' Meeting, Brussels
April	24–5	Asia–Europe Experts Meeting on Technological Cooperation, Beijing
	25	2nd ASEM EMM Coordinators Preparatory Meeting, The Hague
	30	2nd Working Group Preparatory Meeting for FinMM, Washington DC
May	27	Meeting of Group of Experts on setting up the Asia–Europe Environmental Centre, Bangkok
June	2–6	Symposium on Multi-Media and the Future of Electronic Media, Mainz
	4	Symposium on the study of economic synergy, Tokyo
	4	Business Forum Task Force on Infrastructure, Paris
	4	2nd TFAP Shepherds' Meeting, Tokyo
	5–6	SOMTI II, Tokyo
	7	3rd ASEM EMM Coordinators Preparatory Meeting, Tokyo
	20	ASEM Customs Meeting, Vienna
July	8–10	ASEM business conference, Jakarta

	21	4th ASEM EMM Coordinators' Preparatory Meeting, Luxembourg
	26	Coordinators' Meeting, Kuala Lumpur
	28–9	Working Group on IPAP 2, Luxembourg
September	3	Symposium on infrastructure financing, Frankfurt
	3–4	3rd Working Group Preparatory Meeting for FinMM, Washington DC
	4	Coordinators' Meeting (for economic ministers) Luxembourg
	19	1st Finance Ministers' Meeting, Bangkok
	25	3rd TFAP Shepherds' Meeting, Makuhari
	26	ASEM Senior Officials' Meeting, Hong Kong
	27–9	EMM, Makuhari, Japan
	28	Coordinators' Meeting, Makuhari, Japan
October	23	Meeting of cultural operators, France
	24–5	Meeting of ASEF Board of Governors, Luxembourg
	27	Meeting of Group of Experts on setting up Asia–Europe Environmental Centre, Bangkok
	30–1	SOM, Luxembourg
November	13–14	2nd AEBF, Bangkok
December	11–13	ASEM Symposium on Human Rights and the Rule of Law, Lund
	19	4th TFAP Shepherds' Meeting, Manila

1998

January	13	Coordinators' Meeting, Tokyo
	14	5th TFAP Shepherds' Meeting, Tokyo
	16	AEBF Joint Standing Committees' Meeting, Paris
	27–8	Senior Experts' Meeting on AEETC, The Hague
February	3–4	6th TFAP Shepherds' Meeting, Brussels
	5	Meeting of ASEM Finance Deputies, London
	5–6	Europe–Asia Cultural Forum, Paris
	5–6	SOMTI III, Brussels
	6	2nd Meeting of Customs Enforcement Working Group, Brussels
	17–18	Meeting of ASEF Board of Governors, Bangkok
	19–20	SOM 3, London
March	2–3	Informal Preparatory Vision Group Meeting, Seoul

	3–4	Environment officials and Technology Transfers Centres, Düsseldorf
	16	AEBF ASEMConnect 2nd Working Committee, Singapore
	16–17	Coordinators' Meeting, Bangkok
	16–17	2nd Customs Working Group on Procedures, Brussels
	17–19	Asia–Europe University Forum and Fair, Kuala Lumpur
	18	ASEM University Dialogue Meeting, Kuala Lumpur
	19–22	Symposium on Societies in Transition, London
April	1	ASEM2 Coordinators' Meeting, London
	2	SOM 4, London
	2–3	3rd AEBF, London
	3–4	ASEM 2 London
	5–6	1st meeting of Vision Group, Cambridge
May	1–10	Asian Film Festival, London
	11–12	Seminar on the Conservation of the Built Heritage, London
	15–17	Asia–Europe Classroom Seminar, Copenhagen
	25–9	Young Leaders' Symposium 2, Vienna
	28–30	ASEM Forum for SMEs, Naples
June	1	3rd Asia–Europe Lecture by HE Mr Jean-Claude Juncker, Prime Minister of Luxembourg: 'Europe: A Vision for the 21st Century'
	5–6	SOMTI III, Brussels
	15–16	Preparatory Meeting on Child Welfare, Manila
	25–6	AEETC Pilot Phase Guidance Group Meeting, Bangkok
	29	ASEM Trust Fund becomes operational
July	2–3	Vision Group, Singapore
	8	ASEM Trust Fund Review Meeting, Brussels
	10	European Monetary Union roadshow, Hong Kong
	12–24	1st ASEF Summer School for Undergraduates, Reutlingen (Germany)
	24	IPAP IEG Shepherds' Meeting, Bangkok
	24	SOMTI Coordinators' Meeting, Bangkok
	26	Coordinators' Meeting, Manila

September	30	TFAP Thematic Meeting on Standards and Conformity, Accreditation, Certification, Testing and Technical Regulations, Brussels
October	3–4	Vision Group, Rome
	5	Financial Officials' Core Group Meeting, Washington D.C.
	6	ASEF Meeting of Publishers, Frankfurt
	6–8	Child Welfare Experts' Meeting, London
	7–9	Inaugural Workshop of the Programme for Europe–Asia Research Linkage (PEARL), Seoul
	9–10	EMM, Berlin
	12	ASEF Colloquium for Journalists, Singapore
	25	ASEF Board of Governors Meeting, The Hague
	26–7	Seminar on Labour Relations, The Hague
	27–8	SOM IV, Bangkok
	28	ASEF Board of Governors Meeting, The Hague
November	13–16	1st ASEF Young Parliamentarians' Meeting, Cebu
	20–1	'Human Rights and Human Responsibilities' Colloquium, Hanover
	23–4	1st IPAP IEG Meeting, Evian
	26–27	AEETC 2nd Pilot Phase Guidance Group Meeting, Bangkok
	27	SOMTI Coordinators, Geneva
December	2	Asia–Europe Classroom Homepage launched
	18	2nd Financial Deputies' Meeting, Vienna
	18	1st AEBF Steering Committee, Seoul

1999

January	8–9	Vision Group, Tokyo
	15–16	Finance Ministers' Meeting, Frankfurt
	20	ASEM Trust Fund Review Meeting, Bangkok
	20–2	Experts' Meeting on Protection and Promotion of Cultural Heritage, Hanoi
	21–2	1st Asia–Europe Experts' Meeting on Protection and Promotion of Cultural Heritage, Hanoi
	29	Coordinators' Meeting, Berlin
February	3–5	TFAP Meeting on SPS Sector, Chiang Mai
	5–6	Customs Working Group on Enforcement, Brussels

	6–7	Vision Group, Lisbon
	11–12	2nd IPAP IEG meeting, Singapore
	11–13	4th SOMTI, Singapore
	23–5	Seminar on Simplification and Harmonisation of Customs Procedures, Manila
	26	Customs Working Group on Procedure, Manila
March	1	ASEF EMU Roadshow, Singapore
	5–7	Asian Film Festival of Deauville (France)
	8–9	Conference on States and Markets, Copenhagen
	10–12	TFAP Meeting on Standards and Conformity Assessment, Seoul
	18–20	ASEM Seminar on Combination of Traditional and Modern Medicine for Public Health Care, Hanoi
	21	ASEF Cultural Managers' Training Seminar, Barcelona
	26–8	Conference on Asian Crisis, Democracy and Human Rights, Germany
	27–8	SOM, Berlin
	28–9	2nd FMM, Berlin
	29	AEETC officially opened, Pathumthani, Thailand
	29–30	AEETC Pilot Phase Guidance Group Meeting, Thailand
April	11	Asia–Europe Classroom Exhibition, Berlin
	13–14	ASEF Meeting of Cultural and Educational TV Channels, Cannes
	26	Financial Officials' Core Group Meeting
	30	2nd Europe–Asia Forum, Munich
May	2–3	Asia–Europe Workshop on Education in the 21st Century, Luxembourg
	12–14	ASEF Colloquium for Journalists 'A Preview of the Indonesian Elections', Jakarta
	17–18	ASEF Board of Governors meeting, Beijing
	19–21	Asia–Europe Conference on Cultural Industries and Cultural Development, Beijing
	24–8	AEYL Symposium, Korea
June	7–9	Europe and Asia: A New Vision for the Partnership, Wilton Park

	21–2	AEETC Pilot Phase Guidance Group Meeting, Germany
	22	ASEM Trust Fund Review Meeting, London
	23	ASEM Customs Directors-General and Commissioners' Meeting, Brussels
	24–5	TFAP Thematic Meeting on Intellectual Property Rights, Paris
	28–9	2nd Informal ASEM Seminar on Human Rights, Beijing
July	4–6	Workshop on Sustainable Forest Management and People-to-People Exchange, Joensuu, Finland
	5–6	IPAP IEG meeting, Belgium
	5–7	'A New Round of Multilateral Trade Negotiation: An Asia–Europe Perspective', Brussels
	7–8	SOMTI V, Brussels
August 22–5 *September*		2nd ASEF Summer School, Beijing
September	14–15	Seminar on Public Procurement, Germany
	29	AEBF IV, Seoul
October	1	IPAP Decision Makers' Roundtable, Korea
	2–30	Cities on the Move exhibition, Bangkok
	4–5	Seminar on Industrial Districts and Technology Transfer, Bari
	4–6	TFAP Meeting on Standards and Conformity, Brussels
	8–10	Asia–Europe Young Entrepreneurs Forum, Berlin
	9–10	EMM II, Berlin
	14–15	Science and Technology Ministers' Meeting, Beijing
	25–6	ASEF Board of Governors Meeting, Copenhagen
	27	Symposium on Images of Asia in Europe and Images of Europe in Asia, Copenhagen
November	2–4	SOM, Finland
	23–4	TFAP Meeting on SPS Sector, China
	24	Conference on Asia and the Common Foreign and Security Policy, Brussels (EP)
	25–7	Meeting on the Formation of an ASEM Education Hub Network, Fontainebleau
December	30–3	3rd WTO Ministerial Conference, Seattle
	9–10	AEETC Pilot Phase Guidance Group Meeting, Japan

	18	Finance Deputies' Meeting, Vienna

2000

January		Singapore TV, 'Building Bridges – The New Europe and the New Asia'
January-October:		Asia–Europe Young Artists' Painting Competition 'The New Millennium in My Dreams'
February	3–4	ASEM Trust Fund Review Meeting, Indonesia
	4–5	Customs' Working Group on Enforcement, Brussels
	19	AEF 2nd Symposium, 'Fusion or Friction?', Tokyo?
February 28–1 *March*		TFAP meeting on standards and conformity, Thailand
March	16–18	TFAP Thematic Meeting on IPR, Bangkok
	29–31	Asia–Europe Workshop on Copyright Trading for Book Publishers, Beijing
March 31–3 *April*		2nd ASEF Young Parliamentarians' Meeting, Lisbon
April	14–15	3rd Europe–Asia Forum, Singapore
	14–15	Customs' Working Group on Procedure, Brussels
May	2–3	Education for the 21st Century, Luxembourg
	2–3	SOM, Lisbon
	4–5	ASEF Board of Governors, Vienna
	4–6	Child Welfare Meeting of Police and Enforcement Agencies, Korea
	11–12	IPAP IEG meeting, Seoul
	12–13	SOMTI, Seoul
	18–21	Asia–Europe Youth Forum, Brussels
	24	European Parliamentarians visit ASEF, Singapore
June	12–16	4th Asia–Europe Young Leaders' Symposium, Limerick
	19–20	3rd Informal ASEM Seminar on Human Rights, Paris
July	6–7	AEETC Pilot Phase Guidance Group Meeting, Korea
	10–11	Conference, 'Seoul Summit: The Way Ahead for the Asia–Europe Partnership', Seoul
	26	Lecture by Javier Solana, Singapore
August 26–10 *September*		Asia–Europe Youth Work Camp 2000, Shandong
August	30	Asia–Europe Roundtable: Rights in Transition, Singapore
September	11–14	TFAP meeting on SPS Sector, The Hague
	13	ASEM Trust Fund Review Meeting, France

	14	Finance Deputies' Meeting, France
	18–19	The Role of the Individual vis-à-vis the Family, Society and State in Asia and Europe, Vienna
	18–20	SOM, Seoul
	29–30	AEBF, Austria
	30	Conference on Trade, Investment and Competition, Austria
October	2–4	TFAP Meeting on Standards and Conformity
	16	ASEF Board of Governors, Seoul
	20–21	ASEM 3, Seoul

2001

January	14–27	4th ASEF Summer School, Singapore
March	12	ASEF Future Strategies, Singapore
	16	Roundtable, Singapore
	18–31	2nd Asia–Europe Youth Camp, Manila
April	12–28	Focus on Asia–Europe Documentaries, Singapore
May	4–5	Europe–Asia Forum, Berlin
	23–6	Gender Agenda: Asia–Europe Dialogue, Chiba (Japan)
	28–9	ASEM Roundtable on Globalisation, Seoul
May–August		Asia–Europe Young Volunteer Exchange
June	9–17	2nd Asia–Europe Film Festival, Shanghai
July	12–13	4th Informal ASEM Seminar on Human Rights, Jakarta
July 22–4 August		5th ASEF Summer School, Arrabida, Portugal
August 27–9 September		3rd Asia–Europe Youth Camp, Bangkok
September	2-5	Asia–Europe Classroom (AEC) International Teachers' Conference, Singapore
	12-13	'New Economy and the Perspectives of Asia–Europe Economic and Trade Cooperation', Beijing
	18-20	Asia–Europe Seminar on Ethnic Cultures Promotion, Thailand
October	21-3	Asia–Europe Seminar on Music Industry in the New Economy, Paris

November   1−4   3rd Asia–Europe Young Parliamentarians' Meeting, Bali

               5−7   Asia–Europe Seminar on Man, Cultural Heritage and Tourism, Hanoi

               26−8   Asia–Europe Seminar on Cultural Heritage Training, Madrid

Bibliography

Acharya, Amitav (1999a), 'A Concert of Asia?', *Survival*, **41** (3), 84–101.

Acharya, Amitav (1999b), 'Realism, Institutionalism, and the Asian Economic Crisis', *Contemporary Southeast Asia*, **21** (1), 1–29.

Acharya, Amitav (1999c), 'Southeast Asia's Democratic Moment', *Asian Survey*, **39** (3), 418-32.

Acharya, Amitav (2000), *The Quest for Identity: International Relations in Southeast Asia*, Singapore: Oxford University Press.

Adler, Emanuel (1997), 'Imagined (Security) Communities: Cognitive Regions in International Relations', *Millennium*, **26** (2), 249-77.

Aggarwal, Vinod K. (2000), 'The Wobbly Triangle: Europe, Asia and the US after the Asian Crisis', in Maria Weber (ed.), *After the Asian Crises: Perspectives on Global Politics and Economics*, London: Macmillan, pp. 173–98.

Akaha, Tsuneo (1998), 'International Cooperation in Establishing a Regional Order in Northeast Asia', *Global Economic Review*, **27** (1), 3–26.

Amersfoort, Philippe van (1998), 'An European Union Perspective on Democracy, Human Rights and Economic Development in Asia', in Willem van der Geest and Beate Tränkmann (eds), *Democracy, Human Rights and Economic Development: Conflict or Complement?*, Brussels: European Institute for Asian Studies, pp. 131–41.

Anderson, Benedict (1991, 1983), *Imagined Communities: Reflections on the Origin and Spread of Nationalism*, London: Verso.

Anderson, Benedict (1998), *The Spectre of Comparisons: Nationalism, Southeast Asia and the World*, London: Verso.

Armstrong, David (1998), 'Globalization and the Social State', *Review of International Studies*, **24** (4), 461-78.

Arts, Bas (1998), *The Political Influence of Global NGOs: Case Studies in Climate and Biodiversity Conventions*, Utrecht: International Books.

Asia Strategy Project (1999), *Our Future with Asia: Proposal for a Swedish Asia Strategy*, Stockholm: Ministry of Foreign Affairs.

Bibliography

Australian Parliament (1997), *Australia and the European Union: A Parliamentary Perspective*, Canberra: Australian Parliament.

Baker, Nikki (1998), 'Restructuring Foreign and Defence Policy: Strategic Uncertainty and the Asia-Pacific Middle Powers', in Anthony McGrew and Christopher Brook (eds), *Asia Pacific in the New World*, London: Routledge, pp. 189–208.

Barlow, Colin (ed.) (1999), *Institutions and Economic Change in Southeast Asia*, Cheltenham, UK and Northampton, MA, USA: Edward Elgar.

Beeson, Mark and Richard Robison (2000), 'Introduction: Interpreting the Crisis', in Richard Robison, Mark Beeson, Kanishka Jayasuriya and Hyuk-Rae Kim (eds), *Politics and Markets in the Wake of the Asian Crisis*, London: Routledge, pp. 3–24.

Berger, Mark T. and Douglas A. Borer (1997), 'Conclusion: The Coming of the Pacific Century: The Cold War and After in the Asia-Pacific', in Mark T. Berger and Douglas A. Borer (eds), *The Rise of East Asia: Critical Visions of the Pacific Century*, London: Routledge, pp. 288–301.

Berger, Mark T. and Douglas A. Borer (eds) (1997), *The Rise of East Asia: Critical Visions of the Pacific Century*, London: Routledge.

Berger, Peter L. and Thomas Luckmann (1976, 1967), *The Social Construction of Reality*, London: Penguin.

Bhagwati, Jagdish (1992), 'Regionalism Versus Multilateralism', *The World Economy*, **15** (5), 535–55.

Bobrow, Davis B. (1999), 'The US and ASEM: Why the Hegemon Didn't Bark', *The Pacific Review*, **12** (1), 103–28.

Booth, Ken and Steve Smith (eds) (1995), *International Relations Theory Today*, Cambridge: Polity Press.

Bowles, Paul (1997, 1996), 'Regional Blocs: Can Japan be the Leader?', in Robert Boyer and Daniel Drache (eds), *States against Markets*, London: Routledge, pp. 155–69.

Brennan, Brid (2000), 'The Spirit of Seoul', ASEM Watch Number 60.

Breslin, Shaun (1999), 'China: The Challenges of Reform, Region-Building and Globalization', in Jean Grugel and Wil Hout (eds), *Regionalism Across the North-South Divide: State Strategies and Globalization*, London: Routledge, pp. 95–112.

Bridges, Brian (1999a), 'Europe and the Asian Financial Crisis', *Asian Survey*, **39** (3), 456–67.

Bridges, Brian (1999b), *Europe and the Challenge of the Asia Pacific*, Cheltenham, UK and Northampton, MA, USA: Edward Elgar.

Brook, Christopher (1998), 'Regionalism and Globalism', in Anthony McGrew and Christopher Brook (eds), *Asia Pacific in the New World*, London: Routledge, pp. 230–46.

Buzan, Barry, Morten Kelstrup, Pierre Lemaitre, Elzbieta Tramer and Ole Waever (1990), *The European Security Order Recast*, London: Pinter.

Buzan, Barry (1991), 'New Patterns of Global Security in the Twenty-First Century', *International Affairs*, **67** (3), 431–51.

Buzan, Barry (1998), 'The Asia-Pacific: What Sort of Region in What Sort of World?', in Anthony McGrew and Christopher Brook (eds), *Asia-Pacific in the New World Order*, London: Routledge, pp. 67–87.

CAEC (1997), *The Rationale and Common Agenda for Asia-Europe Cooperation*, Tokyo: Japan Centre for International Exchange.

Calder, Kent E. (1993), *Strategic Capitalism: Private Business and Public Purpose in Japanese Industrial Finance*, Princeton: Princeton University Press.

Calhoun, Craig (1998/1994), 'Social Theory and the Politics of Identity', in Craig Calhoun (ed.), *Social Theory and the Politics of Identity*, Oxford: Oxford: Blackwell, pp. 9–36.

Cammack, Paul and Gareth Richards (1999), 'ASEM and Interregionalism', *Journal of the Asia Pacific Economy*, **4** (1), 1–12.

Campbell, David (1998, 1992), *Writing Security: United States Foreign Policy and the Politics of Identity*, Manchester: Manchester University Press.

Camroux, David and Christian Lechervy (1996), 'Close Encounter of a Third Kind? The Inaugural Asia–Europe Meeting of March 1996', *The Pacific Review*, **9** (3), 441–52.

Carver, Terrell (1999), 'ASEM: Political Cooperation in a Globalized Framework', paper presented at the Korean Political Science Association, *International Conference on ASEM 2000: New Cooperation between Asia and Europe in the 21st Century* (2–3 December).

Chan, Joseph (1998), 'Asian Values and Human Rights: An Alternative View', in Larry Diamond and Marc F. Plattner (eds), *Democracy in East Asia*, Baltimore: Johns Hopkins University Press, pp. 28–41.

Chatterjee, Partha (1991), 'Whose Imagined Community?', *Millennium*, **20** (3), 521–6.

Checkel, Jeffrey T. (1999), 'Social Construction and Integration', *Journal of European Public Policy*, **6** (4), 542–57.

Cheeseman, Graeme (1999), 'Asian–Pacific Security Discourse in the Wake of the Asian Economic Crisis', *The Pacific Review*, **12** (3), 333–56.

Chia, Siow Yue and Lee Tsao Tan (eds) (1997), *ASEAN and EU: Forging New Linkages and Strategic Alliances*, Singapore: Institute of Southeast Asian Studies.

Chin, Christine B.N. and James H. Mittelman (1997), 'Conceptualisting Resistance to Globalisation', *New Political Economy*, **2** (1), 25–37.

Christiansen, Thomas, Knud Erik Jørgensen and Antje Wiener (1999), 'The Social Construction of Europe', *Journal of European Public Policy*, **6** (4), 528–41.

Cohen, Anthony P. (1985), *The Symbolic Construction of Community*, London: Tavistock.

Colbert, Evelyn (1992), 'Southeast Asian Regional Politics: Toward a Regional Order', in W. Howard Wriggins (ed.), *Dynamics of Regional Politics: 4 Systems on the Indian Ocean Rim*, New York: Columbia University Press, pp. 213–73.

Coleman, William D. and Geoffrey R.D. Underhill (eds) (1998), *Regionalism and Global Economic Integration*, London: Routledge.

Connolly, William (1991), *Identity/Difference*, Ithaca: Cornell University Press.

Cooper, Andrew F., Richard Higgott and Kim Richard Nossal (1993), *Relocating Middle Powers: Australia and Canada in a Changing World Order*, Vancouver: University of British Columbia Press.

Cox, Robert W. (1981), 'Social Forces, States and World Orders: Beyond International Relations Theory', *Millennium*, **10** (2), 126–55.

Cox, Robert (1997), 'A Perspective on Globalization', in James H. Mittelman (ed.), *Globalization: Critical Perspectives*, Boulder: Lynne Rienner, pp. 21–30.

Dent, Christopher M. (1997–8), 'The ASEM: Managing the New Framework of the EU's Economic Relations with East Asia', *Pacific Affairs*, **70** (4), 495–516.

Dent, Christopher M. (1999a), *The European Union and East Asia: An Economic Relationship*, London: Routledge.

Dent, Christopher M. (1999b), 'The EU–East Asia Economic Relationship: The Persisting Weak Triadic Link', *European Foreign Affairs Review*, **4** (3), 371–94.

Desthieux, Nathalie and Philippe Saucier (1999), 'Regional Integration and Intra-Industry Trade: A Comparison between Asia and Europe', in Sang-Gon Lee and Pierre-Bruno Ruffini (eds), *The Global Integration of Europe and East Asia: Studies of International Trade and Investment*, Cheltenham, UK and Northampton, MA, USA: Edward Elgar, pp. 95–112.

Devetak, Richard and Richard Higgott (1999), 'Justice Unbound? Globalization, States and the Transformation of the Social Bond', *International Affairs*, **75** (3), 483–98.

Diez, Thomas (1999), 'Speaking 'Europe': The Politics of Integration Discourse', *Journal of European Public Policy*, **6** (4), 598–613.

Dinan, Desmond (1994), *Ever Closer Union?*, Boulder: Lynne Rienner.

Dios, Emmanuel de, Alfredo C. Robles Jr. and Joseph Sedfrey S. Santiago (1996), 'The Philippine Stake in the Asia–Europe Meeting', *Euros Update*, European Studies Programme at the University of the Philippines Center for Integrative and Development Studies, No. 1.

Dixon, Chris (1991), *South East Asia in the World-Economy*, Cambridge: Cambridge University Press.

Dobson, Hugo J. (1999), 'Regional Approaches to Peacekeeping Activities: The Case of the ASEAN Regional Forum', *International Peacekeeping*, **6** (2), 152–71.

Doty, Roxanne Lynn (1997), 'Aporia: A Critical Exploration of the Agent-Structure Problematique in International Relations Theory', *European Journal of International Relations*, **3** (3), 365–92.

Drifte, Reinhard (1996), 'The EU's Stake in KEDO', EIAS Briefing Paper 96/01, Brussels: EIAS.

Drifte, Reinhard (1998a), *Japan's Foreign Policy for the Twenty-First Century: From Economic Superpower to What Power?*, London: Macmillan.

Drifte, Reinhard (1998b), 'A Review of EU–Japan Relations', EIAS Briefing Paper 98/06, Brussels: EIAS.

Drysdale, Peter and David Vines (eds) (1998), *Europe, East Asia and APEC: A Shared Global Agenda?*, Cambridge: Cambridge University Press.

Dunne, Timothy (1995), 'The Social Construction of International Society', *European Journal of International Relations*, **1** (3), 367–89.

Dupont, Alan (1999), 'Transnational Crime, Drugs, and Security in East Asia', *Asian Survey*, **39** (3), 433–55.

Edwards, Geoffrey, and Elfriede Regelsberger (eds) (1990), *Europe's Global Links*, London: Pinter.

European Commission (1994), *Towards a New Asia Strategy*, Brussels, COM (94) 427 final.

European Commission (1996), *Creating a New Dynamic in EU–ASEAN Relations*, Brussels, COM (96) 314.

European Commission (1997a), Working Document *Perspectives and Priorities for the ASEM Process*, Brussels SEC (97) 1239 final.

European Commission (1997b), *Europe–Asia Strategy in the Field of the Environment*, Brussels, COM (97) 890 final.

European Commission (2000), *Perspectives and Priorities for the ASEM Process (Asia–Europe Meeting) into the New Decade*, Brussels, COM (241) final.

European Parliament (1998), 'The ASEM Perspectives and Priorities', Brussels, REXT 100 EN 4–1998.

European Parliament (1999), Report on the Commission Working Document on Perspectives and Priorities for the ASEM Process', Brussels, A4–0197/99, PE 229.876.fin, 20 April.

European Parliament (2000), European Parliament resolution on the third Asia–Europe Meeting (ASEM 3) in Seoul, 20–21 October, Brussels.

Evian Group (2000), 'Building Constituencies for a Global Liberal Trade Agenda', Chair's Statement at Evian Group Meeting, Seoul, 21–22 October.

Falk, Richard (1999), 'Regionalism and World Order After the Cold War', in Björn Hettne, Andras Inotai and Osvaldo Sunkel (eds), *Globalism and the New Regionalism*, London: Macmillan, pp. 228–49.

Farrands, Chris (1996), 'Society, Modernity and Social Change: Approaches to Nationalism and Identity', in Jill Krause and Neil Renwick (eds), *Identities in International Relations*, London: Macmillan, pp. 1–21.

Fawcett, Lisa and Andrew Hurrell (eds) (1995), *Regionalism in World Politics*, Oxford: Oxford University Press.

Ferdinand, Peter (1999), 'Democratisation, Good Governance and Good Government in Asia', EIAS Briefing Paper 99/05, Brussels: European Institute for Asian Studies.

Ferguson, R. James (1996), 'Finding the Missing Relationship: Asia, Europe and Open Regionalism', paper presented at the JAIR–ISA Conference, Makuhari, 20–22 September.

Finger, Matthias (1994a), 'Environmental NGOs in the UNCED Process', in Thomas Princen and Matthias Finger (eds), *Environmental NGOs in World Politics*, London: Routledge, pp. 186–213.

Finger, Matthias (1994b), 'NGOs and Transformation: Beyond Social Movement Theory', in Thomas Princen and Matthias Finger (eds), *Environmental NGOs in World Politics*, London: Routledge, pp. 48–66.

Flynn, Gregory and Henry Farrell (1999), 'Piecing Together the Democratic Peace: The CSCE, Norms, and the "Construction" of Security in Post-Cold War Europe', *International Organization*, **53** (3), 505–35.

Fodella, Gianni (1997), 'Economic and Technical Cooperation between Europe and East Asia: A Policy to Form the Appropriate Human Resources Needed for Implementing the Task', paper presented at the Manila Forum on Culture, Values and Technology, 10–12 December.

Forster, Anthony (1999), 'The European Union in South East Asia: Continuity and Change in Turbulent Times', *International Affairs*, **75** (4), 743–58.

Freeman, Michael (1998), 'Asia, Europe and Human Rights: Dialogue or Confrontation', paper presented at the conference on 'Assessing the Asian Crisis: Economics, Politics and Society', Institute for Development Policy and Management, University of Manchester, 7 April.

Friedberg, Aaron L. (2000), 'Will Europe's Past be Asia's Future?', *Survival*, **42** (3), 147–59.

Friedman, Edward (1994), 'Democratization: Generalizing the East Asian Experience', in Edward Friedman (ed.), *The Politics of Democratization: Generalizing Asian Experiences*, Boulder: Westview, pp. 19–57.

Friedman, Jonathan (1993, 1990), 'Being in the World: Globalization and Localization', in Mike Featherstone (ed.), *Global Culture: Nationalism, Globalization and Modernity*, London: Sage, pp. 311–28.

Fukasaku, Kiichiro (ed.) (1995), *Regional Cooperation and Integration in Asia*, Paris: OECD.

Gamble, Andrew and Anthony Payne (eds) (1996), *Regionalism and World Order*, Basingstoke: Macmillan.

Garnaut, Ross (1998), 'The East Asian Crisis', in Ross H. McLeod and Ross Garnaut (eds), *East Asia in Crisis: From Being a Miracle to Needing One?*, London: Routledge, pp. 3–30.

Giddens, Anthony (1984), *The Constitution of Society: Outline of the Theory of Structuration*, Berkeley: University of California Press.

Gill, Stephen (ed.) (1997), *Globalization, Democratization and Multilateralism*, London: Macmillan.

Gill, Stephen (2000), 'Toward a Postmodern Prince? The Battle in Seattle as a Moment in the New Politics of Globalization', *Millennium*, **29** (1), 131–40.

Gill, S. and J.H. Mittelman (1997), *Innovation and Transformation in International Studies*, Cambridge: Cambridge University Press.

Gills, Barry K. (1997), 'Globalization' and the 'Politics of Resistance', *New Political Economy*, **2** (1), 11–24.

Gilson, Julie (1999), 'Japan's Role in the Asia–Europe Meeting: Establishing an Interregional or Intraregional Agenda?', *Asian Survey*, **39** (5), 735–52.

Gilson, Julie (2000), *Japan and the European Union: A Partnership for the Twenty-First Century?*, London: Macmillan.

Gilson, Julie (2001), 'Breaking the Triangle? The U.S. Ghost at the ASEM Feast', in Bert Edström (ed.), *Interdependence in the Asia Pacific*, Stockholm: Swedish Institute of International Affairs, pp. 155–72.

Glarbo, Kenneth (1999), 'Wide-Awake Diplomacy: Reconstructing the Common Foreign and Security Policy of the European Union', *Journal of European Public Policy*, **6** (4), 634–51.

Godement, François (1997), *The New Asian Renaissance: From Colonialism to the Post-Cold War*, translated by Elisabeth J. Parcell, London and New York: Routledge.

Godement, François (1999), *The Downsizing of Asia*, London: Routledge.

Godement, François (2000), 'A New Relationship between the West and Pacific Asia?', in Gerald Segal and David S.G. Goodman (eds), *Towards Recovery in Pacific Asia*, London: Routledge, pp. 119–31.

Grugel, Jean and Wil Hout (eds) (1999), *Regionalism Across the North-South Divide: State Strategies and Globalization*, London: Routledge.

Haas, Ernst B. (1964), *Beyond the Nation State*, Stanford: Stanford University Press.

Haas, Peter (1992), 'Introduction: Epistemic Communities and International Policy Coordination', *International Organization*, **46** (1), 1–35.

Hall, John A. (1995), 'In Search of Civil Society', in John A. Hall (ed.), *Civil Society: Theory, History, Comparison*, Cambridge: Polity Press, pp. 1–31.

Hänggi, Heiner (1998), 'Small State as a Third State: Switzerland and Asia–Europe Interregionalism', in Laurent Goetschel (ed.), *Small States Inside and Outside the European Union: Interests and Policies*, Boston: Kluwer, pp. 79–95.

Hänggi, Heiner (1999), 'ASEM and the Construction of the New Triad', *Journal of the Asia Pacific Economy*, **4** (1), 56–80.

Harris, Stuart (2000), 'Asian Multilateral Institutions and their Response to the Asian Economic Crisis: The Regional and Global Implications', *The Pacific Review*, **13** (3), 495–516.

Hernandez, Carolina (1997), 'The Societal Dimension', in CAEC *The Rationale and Common Agenda for Asia–Europe Cooperation*, Tokyo: Japan Centre for International Exchange, pp. 87–92.

Hettne, Björn (1999), 'Globalization and the New Regionalism: The Second Great Transformation', in Björn Hettne, Andras Inotai and Osvaldo Sunkel (eds), *Globalism and the New Regionalism*, London: Macmillan, pp. 1–24.

Hettne, Björn, Andras Inotai and Osvaldo Sunkel (eds) (1999), *Globalism and the New Regionalism*, London: Macmillan.

Hewitt, John P. (1997), *Self and Society*, Needham Heights, MA: Allyn and Bacon.

Higgott, Richard (1993), 'Economic Cooperation: Theoretical Opportunities and Practical Constraints', *The Pacific Review*, **6** (2), 103–17.

Higgott, Richard (1994), 'Ideas, Interests and Identity in the Asia Pacific', *The Pacific Review*, **7** (4), 367–80.

Higgott, Richard (1998a), 'The Pacific and Beyond: APEC, ASEM and Regional Economic Management', in Grahame Thompson (ed.), *Economic Dynamism in the Asia–Pacific: The Growth of Integration and Competitiveness*, London: Routledge, pp. 335–55.

Higgott, Richard (1998b), 'The Asian Economic Crisis: A Study in the Politics of Resentment', *New Political Economy*, **3** (3), 333–56.

Higgott, Richard (1999), 'The Political Economy of Globalisation in East Asia', in Kris Olds, Peter Dicken and Philip F. Kelly (eds), *Globalisation and the Asia Pacific: Contested Territories*, London: Routledge, pp. 91–106.

Higgott, Richard (2000), 'ASEM and the Evolving Global Order', in Chong Wha Lee (ed.), *The Seoul 2000 Summit: The Way Ahead for the Asia–Europe Partnership*, Seoul: Korea Institute for International Economic Policy, pp. 11–47.

Higgott, Richard, Richard Leaver and John Ravenhill (eds) (1993) *Pacific Economic Relations in the 1990s: Cooperation or Conflict?*, St Leonards: Allen and Unwin.

Hirst, Paul and Grahame Thompson (1995), 'Globalization and the Future of the Nation State', *Economy and Society*, **24** (3), 408–42.

Hirst, Paul and Grahame Thompson (1996), *Globalisation in Question: The International Economy and the Possibilities of Governance*, Cambridge: Polity Press.

Hook, Glenn, Julie Gilson, Christopher W. Hughes and Hugo Dobson (2001), *Japan's International Relations: Economics, Politics, Security*, London: Routledge.

Hsuing, James C. (ed.) (1993), *The Asia–Pacific in the New World Politics*, Boulder: Lynne Rienner.

Huntington, Samuel (1993), 'The Clash of Civilizations?', *Foreign Affairs*, **72** (3), 22–49.

Hveem, Helge (1999), 'Political Regionalism: Master or Servant of Economic Internationalization', in Björn Hettne, Andras Inotai and Osvaldo Sunkel (eds), *Globalism and the New Regionalism*, London: Macmillan, pp. 85–115.

Inoguchi, Takashi and Daniel I Okimoto (eds) (1988), *The Political Economy of Japan Volume 2: The Changing International Context*, Stanford: Stanford University Press.

International Monetary Fund (1999), *IMF Annual Report 1998*, Washington DC.

Iokibe, Makoto (1998), 'Japan's Democratic Experience', in Larry Diamond and Marc F. Plattner (eds), *Democracy in East Asia*, Baltimore: Johns Hopkins University Press, pp. 79–95.

Jameson, Frederic and Miyoshi Masao (eds) (1998), *The Cultures of Globalization*, Durham: Duke University Press.

Jepperson, Ronald, Alexander Wendt and Peter Katzenstein (1996), 'Norms, Identity and Culture in National Security', in Peter J. Katzenstein (ed.), *The Culture of National Security: Norms and Identity in World Politics*, New York: Columbia University Press, pp. 33–75.

Jessop, Bob (1999), 'Reflections on Globalization and Its (Il)Logic', in Kris Olds, Peter Dicken and Philip F. Kelly (eds), *Globalization and the Asia Pacific: Contested Territories*, London: Routledge, pp. 19–38.

Jung, Ku-Hyun and Jean-Pierre Lehmann (1997), 'The Economic and Business Dimension', in CAEC, *The Rationale and Common Agenda for Asia–Europe Cooperation*, Tokyo: Japan Centre for International Exchange, pp. 49–73.

Katzenstein, Peter (ed.) (1996), *The Culture of National Security: Norms and Identity in World Politics*, New York: Columbia University Press.

Kausikan, Bilahari (1998), 'The "Asian Values" Debate: A View from Singapore', in Larry Diamond and Marc F. Plattner (eds), *Democracy in East Asia*, Baltimore: Johns Hopkins University Press, pp. 17–27.

Keating, Michael (1997), 'The Political Economy of Regionalism', in Michael Keating and John Loughlin (eds), *The Political Economy of Regionalism*, London: Frank Cass, pp. 17–40.

Keating, Michael and John Loughlin (eds) (1997), *The Political Economy of Regionalism*, London: Frank Cass.

Keohane, Robert O. (1986), 'Reciprocity in International Relations', *International Organization*, **40** (1), 1–27.

Keohane, Robert O., Joseph S. Nye and Stanley Hoffmann (eds) (1993), *After the Cold War: International Institutions and State Strategies in Europe, 1989–1991*, Cambridge: Harvard University Press.

Kim, Jong Kil (1999), 'Economic Growth of ASEAN in the Context of East Asian Development', in Sang-Gon Lee and Pierre-Bruno Ruffini (eds), *The Global Integration of Europe and East Asia: Studies of International Trade and Investment*, Cheltenham, UK and Northampton, MA, USA: Edward Elgar, pp. 132–48.

Klotz, Audie (1995), *Norms in International Relations: The Struggle Against Apartheid*, Ithaca: Cornell University Press.

Kowert, Paul (1998), 'Agent versus Structure in the Construction of National Identity', in Vendulka Kubálková, Nicholas Onuf and Paul Kowert (eds), *International Relations in a Constructed World*, Armonk: M.E. Sharpe, pp 101–22.

Kratochwil, Friedrich V. (1989), *Rules, Norms and Decisions: On Conditions of Practical and Legal Reasoning in International Relations and Domestic Affairs*, Cambridge: Cambridge University Press.

Kratochwil, Friedrich V. (2000), 'Constructing a New Orthodoxy? Wendt's "Social Theory of International Politics" and the Constructivist Challenge', *Millennium*, **29** (1), 73–102.

Kubálková, Vendulka (1998), 'The Twenty Years' Catharsis: E.H. Carr and IR', in Vendulka Kubálková, Nicholas Onuf and Paul Kowert (eds), *International Relations in a Constructed World*, Armonk: M.E. Sharpe, pp. 25–57.

Kwan, C.H. (1994), *Economic Interdependence in the Asia–Pacific Region: Towards a Yen Bloc*, London: Routledge.

Lach, Donald (1965), *Asia in the Making of Europe*, vol. I, Chicago and London: University of Chicago Press.

Lähteenmäki, Kaisa and Jyrki Käkönen (1999), 'Regionalization and its Impact on the Theory of International Relations', in Björn Hettne, Andras Inotai and Osvaldo Sunkel (eds), *Globalism and the New Regionalism*, London: Macmillan, pp. 203–27.

Lawson, Stephanie (1996), 'Cultural Relativism and Democracy: Political Myths about "Asia" and the "West"', in Richard Robison (ed.), *Pathways to Asia*, St Leonards: Allen and Unwin, pp. 108–28.

Lechervy, Christian (1998), 'L'Europe face à l'Asie, 'l'Asie face à l'Europe: de la *realpolitik* à la recherche d'un nouvel universalisme', *Aséanie*, **1** (mars), 15–41.

Lee, Chong Wha (1998), 'ASEM Investment Promotion Action Plan (IPAP) Revisited: Establishing the Groundwork for Regional Investment Initiative', Working Paper 98–06, Seoul, Korea Institute for International Economic Policy (KIEP).

Lee, Sahng-Gyoun (1999), 'EMU and Asia–Europe Economic Relations: Implications and Perspectives', *Journal of East Asian Affairs*, **8** (1), 51–72.

Lee, Sang-Gon and Pierre-Bruno Ruffini (eds) (1999), *The Global Integration of Europe and East Asia: Studies of International Trade and Investment*, Cheltenham, UK and Northampton, MA, USA: Edward Elgar.

Leifer, Michael (2000), 'Regional Solutions to Regional Problems?', in Gerald Segal and David S.G. Goodman (eds), *Towards Recovery in Pacific Asia*, London: Routledge, pp. 108–18.

Lindstrom, Lamont (1996), 'Cargoism and Occidentalism', in James G. Carrier (ed.), *Occidentalism: Images of the West*, Oxford: Clarendon, pp. 33–60.

Mahathir Mohamad (1999), *A New Deal for Asia*, Selangor Darul Ehsan: Pelanduk.

Mahncke, Dieter (1997), 'Relations Between Europe and South-East Asia: The Security Dimension', *European Foreign Affairs Review*, **2** (3), 291–305.

Mak, J.N. (1998), 'The Asia–Pacific Security Order', in Anthony McGrew and Christopher Brook (eds), *Asia Pacific in the New World*, London: Routledge, pp. 88–120.

March, James G. and Johan P. Olsen (1989), *Rediscovering Institutions*, New York: Free Press.

Maswood, Javed (1998), 'The Rise of the Asia–Pacific', in Anthony McGrew and Christopher Brook (eds), *Asia–Pacific in the New World Order*, London: Routledge, pp. 57–66.

Mattli, Walter (1999), *The Logic of Regional Integration: Europe and Beyond*, Cambridge: Cambridge University Press.

Maull, Hanns and Akihiko Tanaka (1997), 'The Geopolitical Dimension', in CAEC, *The Rationale and Common Agenda for Asia–Europe Cooperation*, Tokyo: Council for Asia–Europe Cooperation, pp. 31–40.

Maull, Hanns, Gerald Segal and Jusuf Wanandi (eds) (1998), *Europe and the Asia Pacific*, London: Routledge.

Mauzy, Dianne (1997), 'The Human Rights and "Asian Values" Debate in Southeast Asia: Trying to Clarify the Key Ideas', *The Pacific Review*, **10** (2), 210–36.

McDougall, Derek (1998), *Australian Foreign Relations: Contemporary Perspectives*, South Melbourne: Longman.

McGrew, Anthony (1998), 'Restructuring Foreign and Defence Policy: The USA', in Anthony McGrew and Christopher Brook (eds), *Asia Pacific in the New World*, London: Routledge, pp. 158–88.

McMahon, Joseph D. (1998), 'ASEAN and the Asia–Europe Meeting: Strengthening the European Union's Relationship with South-East Asia?', *European Foreign Affairs Review*, **3** (2), 233–51.

Mead, George Herbert (1934), *Mind, Self and Society*, Chicago: University of Chicago Press.

Miller, Constanze and Dominik Meier (1998), 'Issues of Democracy and Legitimacy in Asia', in Willem van der Geest and Beate Tränkmann (eds), *Democracy, Human Rights and Economic Development: Conflict or Complement?*, Brussels: European Institute for Asian Studies, pp. 43–56.

Milner, Anthony (2000), 'What Happened to "Asian Values"?', in Gerald Segal and David S. G. Goodman (eds), *Towards Recovery in Pacific Asia*, London: Routledge, pp. 56–68.

Minton, Zanny (1999), 'From EMU to AMU? The Case for Regional Currencies', *Foreign Affairs*, **78** (4), 8–13.

Mistry, Percy (1999), 'The New Regionalism: Impediment or Spur to Future Multilateralism?', in Björn Hettne, Andras Inotai and Osvaldo Sunkel (eds), *Globalism and the New Regionalism*, London: Macmillan, pp. 116–54.

Mitchell, Bernard (1996), 'Regions in the Global Political Economy: Beyond the Local-Global Divide in the Formation of the Eastern Asian Region', *New Political Economy*, **1** (3), 335–53.

Mittelman, James H. (1996), 'Rethinking the "New Regionalism" in the Context of Globalization', *Global Governance*, **2**, 189–213.

Mittelman, James H. (ed.) (1997), *Globalization: Critical Reflections*, Boulder: Lynne Rienner.

Mittelman, James H. (1999), 'Rethinking the 'New Regionalism' in the Global Context', in Björn Hettne, Andras Inotai and Osvaldo Sunkel (eds), *Globalism and the New Regionalism*, London: Macmillan, pp. 25–53.

MOFA (1998), *Diplomatic Bluebook 1997*, Tokyo: Ministry of Foreign Affairs.

Moravcsik, Andrew (1998), *The Choice for Europe: Social Purpose and State Power from Messina to Maastricht*, Ithaca: Cornell University Press.

Morris, Jonathan (1991), *Japan and the Global Economy*, London: Routledge.

Neumann, Iver B. (1999), *Uses of the Other: 'The East' in European Identity Formation*, Manchester: Manchester University Press.

Nicoll, William and Trevor C. Salmon (1994, 1990), *Understanding the New European Community*, New York: Harvester Wheatsheaf.

O'Brien, Robert, Anne Marie Goetz, Jan Aart Scholte and Marc Williams (2000), *Contesting Global Governance: Multilateral Economic Institutions and Global Social Movements*, Cambridge: Cambridge University Press.

Ohmae, Kenichi (1990), *The Borderless World*, London: Collins.

Okfen, Nuria (1999), *Das Asia–Europe Meeting – Eine neue Partnerschaft?*, Braunschweig: Institut für Sozialwissenschaften.

Onuf, Nicholas (1985) *World of Our Making: Rules and Rule in Social Theory and International Relations*, Columbia: University of South Carolina Press.

Paik, Yongsun (1998), 'Open Regionalism: An Alternative to the Regional Trading Bloc in East Asia', *Global Economic Review*, **27** (1), 48–62.

Palmujoki, Eero (1997), 'EU–ASEAN Relations: Reconciling Two Different Agendas', *Contemporary Southeast Asian Studies*, **19** (3), 269–87.

Pape, Wolfgang (1997), 'Values and Religion in Relations to Progress', paper at the Manila Forum on Culture, Values and Technology, Manila 10–12 December.

Patten, Chris (1998), *East and West*, London: Macmillan.

Pei, Minxin (1998), 'The Fall and Rise of Democracy in East Asia', in Larry Diamond and Marc F. Plattner (eds), *Democracy in East Asia*, Baltimore: University of Johns Hopkins Press, pp. 57–78.

Pelkmans, Jacques and Annette Balaoing (1996), 'Europe Looking Further East: Twinning European and Multilateral Interests', paper presented at the Transatlantic Workshop: Towards Rival Regionalism? US and EU Regional Economic Integration Policies and the Risk of a Transatlantic Regulatory Rift, EIAS, Ebenhausen, 4–6 July.

Pelkmans, Jacques and Hiroko Shinkai (eds) (1997), *ASEM: How Promising a Partnership?*, Brussels: European Institute for Asian Studies.

Peña, Fortunato T. de la (1997), 'The Role of SMEs in Technology Exchange between Asia and Europe', paper presented at the Manila Forum on Culture, Values and Technology, Shangri-La's EDSA Plaza Hotel, 10–12 December.

Pieterse, Jan Nederveen (1997), 'Globalization and Emancipation: From Local Empowerment to Global Reform', *New Political Economy*, **2** (1), 79–92.

Preeg, Ernest H. (1998), 'APEC, ASEM and the New Transatlantic Agenda (TAFTA?): An Unequal Interacting Triad', in Jacques Pelkmans and Hiroko Shinkai (eds), *APEC and Europe*, Brussels: European Institute for Asian Studies, pp. 74–90.

Princen, Thomas (1994), 'NGOs: Creating a Niche in Environmental Diplomacy', in Thomas Princen and Matthias Finger (eds), *Environmental NGOs in World Politics*, London: Routledge, pp. 29–47.

Princen, Thomas and Matthias Finger (eds) (1994), *Environmental NGOs in World Politics*, London: Routledge.

Randel, Judith and Tony German (1999a), 'Japan', in Ian Smillie and Henny Helmich (eds), *Stakeholders: Government–NGO Partnerships for International Development*, London: Earthscan Publications, pp. 149–58.

Randel, Judith and Tony German (1999b), 'European Union', in Ian Smillie and Henny Helmich (eds), *Stakeholders: Government–NGO Partnerships for International Development*, London: Earthscan Publications, pp. 263–577.

Ravenhill, John (1995), 'Competing Logics of Regionalism in the Asia-Pacific', *Journal of European Integration*, **18** (2–3), 179–99.

Ravenhill, John (1996), 'Economic Interdependence in East Asia: Its Growth and Effects on the Australian–US Relationship', in Roger Bell, Tim McDonald and Alan Tidwell (eds), *Negotiating the Pacific Century:*

The 'New' Asia, the United States and Australia, St Leonard's: Allen and Unwin, pp. 170–90.Ravenhill, John (1998), 'The Growth of Intergovernmental Collaboration in the Asia–Pacific Region', in Anthony McGrew and Christopher Brook (eds), *Asia Pacific in the New World*, London: Routledge, pp. 247–70.

Richards, Gareth A. and Colin Kirkpatrick (1999), 'Reorienting Interregional Cooperation in the Global Political Economy: Europe's East Asia Policy', *Journal of Common Market Studies*, **37** (4), 683–710.

Richards, Gareth Api (2000), 'ASEM and the New Politics of Development: Restructuring Social Policy After the Crisis', paper presented to the Trade and Economy Forum: 'The Impact of Neo-Liberal Globalization and the Struggles for People's Alternatives', ASEM People's Forum, Seoul, 18–19 October.

Risse-Kappen, Thomas (1996), 'Exploring the Nature of the Beast: International Relations Theory and Comparative Policy Analysis Meet the European Union', *Journal of Common Market Studies*, **34** (1), 53–80.

Robison, Richard (1996), 'Looking North: Myths and Strategies', in Richard Robison (ed.), *Pathways to Asia*, St Leonards: Allen and Unwin, pp. 3–28.

Rodan, Gary and Kevin Hewison (1996), 'A "Clash of Cultures" or the Convergence of Political Ideology?', in Richard Robison (ed.), *Pathways to Asia*, St Leonards: Allen and Unwin, pp. 29–55.

Rosamond, Ben (1997), 'Reflexive Regionalism? Global Life and the Construction of European Identities', paper presented at the Annual Convention of the International Studies Association, Toronto, 18–22 March.

Rosamond, Ben (1999), 'Discourses of Globalization and the Social Construction of European Identities', *Journal of European Public Policy*, **6** (4), 652–68.

Rothacher, Albrecht (1983), *Economic Diplomacy between the European Community and Japan 1959–1989*, Aldershot: Gower.

Rozman, Gilbert (1992), *Japan's Response to the Gorbachev Era, 1985–1991: A Rising Superpower Views a Declining One*, Princeton: Princeton University Press.

Ruggie, John G. (1998), *Constructing the World Polity*, London: Routledge.

Rüland, Jürgen (1996), *The Asia–Europe Meeting (ASEM): Towards a New Euro–Asian Relationship?*, Rostock: Institut für Politik- und Verwaltungswissenshaften.

Said, Edward (1995, 1978), *Orientalism: Western Conceptions of the Orient*, London: Penguin.

Sampson, Edward E. (1993), *Celebrating the Other: A Dialogic Account of Human Nature*, New York: Harvester Wheatsheaf.

Sandholtz, Wayne and John Zysman (1989), '1992: Recasting the European Bargain', *World Politics*, **42** (1), 95–128.

Santer, Jacques (1998), 'Asia and Europe: The Road from Bangkok to London and Beyond', *The Inaugural Asia–Europe Lecture*, Singapore: Asia–Europe Foundation, 13 January.

Sardar, Zia, Ashis Nandy and Merryl Wyn Davies (1993), *Barbaric Others: A Manifesto on Western Racism*, London: Pluto.

SarDesai, D.R. (1997), 4th ed., *Southeast Asia: Past and Present*, Boulder: Westview Press.

Schmit, Leo (1996), 'The Deployment of Civil Energy in Indonesia', in Chris Hann and Elizabeth Dunn (eds), *Civil Society: Challenging Western Models*, London: Routledge, pp. 178–98.

Scholte, Jan Aart (1993), *International Relations of Social Change*, Buckingham: Open University Press.

Scholte, Jan Aart (1996), 'Globalisation and Collective Identities', in Jill Krause and Neil Renwick (eds), *Identities in International Relations*, London: Macmillan, pp. 38–78.

Scholte, Jan Aart (2000), 'Cautionary Reflections on Seattle', *Millennium*, **29** (1), 115–22.

Schreurs, Miranda (1998), 'Environmental Cooperation in Northeast Asia', *Global Economic Review*, **27** (1), 88–101.

Searle, John (1995), *Construction of Social Reality*, New York: The Free Press.

Segal, Gerald (1997a), 'Thinking Strategically about ASEM: The Subsidiarity Question', *The Pacific Review*, **10** (1), 124–34.

Serradell, Victor Pou (1996), 'The Asia–Europe meeting (ASEM): A Historical Turning Point in Relations between the Two Regions', *European Foreign Affairs Review*, **1** (2), 185–210.

Shapiro, Michael (1981), *Language and Political Understanding: The Politics of Discursive Practices*, New Haven: Yale University Press.

Shaw, Jo (1999), 'Postnational Constitutionalism in the European Union', *Journal of European Public Policy*, **6** (4), 579–97.

Shin, Dong-Ik and Gerald Segal (1997), 'Getting Serious about Asia–Europe Security Cooperation', *Survival*, **39** (1), 138–55.

Sikkink, Kathryn (1991), *Ideas and Institutions: Developmentalism in Latin America and Argentina*, Ithaca: Cornell University Press.

Simon, Sheldon W. (1995), 'The Parallel Tracks of Asian Multilateralism', in Michael W. Everett and Mary A. Somerville (eds), *Multilateral Activities in South East Asia*, Washington DC: National Defense University Press, pp. 11–30.

Smillie, Ian (1999), 'At Sea in a Sieve? Trends and Issues in the Relationship between Northern NGOs and Northern Governments', in

Ian Smillie and Henny Helmich (eds), *Stakeholders: Government–NGO Partnerships for International Development*, London: Earthscan Publications, pp. 7–35.

Smith, Heather (1998), 'Korea', in Ross H. McLeod and Ross Garnaut (eds), *East Asia in Crisis: From Being a Miracle to Needing One?*, London: Routledge, pp. 66–84.

Smith, Michael (1998), 'The European Union and the Asia Pacific', in Anthony McGrew and Christopher Brook (eds), *Asia Pacific in the New World*, London: Routledge, pp. 289–315.

Soesastro, Hadi (1997), 'APEC: An ASEAN Perspective', in Donald C. Hellmann and Kenneth B. Pyle (eds), *From APEC to Xanadu: Creating a Viable Community in the Post-Cold War Pacific*, Armonk: M.E.Sharpe, pp. 174–94.

Soesastro, Hadi and Simon Nuttall (1997), 'The Institutional Dimension', in CAEC, *The Rationale and Common Agenda for Asia–Europe Cooperation*, Tokyo: Japan Centre for International Exchange, pp. 75–85.

Solingen, Etel (1998), *Regional Orders at Century's Dawn: Global and Domestic Influences on Grand Strategy*, Princeton: Princeton University Press.

Somers, Margaret R. (1994), 'The Narrative Constitution of Identity: A Relational and Network Approach', *Theory and Society*, **23**, 605-49.

Spell, Sabine (2000), *Japanese Automobile Lobbying in Brussels: The Role of the Japanese Motor Industry*, Unpublished PhD thesis, University of Stirling.

Stokhof, Wim and Paul van der Velde (1999), *ASEM: The Asia–Europe Meeting – A Window of Opportunity*, London: Kegan Paul.

Stone Sweet, Alec and Wayne Sandholtz (1997), 'European Integration and Supranational Governance', *Journal of European Public Policy*, **4** (3), 297-317.

Stubbs, Richard (2000), 'Signing on to Liberalization: AFTA and the Politics of Regional Economic Cooperation', *The Pacific Review*, **13** (2), 297-318.

Tanaka, Toshiro (1999), 'Asia-Europe Relations: The Birth and Development of ASEM', *Keio Journal of Politics*, **10**, 31–51.

Tang, J.H.T. (1995), 'Human Rights in the Asia-Pacific Region: Competing Perspectives, International Discord, and the Way Ahead', in J.H.T. Tang (ed.), *Human Rights and International Relations in the Asia–Pacific Region*, London: Pinter, pp. 1–9.

Taylor, Charles (1989), *Sources of Self*, Boston: Harvard University Press.

Thakur, Ramesh (1995), 'From Collective to Cooperative Security? The Gareth Evans Vision of the United Nations', in Stephanie Lawson (ed.),

The New Agenda for Global Security: Cooperating for Peace, St. Leonards: Allen and Unwin, pp. 19–38.

Thibault de Silguy, Yves (1998), *La Crise financière en Asie*, SPEECH/98/12, Brussels: European Parliament.

Ton Sinh Thanh (1998), 'The Asia–Europe Meeting: ASEAN and EU Perspectives', paper for Carleton University, Ottawa, April.

UNCTAD and the European Commission (1996), Investing in Asia's Dynamism: European Union Direct Investment in Asia, Interim version, March, UNCTAD Division on Transnational Corporation and Investment.

US Department of State (2000), *World Military Expenditures and Arms Transfers, 1998*, Washington DC: Bureau of Verification and Compliance.

Vatikiotis, Michael R. J. (1996), *Political Change in Southeast Asia: Trimming the Banyan Tree*, London: Routledge.

Verdi, Simonetta (1999), 'Political and Security Cooperation, Membership Enlargement and the Global Information Society: Agenda Solutions for ASEM III', Working Paper 99–18, Seoul: Korea Institute for International Economic Policy (KIEP).

Vincent, R.J. (1999, 1986), *Human Rights and International Relations*, Cambridge: Cambridge University Press.

Vines, David (1999), 'Global Economic Institutions from the Southeast Asian Perspective', in Colin Barlow (ed.), *Institutions and Economic Change in Southeast Asia*, Cheltenham, UK and Northampton, MA, USA: Edward Elgar, pp. 150–64.

Watanabe, Akio (1993), 'Asia-Pacific Regionalism and Japanese Diplomacy', in Yoko Sazanami, Terumasa Nakanishi, Miyohei Shinohara, Hiroaki Fukami, Akio Watanabe and Saburo Okita (eds), *The Global Trend Toward Regional Integration*, Tokyo: Foreign Press Center, pp. 43–54.

Weiss, Linda (1999) 'Sources of the East Asian Advantage: An Institutional Analysis', in Richard Robison (ed.) *Pathways to Asia: The Politics of Engagement*, St Leonards: Allen and Unwin, pp. 171–204.

Weldes, Jutta, Mark Laffey, Hugh Gusterson and Raymond Duvall (eds) (1999), *Cultures of Insecurity: States, Communities, and the Production of Danger*, Minneapolis: University of Minnesota Press.

Wendt, Alexander and Raymond Duvall (1989), 'Institutions and International Order', in Ernst-Otto Czempiel and James N. Rosenau (eds), *Global Changes and Theoretical Challenges: Approaches to World Politics for the 1990s*, Lexington: Lexington Books, pp. 52–73.

Wendt, Alexander (1992), 'Anarchy is What States Make of It: The Social Construction of Power Politics', *International Organization*, **46** (2), 391–425.

Wendt, Alexander (1994), 'Collective Identity Formation and the International State', *American Political Science Review*, **88** (2), 384–96.

Wendt, Alexander (1999), *Social Theory of International Politics*, Cambridge: Cambridge University Press.

Wesley, Michael (1997), The Politics of Exclusion: Australia, Turkey and Definitions of Regionalism', *The Pacific Review*, **10** (4), 523-55.

Woods, Ngaire (ed.) (2000), *The Political Economy of Globalization*, London: Macmillan.

Woolcock, Stephen (1996), 'Regional Integration and the Multilateral Trading System', in Till Geiger and Dennis Kennedy (eds), *Regional Trade Blocs, Multilateralism, and the GATT: Complementary Paths to Free Trade?*, London: Pinter, pp. 115–30.

World Bank (1995), *World Development Record*, Oxford.

World Bank (1997), *World Development Record*, Oxford.

Wriggins, W. Howard (ed.) (1992), *Dynamics of Regional Politics: 4 Systems on the Indian Ocean Rim*, New York: Columbia University Press, pp. 213–73.

Yahuda, Michael (1997, 1996), *The International Politics of the Asia–Pacific, 1945–1995*, London: Routledge.

Yamakage Susumu (1980), *ASEAN's Political Co-operation 1967–1977*, Kyoto: Center for Southeast Asian Studies.

Yeo, Lay Hwee (1997), 'The Bangkok ASEM and the Future of Asia-Europe Relations', *Southeast Asian Affairs*, 33–45.

Yeo Lee Hwee (2000), 'ASEM: Looking Forward', *Contemporary Southeast Asia*, **22**, 113–44.

Yeung, May T., Nicholas Perdikis and William A. Kerr (1999), *Regional Trading Blocs in the Global Economy*, Cheltenham, UK and Northampton, MA, USA: Edward Elgar.

Yoshida, Masami, Ichiro Akimune, Masayuki Nohara and Kimitoshi Sato (1994), 'Regional Economic Integration in East Asia: Special Features and Policy Implications', in Vincent Cable and David Henderson (eds), *Trade Blocs? The Future of Regional Integration*, London: The Royal Institute for International Affairs, pp. 59–108.

Young, Oran (1991), 'Political Leadership and Regime Formation: On the Development of Institutions in International Society', *International Organization*, **45** (3), 281–308.

Young, Oran (1999), 'Comment on Andrew Moravscik, 'A New Statecraft? Supranational Entrepreneurs and International Cooperation', *International Organization*, **53** (4), 805–09.

Youngs, Gillian (1996), 'Beyond the "Inside/Outside" Divide', in Jill Krause and Neil Renwick (eds), *Identities in International Relations*, London: Macmillan, pp. 22–37.

Zakaria, Haji Ahmad (1999), 'The Political Future of ASEAN after the Asian Crisis', *International Affairs*, **75** (4), 759–78.

Zhang, Yunling (1997), 'China and APEC: Interests, Opportunities, and Challenges', in Donald C. Hellmann and Kenneth B. Pyle (eds), *From APEC to Xanadu: Creating a Viable Community in the Post-Cold War Pacific*, Armonk: M.E.Sharpe, pp. 195–202.

WEBSITES

www.amnesty.org.uk
www.apecsec.org.sg
www.asean.or.id
www.aseansec.org
www.asef.org
www.asem2.fco.gov.uk
www.asem3.org
www.asemconnect.com.sg
www.asem.inter.net.th
www.asem.vie.net
www.asia-invest.com
www.caec-asiaeurope.org
www.channelnewsasia.com
www.cordis.lu/asem/home.html
www.eias.org
www.eujapan.com
www.europa.eu.int
www.eurostat.cec.be
www.infoasia.co.jp
www.jaring.my
www.jcie.or.jp
www.mofa.go.kr
www.mofat.go.kr/aevg
www.mofat.go.kr/asem3/eng/pour
www.oneworldaction.co.uk
www.tni.org/asia
www.worldbank.org/rmc/asem/

Index